Language and Literature

An Introductory Reader in Stylistics

Edited by
RONALD CARTER

London and New York

First published in 1982 by the Academic Division of
Unwin Hyman Ltd
Second impression 1984
Third impression 1988

Reprinted in 1991 by

Routledge

11 New Fetter Lane, London EC4P 4EE
29 West 35th Street, New York, NY 10001

© George Allen & Unwin (Publishers) Ltd, 1982

British Library Cataloguing in Publication Data

Language and literature: an introductory reader
in stylistics. – (Aspects of English)
1. English language – Style
I. Carter, Ronald   II. Series
808   PE1421
ISBN 0-415-07889-X (pbk)

Library of Congress Cataloging in Publication Data

Main entry under title:
Language and literature.
(Aspects of English)
Bibliography: p.
Includes index.
Contents: The conditional presence of Mr Bleaney / by
H. G. Widdowson – Deixis / by Mary Mason – Othello in person / by
H. G. Widdowson – [etc.]
1. English language – Style – Addresses, essays, lectures.   2. Style,
Literary – Addresses, essays, lectures.   I. Carter, Ronald.
PE1421.L29   808'.0427   82-4000
AACR2
ISBN 0-415-07889-X (pbk)

Set in 10 on 11 point Times by D. P. Media Ltd, Hitchin, Hertfordshire
and printed and bound in Great Britain by
Biddles Ltd, Guildford and King's Lynn

Language and Literature

Contents

Acknowledgements

Books like this are collective enterprises and thanks are owed to many. In the first place must come the contributors themselves, who have not only provided the material of the book but who have also patiently endured several adjustments to the book's format and have co-operated fully throughout a long gestation. Thanks also go to Deirdre Burton, who worked with me on large parts of the book and to whom I owe more ideas on stylistics and its teaching than can be given due credit here. To two of the founding fathers of stylistics in Britain – John Sinclair and Henry Widdowson (and they are not *that* old) – I owe also considerable debts. John Sinclair, as general editor, gave considerable support for the book and much useful advice; Henry Widdowson commented in detail on draft chapters, wisely pointing out weaknesses and recommending improvements. I have also benefited greatly from conversations and practical teaching demonstrations with my colleague Bill Nash and must thank Norma Hazzledine for, as always, organising me sufficiently to get the book put together and for her endless patience, hard work and skill in typing the manuscript. Michael Stubbs and Margaret Berry have always been able to supply answers to tricky linguistic questions I have not been able to answer. The kindness and friendship of these people and others in the English Studies Department of Nottingham University must not go unrecorded.

In case it be thought otherwise, I did do *some* of the work on this book myself and assume responsibility for what remains. In this work I owe more than can sometimes be imagined or adequately recompensed to my children, Matthew, Jennifer and Claire and to my wife, Jane Carter, for support which goes beyond the merely academic.

Acknowledgement is due to the copyright holders for their kind permission to reprint the following extracts: Faber & Faber Ltd for *Mr Bleaney* in *The Whitsun Weddings* by Philip Larkin, *Preludes I* from *Collected Poems 1909–1962* by T. S. Eliot (acknowledgement is also due to Harcourt Brace Jovanovich, Inc.) and 'O where are you going? said rider to rider' from *Five Songs* in *Collected Poems* by W. H. Auden (acknowledgement also due to Random House, Inc.); Jonathan Cape Ltd., for *Cat in the Rain* from *The First Forty-Nine Stories* (also reproduced with the permission of Charles Scribner's Sons and the Executors of the Ernest Hemingway Estate) and the extract from *A Portrait of the Artist as a Young Man* by James Joyce (with the permission of the Executors of the James Joyce Estate and Viking Penguin, Inc.); extracts from *Daughters of the Vicar* and *Odour of Chrysanthemums* from *The Collected Short Stories of D. H. Lawrence* reprinted with the permission of William Heinemann Ltd, Lawrence Pollinger Ltd, Viking Penguin, Inc., and the Estate of the late Mrs Frieda Lawrence Ravagli.

Notes on Contributors

RONALD CARTER (editor) is currently lecturer in English studies at the University of Nottingham. His main interests are in stylistics and linguistics and education. He has published books on W. H. Auden and edited *Literary Text and Language Study* (with Deirdre Burton; Edward Arnold, 1982) and *Linguistics and the Teacher* (Routledge & Kegan Paul, 1982). He has published a number of articles on the above topics and on literary criticism and twentieth-century literature.

GILLIAN ALEXANDER is a postgraduate research student in English language in the Department of English Language and Literature at the University of Birmingham. She has written an MA thesis on metaphor and linguistics and is currently preparing a doctorate on 'Linguistic processes in recent women's writing'. She has taught linguistics in a college of education and at the universities of Birmingham and Loughborough.

DEIRDRE BURTON is currently lecturer in English language at the University of Birmingham. Her main research and teaching interests are in sociolinguistics, discourse analysis and the philosophy of language. She has written a book called *Dialogue & Discourse: a sociolinguistic approach to modern drama dialogue and naturally-occurring conversation* (Routledge & Kegan Paul, 1980), and is currently working on a book concerned with the sociolinguistics of everyday life – essays from a feminist perspective.

CHRIS KENNEDY is lecturer in English at the University of Birmingham with particular responsibility for courses in applied linguistics and English as a foreign language for intending teachers. He has lectured in Malaysia, Nigeria, Colombia and Germany. He has published widely on English language teaching and is editor of *English Language Research Journal*.

MARY MASON has taught English language and literature in secondary schools in England and Bulgaria and is at present engaged in teacher training in the Faculty of Education, City of Birmingham Polytechnic. She is interested in the application of studies of syntax to an interpretation of literary texts and has published an article related to the one included in this volume entitled 'Syntax as a point of entry to Dylan Thomas' "Fern Hill"' (*Midlands Association for Linguistic Studies Journal*, 1980).

WALTER NASH is senior lecturer in English studies at the University of Nottingham. His main academic work includes *Our Experience of Language* (Batsford, 1971), *Designs in Prose* (Longman, 1980) and several articles ranging from literary criticism of Tennyson to aspects of English language teaching. Walter Nash is also a prolific short-story writer and the author of a novel, *Kettle of Roses* (Hutchinson, 1982). He is currently working on a second novel, a book on English usage and a stylistic study of English comedy and humour (Longman)

ALEX RODGER was educated at the University of Edinburgh and at the University of Oxford. Since 1962 he has been head of English studies for foreign students at the University of Edinburgh. His chief interests are poetic and pedagogical stylistics. Publications include: 'Linguistics and the teaching of literature' and 'Linguistic form and literary meaning', both in Fraser, H. and O'Donnell, W. R. (ed.), *Applied Linguistics and the Teaching of English* (Longman, 1969); with Jean N. Ure, ' "Cargoes": a linguistic analysis of a literary text', *Journal of English as a Second Language*, III, 2, 1968, and IV, 1, 1969; 'Methodology of teaching English literature in the context of the foreign learner situation', *Views on Language and Language Teaching* (Cultural Association of Teachers of English, Athens), III, 1, 1977; 'Themes and theses: lexical cohesion and poetic significance in Theodore Roethke's "Child on Top of a Greenhouse" ', *Nottingham Linguistic Circular*, V, 3, 1977.

MICK SHORT is lecturer in English and linguistics at the University of Lancaster where he acted as head of department 1977–80. He has published widely on stylistics and narrative theory, and in 1980 co-founded the Poetics and Linguistics Association of Great Britain. He has lectured in Finland, Tunisia and China. He is the author (with G. N. Leech) of *Style in Fiction* (Longman, 1981).

JOHN SINCLAIR (general editor Aspects of English series) is Professor of Modern English Language at the University of Birmingham. His major research and publications have been in stylistics, linguistics and education, English for special purposes and the analysis of spoken discourse. He has written *A Course in Spoken English: Grammar* (OUP, 1972). He is also the author (with Malcolm Coulthard) of the influential *Towards an Analysis of Discourse: the English Used by Teachers and Pupils* (OUP, 1975).

HENRY WIDDOWSON, MA Cambridge, PhD Edinburgh, is Professor of Education, Department of English as a Foreign Language, University of London. He was previously a British Council officer and then lecturer in the Department of Linguistics, University of Edinburgh. Author of *Teaching Language as Communication* (OUP, 1977), *Stylistics and the Teaching of Literature* (Longman, 1975), *Explorations in Applied Linguistics* (OUP, 1979), he is also an editor of the journal *Applied Linguistics*. He is currently working on aspects of written discourse in literature and other uses of language.

Introduction

The point of this introduction is to acquaint readers with some of the basic issues and questions raised by stylistics in its application to the teaching and study of literature, and to explain some of the purposes and uses for this book. The application of linguistics to literature has aroused much discussion and heated debate, and continues to do so. But, as interest in language study and teaching revives across the whole curriculum, questions are raised concerning appropriate ways in which language can be studied, how it can be integrated with the study of literature, contribute to foreign-language teaching, and so on. This book has as its main objective to explore some ways in which language and literature study can be integrated. The aims are modest and necessarily fairly controlled (see below, Section VI); where feasible, questions of the relevance of this approach to *teaching* and *learning* will be uppermost. Many theoretical questions have therefore to be left unanswered in a book of this kind; but most of the writers in this book – as practitioners of stylistics in their daily work – would argue that practical exploration of the kind suggested here ultimately works to focus issues and principles in usefully tangible ways.

In the six sections that follow I look at language and literature study from a broader theoretical perspective and point to some possible sources of misunderstanding about stylistics. The starting-point for this must be a discussion of some traditional, conventional and, it must be said, dominant models for the study of literature and literary meaning.

I Literary Meaning and the Literary Critic

As an example of what I think is generally understood by literary meaning, and of the particular form of literary criticism with which the kind of stylistic analysis exemplified in this book would be contrasted, I want to cite a short extract from a well-known and widely quoted book of novel criticism by F. R. Leavis. The extract is devoted to characterisation in Henry James's *The Portrait of a Lady* and George Eliot's *Daniel Deronda*:

> It would hardly be said of Isabel Archer that the presentation of her is complete; it is characteristic of James's art to have made her an effective

enough presence for his purpose without anything approaching a 'wealth of psychological detail'. Her peculiar kind of impressiveness, in fact, is conditioned by her not being known inside out, and – we have to confess it – could not have been achieved by George Eliot. For it is fair to say that if James had met a Gwendolen Harbeth (at any rate an American one) he would have seen Isabel Archer; he immensely admired George Eliot's inwardness and completeness of rendering, but when he met the type in actual life and was prompted to the conception of the Portrait of a Lady, he saw her with the eyes of an American gentleman. One must add – an essential point – that he saw her as American.

It is, of course, possible to imagine a beautiful, clever and vital girl, with 'that sense of superior claims which made a large part of her consciousness' (George Eliot's phrase for Gwendolen, but it applies equally to Isabel), whose egotism yet shouldn't be as much open to the criticism of an intelligent woman as Gwendolen's. But it is hard to believe that, in life, she could be as free from qualities inviting a critical response as the Isabel Archer seen by James. (Leavis, 1964, pp. 110–11)

The first question to ask is: what kind of literary meaning is being sought out here? Leavis's primary appeal is to a mode of psychological and moral sensitivity in his readers which is not made explicit, but which is presumed to have derived from a particular life experience ('But it is hard to believe that, in life, she could be as free from qualities . . .'). The meaning sought appears to be connected with accuracy of representing a type in fiction ('that kind of girl') which can be felt to be true – but not too true to lack suggestiveness – as well as with passing judgement on the particular human characteristics depicted. In this respect, Eliot is adjudged to be the more consummate artist.

The second question is this: does Leavis make explicit the criteria whereby he arrives at such pronouncements? The answer is that he offers no operable principles of analysis. No criterion is supplied, for example, for determining how, precisely, Eliot promotes a particular awareness whereas James doesn't. The differences between them and the resulting preference are asserted not demonstrated. For a critic, too, who once wrote 'No treatment of poetry is worth much that does not keep very close to the concrete: there lies the problem of method' (Leavis, 1966:10), there is remarkably little textual substantiation for the points he adduces. As a result his argument here is, in fact, wholly declarative in mood with only very minimal clausal qualification or concession. Where verbs occur which might introduce some modalisation into his points they are either in semi-negative form ('It would hardly be said') or appear in parenthetical asides. In reality, the modals selected work only to underline the certainty and assertiveness of Leavis's discourse ('we *have to* confess it', 'One *must* add'). Furthermore, who is implied by his use of 'we' or 'one'? Presumably, not simply Leavis himself. As Trevor Eaton has put it, commenting on similar prevalent usages in Leavis's literary criticism:

> By this apparently innocent pronoun, he places his student in a dilemma: he either agrees with the assertion, in which case the master wins his point, or he disagrees and is placed on the defensive, for Leavis's tone suggests that non-acceptance entails insensitivity. (Eaton, 1978)

The assumption appears to be that 'we' are a community of readers whose sensitivity, awareness and moral judgement are such as not to require any more explicit reference. As a result, we are forced into the position of accepting connecting links or points of emphasis in his argument ('For', 'an essential point', 'yet', 'it is fair to say', 'in fact') which do not really exist. Throughout Leavis shows no willingness to indicate either the modality or selectivity of his assertions. His commentary is, to a considerable extent, characterised by impressionism, while his critical propositions are embedded.

It is, of course, a little unfair to cite critics' work in extract form or to take only a single example. But I do believe this mode of criticism to be largely representative of Leavis and of his particular orientation towards 'literary meaning' (see also Widdowson, 1975: 72–4, for further objections). Meaning is measured against an ostensibly common life experience; there is only minimal appeal to the medium from which the text is constructed; meaning is established without method. Leavis is not wholly typical of traditional literary criticism, but his 'style' is widely followed, not least by critics such as F. W. Bateson, Helen Vendler and others (see Bibliography) who have objected more strongly to linguistic criticism.[1] Even I. A. Richards and the American 'New Critics', though responsible through their advocacy of practical criticism for greater textual analysis, still tacitly share many of Leavis's assumptions. Where, in this book, reference is made to traditional literary criticism, it is generally to the kind of material and approach analysed here that I am pointing. As I see it, the main dangers are that the standards to which students are trained are those of the literary establishment; the 'classic' works to which they should be exposed are chosen for them by the more 'sensitive' readers. Those who do not develop the necessary sensitivity fall by the wayside or only 'learn' the judgements required of them.

It is important to recognise two more fundamental tenets in the approach to literary criticism of Leavis and his followers. One I have already hinted at. When Leavis undertakes analyses, he works within limits which are prescribed by his sense that a writer's language is a medium *through* which 'felt' life is registered. The critic analyses literary meaning with reference to such touchstones as the writer's openness to the complexity of experience which is reflected and, in the great writers in the tradition, controlled by language. To interrogate the workings of this medium is not the business of the critic. In this scheme language becomes a kind of link between the essentiality of experience and the mature judgement of the writer. It is a precious link and therefore not to be tampered with. Such principles, in so far as they are articulated, do not allow of any consideration of the epistemological status of language. Where language is considered, it is as if it were only an analogy for something else.

The second fundamental tenet is linked with the first. For Leavis and, in fact, for most literary critics of most persuasions, it is a basic proposition that literary texts are sources of meaning in that they make statements about man and man in the world. Such a proposition is so rooted in the empirical and humanistic tradition of much Anglo-American criticism that it is now taken for granted. Criticism after Leavis has to a considerable extent acquiesced in the silences between his lines. We are usually taken to be sensitive and commonsensical enough not to need to have spelled out to us such obvious purposes of reading and criticising literary texts. To this end, language is seen as transparent in its opening on to the world, and writers use this medium to render its meanings. The relationship between language and the text and the world is essentially taken for granted and unproblematic.

This proposition is so basic that it needs to be stated. This is particularly so in the case of this reader, because not all the writers in this volume feel that the proposition *is* basic to what they are doing in their criticism or that it can pass unchallenged. It is important for readers of this book to be alert to assumptions in method, approach and principle, whether hidden or otherwise. The issue of criticism, meaning and language is taken up again in Section IV of this introduction. Two very useful sources of further discussion are Norris (1980) and Belsey (1980).

II Practical Criticism and Practical Stylistics

Since most readers who use this book will understand the term 'practical criticism', or will actually be practising it as part of their literary studies, defining 'practical stylistics' in relation to practical criticism seems to be a sensible starting-point. It is particularly necessary, however, because (although there are some similarities) practical stylistics is in many ways quite different from practical criticism.

Practical stylistics is a process of literary text analysis which starts from a basic assumption that the primary interpretative procedures used in the reading of a literary text are *linguistic* procedures. As readers of literature we are involved first and foremost in a response to language. And we perform this act of interpretative response by reference to what we already know of the language as native users of that language.

But, often, what we know is *only* intuitive. We sense that what we are hearing or reading is odd or belongs to a special register or code of the language (e.g. that it is legal language, or sounds harmonious, or seems to be in no way abnormal at all). Such intuitions and sense impressions are undeniably responses to language, and have formed the basis of much valuable literary criticism. But there is inevitably difficulty in properly accounting for these intuitions. Students of literature frequently say that they are experiencing particular tones, moods or feelings from contact with the text, but often lack the confidence or a method that will give them the confidence, to explore more fully and then explicitly formalise those same feelings. Thus, the *precise* nature of the interpretative processes readers undergo tends to remain obscure to us. The implicit and intuitive nature of our operational knowledge of our native language is, I believe, very much at the root of this obscurity.

There are, of course, serious objections raised to making things more precise. Indeed, we may prefer things to stay as they are and not analyse language. For, if we do so, it is feared, we may destroy the primacy of our intuitions or confuse in some way the nature of our response by subjecting to close scrutiny something which is precious and individual. As we have seen, this is very much a Leavisite position. Although my view is that critics of practical stylistics often misunderstand or misuse the term, many teachers and students of literature feel they are engaging in something which should not be allowed to become too 'scientific'. Within what is practised as practical criticism, appeal is made to language but in the belief that general ideas about the nature of language or general reference to words and their organisation are sufficient. Frequently such reference is to whatever bits of language strike the critic as interesting.

It is, however, a basic principle of a linguistic approach to literary study and criticism that without *analytic* knowledge of the rules and conventions of normal linguistic communication we cannot adequately validate these intuitive interpretations either for ourselves or for others. In other words, I want to argue here for three main points of principle and practice:

(1) that the greater our detailed knowledge of the workings of the language system, the greater our capacity for insightful awareness of the effects produced by literary texts;
(2) that a principled analysis of language can be used to make our commentary on the effects produced in a literary work less impressionistic and subjective;
(3) that because it will be rooted in a *systematic* awareness of language, bits of language will not be merely 'spotted' and evidence gathered in an essentially casual and haphazard manner. Statements will be made with recognition of the fact that analysis of one linguistic pattern requires

reference to, or checking against, related patterns across the text. Evidence for the statements will thus be provided in an overt or principled way. The conclusions can be *attested* and *retrieved* by another analyst working on the same data with the same method. There is also less danger that we may overlook textual features crucial to the significance of the work.

In fact it is essentially its recourse to this systematic and explicit knowledge of communicative and linguistic norms which distinguishes practical stylistics from practical criticism.

Are there any presuppositions underlying work in practical stylistics which need to be clarified? There is perhaps a further point which needs to be underlined. It is that stylistic analysis can provide the means whereby the student of literature can relate a piece of literary writing to his own experience of language and so can extend that experience. It can assist in the transfer of interpretative skills which is one of the essential purposes of literary education. Hence by appealing primarily to what people already know, that is, their own language, there is no reason why practical stylistics cannot provide a procedure for demystifying literary texts. We have here a basis from which to work out for ourselves what, in the fullest sense, is meant. We do not need to rely on the passing down of judgements or information from the literary establishment. We can make our own interpretations and do so in a relatively objective manner.[2] The more confident we become in analysing our language, the better equipped and more confident we shall become in adducing linguistic facts to substantiate our intuitions and use them to make sound literary judgements.

It is this basic presupposition of most work within the field of practical stylistics, then, which engages centrally with the *pedagogy* of the subject. Of all the linguistic approaches to literature, practical stylistics recommends itself as the most suitable introductory mode of analysis for learning about language, the workings of language in literature and for developing the confidence to work systematically towards interpretations of literary texts. It all depends, of course, what you want to do with your analysis, but practical stylistics works in an easily accessible way and has infinite possibilities for extension. Experience of teaching integrated courses in linguistics and literature to first-year undergraduates, English teachers on in-service courses, foreign students of English, and senior-school students suggests that its techniques and aims are fairly readily assimilated. It is important that in many respects it is an extension of practical criticism and thus keeps within what is for most students an existing framework and mode of understanding. It is for this pedagogic reason that readers are advised to begin using this book by first tackling the chapters on practical stylistics.

To conclude this section, it is necessary to draw attention to another main presupposition of work in practical stylistics. This is that in seeking a middle ground between linguistics and literature there is a discernible need to play the game according to literary rules. More often than not, and perhaps understandably, practical stylisticians want to demonstrate to literary critics that their analysis is useful. There is sometimes a purposeful urge to rise to Helen Vendler's much-quoted challenge:

> If linguistics can add to our comprehension of literature, someone trained in linguistics should be able to point out to us, in poems we already know well, significant features we have missed because of our amateurish ignorance of the workings of language. (Vendler, 1966)

In so doing, usefulness tends to become measurable in traditional literary critical terms of judgement, interpretation, evaluation, or advancing our appreciation or understanding of the meaning of the text. The accommodation, therefore, is primarily in the direction of literary criticism which is, after all, in terms of the study of English at all levels, very much the dominant model. Although, as we have just seen, very real differences in approach and method are insisted upon, the very name of the enterprise, 'practical stylistics', reveals a certain parasitism on practical criticism. Henry Widdowson, who has contributed substantially to the development and pedagogy of practical stylistics in this country, sees its role as genuinely integrating:

> By 'stylistics' I mean the study of literary discourse from a linguistics orientation and I shall take the view that what distinguishes stylistics from literary criticism on the one hand and linguistics on the other is that it is a means of linking the two. (Widdowson, 1975: 3)

Perhaps because of this orientation, it is the approach which is accepted with least reservation by literary critics, and which thus leads to an increasing institutionalisation of stylistics as a valuable additional mode of study within departments of English.[3] But readers of this book will realise that there are some linguists and students of language who feel compromised by the orientation of practical stylistics. They argue that it does not really occupy a *middle* ground. It is one of the main aims of this book to demonstrate the usefulness of practical stylistics to students of language and literature. The highest proportion of chapters in the book are practical or literary stylistic. But other chapters in the book will enable students to progress to discussion, examination and testing of one or two alternative linguistic approaches to literature which differ methodologically and ideologically from practical stylistics.

III Interpreting Interpretations

The point of this section is to raise one or two questions about the different kinds of interpretations of texts which are made in the course of the different chapters which comprise this reader. It must be pointed out that not all the contributors regard interpretation as the sole and necessary end-product of literary text analysis. For example, literary texts can provide interesting language problems to solve and can teach us much that is of real value in our understanding of the language system (see also below, Section VI). The interpretation might therefore be of the meaning and function of a stretch of language, and the interpretation might take the form of a precise, sensitive and insightful account of that language. There is no reason on earth why sensitivity and perceptive insight should be the exclusive preserve of interpretations of literary meaning. Even if such linguistic insights are not directly applied to the literary text in question, then, if they are clear and systematic and descriptively adequate, they can be applied by the reader prepared to tackle the necessary details. For example, John Sinclair's chapter provides some important strategies for analysing language. These features of language are found in a number of contexts of use, including poetry; in fact, much of the interest of this chapter consists in the way these strategies are derived from analysis of a piece of poetic discourse. Although his analysis is illuminating in this respect, his primary purpose is not to attempt a detailed analysis of a stretch of Wordsworth's poetry. Instead, he has provided some enabling devices for taking our study of the language of poetry beyond the interpretation of a single text.

Where he has interpreted, too, it is in terms of strictly linguistic terms and categories. The syntactic shape and effects of 'arrest' and 'extension', for example, are described with reference to the job they perform as features of *language*. Direct equation is then made between linguistic form and the linguistic function of that form in the literary text. There is no undue semanticisation of linguistic categories for the purposes of literary critical exegesis.[4] This is, of course, not at all the same thing as saying that insights into literary effects are unimportant. It is to represent the argument that 'the middle ground' of stylistics be marked out by adherence to linguistic principles as well as to literary critical rules. If there is to be effective marriage between the partners of language and literature, then each partner must fully understand and appreciate as far as is possible the concerns, the techniques and the principles of the other. Accommodation and adjustment cannot be only in one direction.

This and analyses like it are, as it were, a 'purer' form of linguistic examination of literary text. The primary responsibility is to descriptive accuracy and fullness in the statements made about language. It can involve describing features of language by locating them in a system of formal differences and relationships. This can in turn involve setting up a model for analysis. The advantage of this for analyses of literary texts is that linguistic observations of features of language become more easily *replicable*. The model can be generated in relation to several texts and, although adjustments will inevitably be entailed, there should always be sufficient detail available to accommodate these modifications. There is thus less risk of linguistic observations tending to be confined to features of single texts and not move beyond them. Such approaches tend to commend themselves to more advanced students in that they can reveal much about the detailed structure of literature and language as interrelating and interrelated systems. A basic presupposition here is that language is patterned in highly interesting ways in literary texts and so they are in a primary sense fascinating sources for the study of language. For further examples of what may be designated *linguistic stylistics*, see Carter and Burton (1982).

On the other hand, as pointed out in Section II, there are those chapters in this reader which proclaim the need to start from defined literary concerns, adducing linguistic facts in support of more explicit and precise definition of those concerns. In doing this writers are following a call made by Crystal (1972):

> One reason why much linguistic analysis of literature has not been well-received is that linguists take texts which seem interesting and problematic to them; they often forget that the text, or the problems, may not be of comparable interest to the critic. The stylistician must thoroughly appreciate the literary critics' problems and position.

I have already discussed the advantages of these approaches. They start from what is most familiar to students of literature and operate according to the most familiar and common-sense-based interpretative strategies of literary meaning in literary texts. I have tried to outline the enormous pedagogical advantages of this view of stylistics. It is, indeed, the most *practical* introductory approach to linking linguistics and literature.

Next, we need to interpret those interpretations which have an even more exclusive focus on the literary text and on literary interpretation, as it is generally and conventionally understood. Alex Rodger's chapter in this volume is not content to examine those bits of literary language organisation or effect which are striking and thus in need of some systematic objectification. Such bits of language may be crucial in laying a basis for an interpretation of a text. But Rodger's chapter goes beyond the provision of a basis. It is an exhaustive analysis of a text and an example of what detailed attention to almost every word of a text can reveal when it is combined with a sharp appreciation of how

literary meanings can be made. As much can be learned about literature, about the way a literary text can work, by following the detail and
process of his interpretation as from the interpretation of Auden's
poem itself.

This last feature of interpretation – or should it be referred to as
interpreting? – is not without importance, and in many respects can be
considered one of the more neglected values of stylistic analysis.[5]
Interpreting what the text means is Alex Rodger's chief concern, I
think. But we are given important and crucial insights into *how* that
text of Auden's means. Depending what value we place on interpretation or, indeed, what we understand by interpreting, and what assumptions we operate with when making an interpretation, it may be that
being as fully explicit as possible about the linguistic *process* of
interpretation, and revealing some of the conditions of meaning under
which interpretations of meaning are made, may be as valuable a
service to literary analysis as linguistic interpretations in themselves.

There are also some intriguing questions raised by Deirdre Burton's
and Gill Alexander's fascinating chapters. This may be one of the most
radical and productive of new directions for stylistic analysis of
literature.

If this 'direction' is thought a long way from the concerns of practical
stylistics, then it should serve as a reminder to some literary critics who
consider 'practical stylistics' *radical* that far more radical processes of
literary text investigation are under way. These do not involve linguistics alone; work by structuralists, semioticians, philosophers of language and social ethnographers is utilised. They are processes which go
so far as to challenge the comfortable notion that there is a stability
between text and the world, that words are the sole sources and
repositories of meaning, and that 'meaning' is carried transparently
from the words of the text to the things of the world and vice versa.
(For further discussion, see Belsey, 1980: esp. chs 1–3.)

It is my view that students of literature need a secure basis for
discussion and interpretation of texts. As I have argued, practical
stylistics offers this clear and operable 'way in', and enables real
advances to be made. But the advanced student can develop even
further by considering the extent to which different kinds of texts can
demand different methods, and how a utilisation of different and
relative methods can lead to an appreciation of the plurality of literary
meanings. To this end, aspects of some current work in stylistics can be
of real advantage.

Stylistic analysis is only one way in which literary texts can be
approached, though I think it is a primary one deserving of wider use.
But it only takes a little thought to realise that it is naive to assume that
there will not be diverse and different approaches within stylistics any
more or less than with any other method of literary study.

IV English Literature and Studying English as a Foreign Language

For many years now English literature study has occupied an uncomfortable place in the pedagogy of teaching English as a foreign or second language. Some of the reasons for this are obvious and understandable. It has often been seen as an optional extra, offering a limited access to some great names, or a 'way in' to discussing aspects of English history or culture. From a linguistic viewpoint the argument is often that literary language is so remote from everyday usage that the student can derive little of practical value from contact with literary texts. After all, learning chunks of Shakespeare or even quotations from modern novelists can hardly enhance students' communicative abilities. Tests of comprehension, translation, or reading have involved samples of literary English, but usually as a basis for discussion, for assessing knowledge of vocabulary or for vaguer reasons such as the need for exposure to the 'best' English.

Recently, though, the issue has been reactivated. The publication of Henry Widdowson's seminal book *Stylistics and the Teaching of Literature* (1975) has shifted attention to both the principles and strategies involved in teaching literature as language *in use*, that is, as an extension to the acquisition of communicative skills. Widdowson bypasses the question of the relatively common but for the foreign learner *difficult* deviations and anomalies found in literary language by advocating the comparison of literary discourse with other conventional discourses. By comparing the way language is used in various forms of discourse, the student begins to recognise and perhaps acquire a sense both of the linguistically appropriate and of the differently marked linguistic conventions of use. With increasing awareness of, and sensitivity to, the conventional use of the 'code' he can then compare this with some of the deviant but communicatively resourceful ways in which the 'code' is frequently employed in literature. An appreciation is thus gained of the expressive scope of writers within and beyond the conventional language codes.[6] From this the student can derive greater confidence not only in handling language in a range of different communicative contexts; learning what can be done with language, becoming sensitive to its communicative potential, enables the student to have insights into the nature of the linguistic organisation of that language.

Two further points in this connection have been well made by Short (forthcoming):

> And we should remember that the foreign student has one very positive advantage over his English counterpart, namely that he is familiar . . . with linguistic terminology and analysis precisely because the teaching of English grammar (unlike in England) has never been expunged from the

foreign learner's curriculum. This means that he is better prepared to cope with the detailed technicality of stylistic description so necessary for him to increase his understanding and awareness. But even if this were not the case it would still seem to me that the arguments for explaining via stylistic analysis and other such tools how texts acquire particular meanings through the applications of the general conventions of use are stronger when teaching English literature overseas than at home, precisely *because* the chances of student misunderstanding are greater, and because the only way of guaranteeing with any certainty that misunderstandings are cleared up is through as explicit an analysis as possible.

Finally, the focus of a literary text in itself provides a context in which the learning of aspects of language can be positively enjoyed. In my experience it is a context particularly valued as students' study of English becomes more advanced, but its benefits are apparent at all levels.

It is my hope that teachers and students of English as a foreign language will find several of the chapters here useful to them in pursuit of the above aims and principles. For further reading and examples of these procedures, see Pincas (1980).

V   A Note on the Uses of Literature for Language Study

This is, indeed, no more than a brief note. The point is an obvious one, but it is one which is stated only too rarely. Literature is an example of language in use, and is a context for language use. Studying the language of literary text *as* language can therefore enhance our appreciation of aspects of the different systems of language organisation. A look at the glossary of terms used will illustrate how much grammar can have been learned by the end of the book. Grammar can be taught not in a rote or abstract way but in relation to the way in which writers can creatively exploit or adhere to grammatical rules in order to produce particular literary-aesthetic effects. This is not the place to debate whether grammar should be taught at all or whether knowledge of language rules has any discernible influence on performance skills. Readers are referred elsewhere for such discussion.[7] My point is simply to underline that the integration of language and literature teaching in English classrooms is long overdue. The writers in this book hope to have provided some impetus to that marriage. A considerable number of exercises and points developed throughout this book relate, therefore, to ways in which literature can help language study in the same way that language study can reinforce the analysis of literary text. As Alex Rodger puts it at the end of his contribution to this volume:

The immense pedagogic value of such an approach is that a communicative focus on the problems of comprehension raised by any poem at all inevitably demands discussion of what is communicatively abnormal and grammatically unorthodox, which in turn necessitates constant appeal to what is normal in these respects, especially in some analogous context-of-communication. This means that work in the practical criticism of poetry can be directly linked to the teaching of basic communication skills.

VI Advice on Using This Book: Conclusion

I have been using terms like 'linguistic tools', 'patterns of language', 'grammatical structures', and so on, very casually so far. Language is, of course, highly organised at all sorts of levels and, at least, in terms of the following: sound patterns (phonology); word structure and inter-relations (lexis); meaning relationships (semantics); the structure of linguistic interaction (discourse); situational constraints (context); and so on. In this book there is a heavy concentration on *syntax*. Writers make occasional reference to other features of organisation where it is interesting, but I wanted there to be, in an introductory book of this kind, a focus on a well-specified, interrelated set of concepts and terminology – something both students and teachers can acquire with ease, and *use* with confidence. So, although contributors to this book happily acknowledge that the language in a text can be described in many different ways and with many different descriptive foci, the level of grammar is chosen as our primary orientation because we know that you will be able to get a very long way by talking about the syntax of any particular piece of text.

We do not therefore claim to say 'everything about a text'. We do not claim the only or best interpretation of a text – though we do claim a reasonable and explicit one. Writers in this volume are fully aware, too, that interpreting and, where appropriate, evaluating literary texts requires reference to features of the literary context other than grammar or, indeed, other levels of language organisation.

Necessarily, in a book concerned with the integration of language and literature, there is no space to cover everything. A decision had to be taken, too, to exclude a historical approach to syntax and thus have a focus which is largely on twentieth-century texts. Furthermore, questions of social and historical background, a writer's biography, influences from and allusions to other writers and texts, aesthetic theories, the writer's 'development', are all important considerations and are ignored here because the focus is a linguistic one. However, as I have argued, traditional literary and practical criticism, while often insightful and stimulating, is tentative about its own methodology. Bewildered students of literature have few safe guidelines to follow when asked to do practical work. The linguistic–syntactic approaches adopted here do lay a basis. It is further a basis without which it becomes very difficult to decide *which* aspects of the broader literary context might be *relevant* to developing the interpretation. This is thus a recognition of what is missing from the book, not an apology for it.

There are two further aspects of the approach which should be recognised. One is that not all the writers in the book undertake the application to their texts of syntactic analysis from precisely the same grammatical model. The basic principles of analysis and application remain the same but the approaches and terminology can differ in one or two details. Two main grammars are adhered to: the more 'traditional' grammar of Quirk *et al.* (1972) and Hallidayan systemic grammar – see Berry (1975) and Sinclair (1972). (See Glossary.) Distinctions in the details of these grammars are made in the Glossary. It is common for stylisticians to draw on those aspects of different grammatical models which furnish the greatest descriptive adequacy for the analytical purposes in hand.[8]

Secondly, it will be noted that in a number of cases analysis is of extracts from a work. The dangers involved in inappropriate contextualisation, for example – assuming that extracts can be self-contained and have meanings in isolation from the total work of which they are a part – must be highlighted. A well-argued case against the use of extracts in the teaching of English as a foreign language can be found in Cook (1980). But in activities such as stylistics – where close verbal analysis is a paramount concern – there is often no practicable alternative to a selective use of extracts.

Another anomaly may be the absence of any clear definition of the term 'style'. This is particularly so in the case of a reader in *stylistics*. There are good reasons for this. For one thing, whole books have been devoted to definitions of style, and this is not the place to attempt to summarise or synthesise the many arguments involved. The Bibliography contains numerous suggestions for following up this complex but fascinating area. I think it is generally recognised that the style of a work can depend on linguistic effects produced at a number of different linguistic levels – often simultaneously – and that one fairly crucial factor is our expectations concerning the literary form or genre deployed. Clearly, a poem of only twelve lines entitled 'Sonnet' draws attention to its semiotic properties as a particular kind of poem. Such expectations and effects are also not wholly the result of linguistic means (see also the chapter by Walter Nash). I have also conspicuously avoided questions concerning the relation of 'ordinary' and 'poetic' or literary language. This is a complex question and one which should be squarely faced sooner or later by all students of literature. It is safe to say, I think, that the contributors to this book do not approach analysis of language in literary texts as if the language itself were anything other than a common property (for further reading see especially Werth, 1976 – where the author argues that a Shakespearian sonnet, a poem by William McGonagall and a leader article in *The Times* all exhibit the same degree of patterning – as well as Pratt, 1977: ch. 2). The most useful point which can be made here, then, is to say that in the following chapters the stylistic effects examined are measurable largely in relation to the level of grammar and its norms and expectancies.

For some assistance in understanding some of the principal terms used to describe stylistic effects and the (largely) grammatical patterns which produce them, reference should be made either to the Glossary or to the Bibliography which is graded according to different degrees of analytical and terminological sophistication. Again, differences in metalanguage will be noticed. But it would be unusual if a dozen different writers adhered to precisely the same terms.

Finally, there is the question of the exercises which are appended to most of the chapters in this book. Although they are 'appended' and need not necessarily be worked through, they have been supplied by the editor or the writer of the chapter and have been designed to grow organically from the analytical points or procedures developed in the chapter. The exercises are extensions to the chapter, and it is hoped that undertaking them will primarily reinforce and extend skills of linguistic–stylistic analysis of literature. In that the chapters provide a graded introduction to stylistics, and should preferably be read in the order in which they are arranged in the book, the exercises related to each chapter offer a similar developmental and progressive approach, though it is, of course, impossible to meet everyone's needs in this respect and some will remain unhappy with the sequencing. So teachers using the book or students working on their own will mostly have to decide for themselves on the appropriateness or otherwise of particular exercises to their own objectives. Although exercises are numbered, the order will not always be the most appropriate one. Some exercises are necessarily more complex and difficult than others. All that can be said is that most of the exercises have been used with first-year undergraduate students of English and that considerable benefits seem to have accrued in terms of (*a*) competence in stylistic analysis of literary text, (*b*) systematic awareness of aspects of the nature and organisation of language and (*c*) providing an impetus to students' own creative uses of language by reference to a controlled base in defined linguistic structures. (For discussion of this principle see Sinclair, 1982.) Lastly, it should be noted that in the case of some chapters (for example, those by Rodger and Burton) exercises have not been separately appended because the authors discuss approaches to further teaching and study within the chapter itself.

Notes: Introduction

1 The debate between Roger Fowler and F. W. Bateson originally conducted in the pages of *Essays in Criticism* is most illuminating in this respect. The relevant papers are conveniently reprinted in Fowler (1971).
2 I use the word 'objective' with a clear awareness that, like the word 'scientific', it is a dangerous shorthand but that there is not space in an introduction of this kind to alert the danger properly. Suffice it to say, therefore, that there is, of course, no such thing as an objective criticism. Objectivity can only be purported because there is an ideology at work in whatever literary critical or linguistic pursuit we follow. For example, in its concern for systematic analysis of the language internal to a text, most 'objective' stylistic criticism might be said to betray a 'subjective' exclusion of a socio-historical dimension. A Marxist critic, for example, could find this approach both profoundly relative and subjective. The term is used here, then, loosely to designate that process of fairly open and retrievable attestation described in Section III where it is argued that a practical stylistic approach is at least *more objective* than that of practical criticism and traditional literary criticism, in general.
3 A good example of this is the complimentary reception by established literary critics of Anne Cluysenaar's *Introduction to Literary Stylistics* (1976). See reviews by Holloway (1976) and Bergonzi (1977).
4 See Pearce (1977: 18–26) for detailed discussion of numerous examples from practical critics and practical stylisticians of equations between linguistic forms and literary meanings which result from the particular linguistic form receiving a semantic label attributable more to the literary job the critic feels the aspect of language to be doing than to its intrinsic linguistic function in the language system.
5 For further discussion of this topic see Widdowson (1979).
6 The question of norms needs careful handling, of course. It may be safer to say that there are norms which vary according to different contexts rather than to postulate any single norm. It is also essential not to ignore the norms of language which a text can create for itself. This latter feature is one of the 'stylistic context' (Riffaterre, 1960).
7 See particularly the debate in *English in Education*, vol. 14, nos 1 and 2 (1980), especially articles by Stork, Mittins, Torbe and Doughty.
8 Examples of the application of transformational–generative grammar to stylistic analysis can be found in Traugott and Pratt (1980).

References: Introduction

Belsey, C. (1980), *Critical Practice*, New Accents series (London: Methuen).
Bergonzi, B. (1977), 'Syntax now', *Critical Quarterly*, vol. 19, no. 2, pp. 31–9.
Berry, M. (1975), *Introduction to Systemic Linguistics*, Vol. I (London: Batsford).
Carter, R. A. and Burton, D. (eds) (1982), *Literary Text and Language Study* (London: Edward Arnold).
Cluysenaar, A. (1976), *An Introduction to Literary Stylistics* (London: Batsford).
Cook, G. (1980), 'The use of literary extracts in the teaching of EFL', in Pincas (1980), pp. 55–74.
Crystal, D. (1972), 'Objective and subjective in stylistic analysis', in Kachru, B. and Stahlke, H. (eds), *Current Trends in Stylistics* (Edmonton, Alberta: Linguistic Research Inc.), pp. 103–13.
Eaton, T. (1978), 'Literary semantics: modality and "style" ', *Journal of Literary Semantics*, vol. VII, no. 1, pp. 5–28.
Fowler, R. (1971), *The Languages of Literature* (London: Routledge & Kegan Paul).

Holloway, J. (1976), 'Laws of language', review in *Times Higher Educational Supplement*, no. 247, 16 July, p. 15.

Leavis, F. R. (1966), *Revaluation* (Harmondsworth: Penguin).

Norris, C. (1980), 'Deconstruction and the limits of sense', *Essays in Criticism*, vol. XXX, no. 4, pp. 281–92.

Pearce, R. (1977), *Literary Texts*, Discourse Analysis Monographs No. 3 (Birmingham: University of Birmingham, English Language Research).

Pincas, A. (ed.) (1980), *English Literature for EFL*, Working Documents No. 2 (London: University of London Institute of Education).

Pratt, M. L. (1977), *Toward a Speech Act Theory of Literary Discourse* (Bloomington, Ind.: Indiana University Press).

Riffaterre, M. (1960), 'Stylistic context', *Word*, vol. XVI, pp. 207–18.

Short, M. (forthcoming), 'Stylistics and the teaching of literature: with an example from James Joyce's *Portrait of the Artist as a Young Man*', in *ELT Documents 110: Literature and Language* (London: British Council).

Sinclair, J. McH. (1972), *A Course in Spoken English: Grammar* (London: OUP).

Sinclair, J. McH. (1982), 'The integration of language and literature in the English curriculum', in Carter, R. A. and Burton, D. (eds), *Literary Text and Language Study* (London: Edward Arnold), pp. 9–27.

Traugott, E. C. and Pratt, M. L. (1980), *Linguistics for Students of Literature* (New York: Harcourt Brace Jovanovich).

Vendler, H. (1966), review of Fowler (ed.), 'Essays on style and language', *Essays in Criticism*, no. 16, pp. 457–63.

Werth, P. (1976), 'Roman Jakobson's verbal analysis of poetry', *Journal of Linguistics*, vol. 12, no. 1, pp. 21–73.

Widdowson, H. G. (1975), *Stylistics and the Teaching of Literature* (London: Longman).

Widdowson, H. G. (1979), 'Interpretative procedures and the importance of poetry', in *Explorations in Applied Linguistics* (London: OUP), pp. 153–62.

Introduction to Chapter 1

Henry Widdowson argues that in the case of Larkin's poem 'Mr Bleaney' an analysis of some features of its grammatical organisation is basic to what it has to say. He notes that a blurring of focus occurs across the text as a result of a compounding of both first- and third-person pronouns ('I' and 'he') and of present and past tenses. This blurring mirrors a sense of confusion and uncertainty in the mind of the poem's persona about how he stands in relation to Mr Bleaney. Widdowson reinforces these points by concentrating on a syntactical ambiguity in the final sentence of the poem. By analysing points of difference in how conditional clauses can be sequenced and structured in English, he shows that the syntax enables us to take the meaning of that final sentence two different ways. He goes on to demonstrate that this reflects an ambivalence in the extent to which the speaker identifies with the events he refers to. Such processes can be seen to be an inextricable part of Larkin's dramatisation of a state of mind in the poem. By demonstrating the 'conditional presence' of Mr Bleaney, an interesting and direct equation is made between categories of syntax and important elements of meaning in the text. The chapter is practical stylistic in orientation and enables the reader to give precise definition to otherwise vague and intuitive literary critical statements such as the persona's 'confused involvement' or 'confident detachment'. This is not a total interpretation of the poem; nor does it set out to give one. It is a cogent illustration of how understanding and being articulate about the rules and patterns of language can provide an explicit description of perceived literary effects.

1 The Conditional Presence of Mr Bleaney

H. G. WIDDOWSON

Imagined medieval monsters like the basilisk were weird and wonderful because they were in part familiar and commonplace. The basilisk, or cockatrice, was part reptile and part domestic fowl, and it had a mysterious effect on men. Metaphors can be thought of as monsters of a linguistic kind created from the elements of ordinary language. They also have a mysterious, if less fatal, effect. We are accustomed to thinking of metaphors as composed of lexical parts. What I propose to do in this paper is to consider hybrids of a syntactic kind which have the same effect of estrangement and oblige us to see a new significance in ordinary language and everyday experience. I shall take as my text a poem by Philip Larkin called 'Mr Bleaney'. My argument will be that an appreciation of this poem depends, in some degree at least, on an understanding of the peculiarities of certain grammatical features. These have to do with person, tense and the conditional clause. Here is the poem:

MR BLEANEY

'This was Mr Bleaney's room. He stayed
The whole time he was at the Bodies, till
They moved him.' Flowered curtains, thin and frayed,
Fall to within five inches of the sill,

5 Whose window shows a strip of building land,
Tussocky, littered. 'Mr Bleaney took
My bit of garden properly in hand.'
Bed, upright chair, sixty-watt bulb, no hook

Behind the door, no room for books or bags –
10 'I'll take it.' So it happens that I lie
Where Mr Bleaney lay, and stub my fags
On the same saucer-souvenir, and try

Stuffing my ears with cotton-wool, to drown
The jabbering set he egged her on to buy.
15 I know his habits – what time he came down,
His preference for sauce to gravy, why

> He kept on plugging at the four aways –
> Likewise their yearly frame: the Frinton folk
> Who put him up for summer holidays,
> 20   And Christmas at his sister's house in Stoke.
>
> But if he stood and watched the frigid wind
> Tousling the clouds, lay on the fusty bed
> Telling himself that this was home, and grinned,
> And shivered, without shaking off the dread
>
> 25   That how we live measures our own nature,
> And at his age having no more to show
> Than one hired box should make him pretty sure
> He warranted no better, I don't know.

The first thing to notice is that two scenes are presented here which have the same spatial setting, in that they both occur in Mr Bleaney's room, but distinct temporal settings. The first scene involves two characters: the landlady and the new lodger. It is presented in theatrical mode with dialogue and description of décor: the flowered curtains and the window with a view of building land appear like stage scenery. The second scene, which begins in the second half of line 10, involves only the lodger. Or so it seems at first sight. Later in the discussion we shall find that we need to revise this view. Meanwhile, let us note that, although the two scenes represent different occasions, they both apparently take place in the present:

> . . . Flowered curtains, thin and frayed
> *Fall* to within five inches of the sill,
>
> Whose window *shows*. . . .
> (Scene 1)
>
> So it *happens* that I *lie*
> . . . and stub my fags
> (Scene 2)

Thus, the first person, whose point of view informs the poem as a whole (the new lodger) is simultaneously present, in both a temporal and spatial sense, in two different periods of time.

But he is also present in two different ways. As I have indicated, the first scene is theatrically described and, although the lodger appears in it, it is presented in terms of his detached observations. In this sense he is apart from the scene. In the second scene, on the other hand, he is a part of it, and now the present tense is used to describe not his observations but his actions. His role shifts from onlooker to participant. So, although the two scenes share the same spatial setting, the first-person lodger's relationship with the setting is different in each case.

I have spoken of two characters: the landlady and the new lodger. There is another character of course: the previous lodger, Mr Bleaney himself. Unlike the others, he is a third-person figure, and furthermore never actually appears in the present. Everything about him is reported in the simple past tense, in both scenes. Thus, his existence is associated with the same spatial setting as the two scenes presented in the poem, but his temporal setting is in the past. Or is it? For just as the present lodger appears in the present in two different ways in the two scenes, so the previous lodger appears in the past in two different ways. In the first scene, reference to him occurs exclusively in the landlady's direct speech, and for the prospective lodger, therefore, his actions are to be noted in detachment, like the details of the room. He is, as it were, part of the scenery. In the second scene, on the other hand, reference to Mr Bleaney and his activities is made by the new lodger in relation to his own activities. Mr Bleaney has come into the reality of the new lodger's own present life. He is associated now with the physical props of the setting with which the lodger is now fully engaged as a participant:

> . . . So it happens that I lie
> Where Mr Bleaney lay, and stub my fags
> On the same saucer-souvenir, and try
>
> Stuffing my ears with cotton-wool, to drown
> The jabbering set he egged her on to buy.

In the first scene, then, the physical setting and Mr Bleaney, though described in the present and past tense respectively, are alike in being dissociated from the lodger, the detached observer. In the second scene, the past existence of Mr Bleaney converges with the present existence of the person replacing him; and aspects of the physical setting (the saucer-souvenir, the jabbering radio set) are a focus of this convergence. First and third persons, present and past time, so clearly distinct in the first scene, become fused in the second. The first-person present of the new lodger merges with the third-person past of the previous one. Mr Bleaney, though not present, is nevertheless a presence in the second scene of the poem.

The consequence of this convergence of person and time reference is worked out in the last two stanzas. And here we come to the significance of the conditional clause. Up to line 20, the syntax of the poem is simple enough and easy to process: it realises a serial presentation of observations about Mr Bleaney and his room. Up to this point, the new lodger still retains his detachment to some degree, expressed in ironic undertones, even though Mr Bleaney has begun to encroach on his individual identity. The syntax of the last two stanzas, however, is complicated in the extreme. And as the syntax changes so does the attitude expressed. These two stanzas consist of one complex sentence whose completion is deferred by one syntactic elaboration after another until the very last three words of the poem. This sentence begins with what appears to be a conditional clause:

> But if he stood and watched the frigid wind. . . .

But *is* it a conditional clause? The initial *if* seems to indicate that it is. On the other hand, there are other facts we must note that indicate that it is not.

If clauses in English are not necessarily adverbial. They can also be nominal.[1] Consider the following examples:

> (1)   If he stood here, he would see the clouds.
> (2)   I do not know if he stood here and saw the clouds.

In the first of these sentences, the *if* clause is adverbial, but in the second it is nominal, functioning as object. Hence *if* can be replaced by *whether* in the second sentence but not in the first. Compare:

> (3)   *Whether he stood here, he would see the clouds.
> (4)   I do not know whether he stood here and saw the clouds.

There are other features which distinguish the two types of *if* clause and which have a direct bearing on the convergence of person and time that I have referred to. First, the normal, or unmarked, order of appearance relative to the other constituents of the sentence is different in each case. Thus, although the adverbial may precede or follow the main clause, the nominal must normally follow subject and verb to complete the main-clause structure of which it is an intrinsic part. Thus, the following, as an alternative version of sentence 2, exhibits a marked and so abnormal ordering:

> (5)   *If he stood here and saw the clouds I do not know.

Such a sentence presents us with an interpretative problem. On the one hand, the fronting of the *if* clause disposes us to think of it as an adverbial but, on the other hand, the normal transitivity of the verb *know* leads us to interpret the clause as its object and the sentence, therefore, as a version of sentence 2. In other words, sequence inclines us to understand the *if* clause as adverbial but structure inclines us to understand it as nominal.

And so it is with the *if* clause of the last two stanzas of this poem. We begin by assuming that it is an adverbial clause of condition since it occurs initially, and we therefore expect the main clause to appear quite promptly afterwards. This appearance is delayed by a prolonged elaboration of the conditional clause itself, and our expectation is dulled by this intervening elaboration which seems to increase in obscurity and inconsequence as it develops. Then comes the main clause to provide the necessary syntactic completion, and it takes us by surprise because it requires us to recategorise everything that has preceded as a nominal clause, a displaced object of the verb *know*. This has the effect of making us reconsider the structure of the syntax and of directing our attention to what is actually being said in the meandering phrases that precede. By initially interpreting the *if* clause as an adverbial we necessarily assign it subsidiary status. But this is inconsistent with the elaboration, which provides more and more information and so approximates more and more to the function of a main clause. The effect of this is that the reader initially assumes a pitch pattern appropriate to a subsidiary clause, and then, as information builds up, he either attempts to contain it within one tone group, which results in a dull monotone tailing off into inconsequence, or he varies the pattern to give independent value to the units of information as if they had main-clause status. The reader, faced with this difficulty, really does not know where he is.

But neither does the lodger. The syntactic complexity is a direct expression of his own confusion, a confusion which has its origins in the convergence of person and time in the earlier lines. This is further borne out by another distinction between adverbial and nominal *if* clauses that has yet to be mentioned. It has to do with the value of the past tense in such constructions. In the case of the nominal clause, as exemplified by sentence 2, the simple past tense is used to make reference to a possible event in past time. This event may or may not have taken place, but the temporal context is firmly fixed in the past. With the adverbial clause, however, matters are somewhat different. In this case, the past tense may be associated either with a temporal context in the past or with a temporal context in the present. Compare sentence 1 with sentence 6:

(1) If he stood here, he would see the clouds.
(6) If he stood here, he would have seen the clouds.

The utterance of sentence 1 expresses the hypothetical possibility of the third person appearing in the present: it refers to a state of affairs alternative to that which actually obtains. Sentence 6, on the other hand, refers to a possible state of affairs in the past. Since in the poem there is no indication in a main clause as to which of these values for the past tense is intended, the ambiguity remains unresolved. We do not know as we read through these last two stanzas whether reference is being made to a possible state of affairs in the past or in the present. We do not know whether the past tense in the expression *lay on the fusty bed* (line 22) has the same value as the expression *Where Mr Bleaney lay* (line 11) or whether it does not rather serve to invoke Mr Bleaney's presence, and so to fuse his identity with that of his successor. For, although all of the activities referred to in the last two stanzas are, by virtue of the *if* clause, represented as hypothetical activities of Mr Bleaney, as phrase follows phrase the reader recognises that what is being expressed are the present lodger's own actual experiences, for why else would he be led to wonder whether Mr Bleaney underwent them?

The *if* clause, then, is in this poem a syntactic hybrid: part adverbial and part nominal. If we read it, in retrospect, by reference to normal structure, we derive something like the following meaning:

> I do not know whether Mr Bleaney stood and watched the
> frigid wind tousling the clouds, etc.

And this sets up a parallel with what is expressed in lines 15 ff. Thus

> I *know* his habits – what time he came down,
> His preference for sauce to gravy, why, etc.

contrasts with

> But if he stood and watched, etc., I *don't* know.

If we read the last verses by reference to sequence, however, retain our adverbial interpretation and ignore the normal structural implications of the last three words, then these words themselves constitute an independent main clause with *know* as an intransitive verb requiring no object:

> I don't know.

This is an expression of resignation to a general state of unknowing, a failure to understand. It is as if the complexity of the preceding lines, after the simple detachment of the earlier parts of the poem, creates a confusion which cannot be resolved. There are, then, two possible ways of interpreting this clause, but it is not a matter of choosing one and rejecting the other. They co-exist. The clause is both adverbial and nominal, and so neither, a newly created syntactic metaphor devised to express precisely a confusion of thought and attitude which could not be otherwise expressed. The meaning depends on the ambiguity remaining unresolved.

I have tried to show how this poem moves from confident detachment to confused involvement, and how this development is mediated through certain peculiarities of language use. The normally distinct categories of first and third person conflate so that the identity of Mr Bleaney is superimposed on that of the present lodger. They begin by occupying different worlds, one in the past and the other in the present, but end up in the same world, both occupants of Mr Bleaney's room. This is a world which is both past and present, both actual and hypothetical, both experienced and observed. Such a world is not one which is given sanction by normal language usage, and so the poet has to create it by devising new linguistic categories which must of their nature be intrinsically ambiguous. In this way he can directly represent a reality in a different dimension from that which is recorded by convention. And this is where the basilisk and Mr Bleaney have their being.

Note: Chapter 1

1   'I do not know if he stood here . . .' could also be classified as a reported clause (see Sinclair, 1972: 30–4). But the point being made here is not affected.

Suggestions for Further Work: Chapter 1

1   As a writing exercise produce an alternative version to 'Mr Bleaney' by changing the tense from present to past throughout the first five stanzas. What new patterns of meaning are produced? Another useful example would be to record and transcribe part of a sports commentary (e.g. football, rugby, tennis) and rewrite it into the simple past tense. What happens to where we are placed in relation to the events of the commentary?

Further, what happens when the contrast is between present tense and perfect tense (e.g. *have* gone)? As an example of this contrast, examine the effects produced in Hopkins's poem 'Heaven-Haven'.

Examine the conflation and interpenetration of past and present in many of Hardy's poems. Good examples are 'The Self-Unseeing', 'The Musical Box', 'At Castle Boterel' and especially 'The Oxen' with its interesting conditionals. For an analysis of shifts in tense and the effects produced by them in Yeats's poem 'Coole Park and Ballylee', see Cluysenaar (1976: 82–4).

Finally, returning to 'Mr Bleaney', compare the poem with Anthony Thwaite's 'Mr Cooper' – a not dissimilar poem, but one written wholly in the past tense. Why?

2   For further investigation of clause structure and sequence on patterns of meaning, the following poems make useful examples: Robert Graves, 'Flying Crooked'; W. H. Auden, 'The Wanderer' and 'Musée des Beaux Arts'. In 'The Wanderer' to what extent do difficulties in resolving which clauses are dependent on each other, and in what order we should take

them, reflect uncertainties as to which actions and events predominate? Is the poem's subject acting for himself, or acted upon, or both simultaneously? In 'Musée des Beaux Arts' why is the subject (Icarus) of the painting which is described in the second stanza positioned in this kind of clause structure:

> . . . and the expensive delicate ship that must have seen
> Something amazing, a boy falling out of the sky,
> Had somewhere to get to and sailed calmly on.

For a discussion of the Graves poem, see Cluysenaar (1976: 57–9).

Finally, on the question of conditional clauses compare that analysed here in 'Mr Bleaney' with those in Larkin's 'Poetry of Departures'. What are the differences and similarities?

On the other hand, compare the structure of clauses in a poem like 'Mr Bleaney' with those in Ted Hughes's poem 'Hawk Roosting'. Here there are just main clauses throughout. Towards the end each clause fits with each line of each stanza. There are no concessions, qualifications, or conditions on what is said. What might be some of the differences in the states of mind being dramatised in the two poems?

References: Chapter 1

Cluysenaar, A. (1976), *Introduction to Literary Stylistics* (London: Batsford).
Sinclair, J. McH. (1972), *A Course in Spoken English: Grammar* (London: OUP).

Introduction to Chapter 2

In this chapter Mary Mason demonstrates how a recognition of one group of related linguistic features can provide the 'point of entry' for literary interpretation. In this case the main focus is on deixis: formal devices in language for indicating how the speaker is related to what he refers to. In this text Mary Mason finds deixis to be central to the effects achieved by Dickens at the opening of *Little Dorrit*. She finds such features contribute above all to a feeling of disorientation. Other linguistic categories such as transitivity reinforce this. She argues that the kinds of meaning established in the opening paragraphs work in varying degrees across the whole novel, and in an examination of the final paragraphs of the text shows how an interpretation of the ending requires recognition of stylistic echoes and recurrences from the opening passage. The chapter is a good example of how seemingly insignificant details of language can, when analysed systematically, be shown to be organised in such a way that whole patterns of meaning depend on them. It is an example of practical stylistics in operation.

2 Deixis: a Point of Entry to *Little Dorrit*

MARY MASON

Writing of the interpretation of a work of art, Leo Spitzer describes how the critic 'may make the trip from language or style to the soul'. He convincingly illustrates how the observation of a tiny point of grammar may lead to the unravelling of a whole world view expressed by a writer through his art. 'This first step', he says, 'is the awareness of having been struck by a detail, followed by a conviction that this detail is connected basically with the work of art' (Spitzer, 1970).

The approach to *Little Dorrit* which I shall describe here follows this pattern. A point of syntax which is normally taken for granted gave me the point of entry to the meaning of the first four paragraphs of *Little Dorrit* and thence to the whole novel.

It shows how a linguistic insight may be of service in illuminating a particular work of art. It does not claim to establish a methodology applicable to all literature. While I am sure that what follows formulates an objective fact about the syntax of the opening section of *Little Dorrit*, I am not aware as yet of any substitute for intuition in relating this fact to the meaning of the novel as a whole.

After elucidating the first four paragraphs of *Little Dorrit*, I shall make a few suggestions about how my interpretation might be articulated into the novel as a whole. I shall conclude by looking in rather less detail at the end of *Little Dorrit*, which approximately 900 pages later depicts a world transformed by the events of the novel from the one described at the beginning. To some extent, this throws some light on the extraordinary beauty of the last words of this novel.

BOOK THE FIRST. POVERTY
CHAPTER I
Sun and Shadow

Thirty years ago, Marseilles lay burning in the sun, one day.

A blazing sun upon a fierce August day was no greater rarity in southern France then, than at any other time, before or since. Everything in Marseilles, and about Marseilles, had stared at the fervid sky, and been stared at in return, until a staring habit had become universal there. Strangers were stared out of countenance by staring white houses, staring white walls, staring white streets, staring tracts of arid road, staring hills from which verdure was burnt away. The only things to be seen not fixedly staring and glaring were the vines drooping under their load of grapes. These did occasionally wink a little, as the hot air barely moved their faint leaves.

There was no wind to make a ripple on the foul water within the harbour, or on the beautiful sea without. The line of demarcation between the two colours, black and blue, showed the point which the pure sea would not pass; but it lay as quiet as the abominable pool, with which it never mixed. Boats without awnings were too hot to touch; ships blistered at their moorings; the stones of the quays had not cooled, night or day, for months. Hindoos, Russians, Chinese, Spaniards, Portuguese, Englishmen, Frenchmen, Genoese, Neapolitans, Venetians, Greeks, Turks, descendants from all the builders of Babel, come to trade at Marseilles, sought the shade alike – taking refuge in any hiding-place from a sea too intensely blue to be looked at, and a sky of purple, set with one great flaming jewel of fire.

The universal stare made the eyes ache. Towards the distant line of Italian coast, indeed, it was a little relieved by light clouds of mist, slowly rising from the evaporation of the sea; but it softened nowhere else. Far away the staring roads, deep in dust, stared from the hill-side, stared from the hollow, stared from the interminable plain. Far away the dusty vines overhanging wayside cottages, and the monotonous wayside avenues of parched trees without shade, drooped beneath the stare of earth and sky. So did the horses with drowsy bells, in long files of carts, creeping slowly towards the interior; so did their recumbent drivers, when they were awake, which rarely happened; so did the exhausted labourers in the fields. Everything that lived or grew, was oppressed by the glare; except the lizards, passing swiftly over rough stone walls, and the cicala, chirping his dry hot chirp, like a rattle. The very dust was scorched brown, and something quivered in the atmosphere as if the air itself were panting.

Blinds, shutters, curtains, awnings, were all closed and drawn to keep out the stare. Grant it but a chink or keyhole, and it shot in like a white-hot arrow. The churches were the freest from it. To come out of the twilight of pillars and arches – dreamily dotted with winking lamps, dreamily peopled with ugly old shadows piously dozing, spitting, and begging – was to plunge into a fiery river, and swim for life to the nearest strip of shade. So, with people lounging and lying wherever shade was, with but little hum of tongues or barking of dogs, with occasional jangling of discordant church bells, and rattling of vicious drums, Marseilles, a fact to be strongly smelt and tasted, lay broiling in the sun one day.

At one level the first four paragraphs pose no problem. It is clearly a very hot day in Marseilles, and the brilliance and heat outside are in stark contrast to the dark and cold of the 'villainous prison' of the fifth paragraph. So much is indicated by the chapter title 'Sun and Shadow'. The problem lies in the fact that the world outside the prison is anything but an agreeable one: it is on the contrary a disturbing and disorienting vision.

This is created – obviously deliberately and for reasons I shall discuss later – by an extraordinary lack of deixis. John Lyons (1968: 275) describes deixis as 'the orientational features of language relative to the time and place of the utterance'. Such features include person, demonstrative and locative expressions, and tense. They are normally crucial at the beginning of a novel since there is no context beyond the writing itself to which the reader may refer.

Yet here, as soon as one expectation is set up by a deictic utterance, it is contradicted by the next. Let us take time first. A novel would normally begin: 'One day thirty years ago . . .', 'one day' indicating the beginning of the story at a point in time chosen by the writer, and 'thirty years ago' relating that point to the time of writing. By separating and reversing these phrases, Dickens takes from us the anticipated focus. Thirty years ago from when? When was the one day? In the second sentence 'then' seems to pinpoint time, but the hope of further definition is dissipated in 'than at any other time, before or since'. Since the 'then' can only pick up the temporal uncertainty of the first sentence, we are left asking: before or since what? And 'any other time' is accorded the same status as 'then'. The peculiarity of the syntax is suggested by the necessary proliferation of commas round these phrases. Also, the ambiguity of the time is not cleared up by the tenses of the verbs. The general past tense is used throughout, so leaving it unclear whether the actions take place over a short or long period: for this we rely on adverbs of time, which are missing (e.g. '. . . with which it never mixed'. Compare '. . . with which it never mixed that day/for weeks/for centuries'.) Where the past perfect is used, the point of reference is uncertain and the action continues in the present anyway ('Everything . . . had stared', 'The stones . . . had not cooled'). One occasion on which if the perfect tense had been used it would have indicated a completed action is: 'from which verdure had been burnt away.' Instead Dickens gives us a timeless copula and adjective: 'was burnt away'.

If time is uncertain in the first two paragraphs, so is place, in that the focus on Marseilles is not made clear. Marseilles, after all, can be a point on a map, a city seen from above, with or without the adjoining land and/or sea, or a city experienced by a person walking through its streets. If this passage were translated into terms of film, the camera would have to be somewhere quite specific. Words can obfuscate, however. As soon as we think we have a clear angle – 'Everything *in* Marseilles . . .' – it is confused by a different perspective: 'and *about* Marseilles'. Then we seem to be a person in the 'streets' of the city, which in the next phrase have become 'roads' in the surrounding countryside. From the third paragraph limits are set: 'towards the Italian coast'. This is vague enough, and indeed literally misty, but it suggests a horizon for the first time. The spatial uncertainty continues with the repeated 'far away' (from where?). In this paragraph, however, the roads which have hitherto led nowhere – they have only 'stared' – lead at last to 'the interior', indefinite enough but less disturbing than nothing.

In each of the first three paragraphs, moreover, the shifting perspective moves from a distant prospect to a close-up. Each time, however, the close-up turns out to have no particular significance: the grapes of paragraph one and the lizard of paragraph three are dead ends. So, indeed, are the stones of the quays in paragraph two, and here the angle is turned (crucially) back to the sky.

Confusion about time and place is compounded by lack of people. There is no person on whom we can focus. The title 'Sun and Shadow' and the first three sentences could be descriptive of a world which had been unpeopled. The first people mentioned are 'strangers', but they are there only to have their humanity go unrecognised, being 'stared out of countenance' by the place. In the second paragraph a sample of all the nations on earth are listed in indeterminate number – plural with no article. As so often in this passage, we feel we might be working towards a point of view since the list begins with (to us) exotic nationalities and, moving through more familiar European ones, arrives at ourselves, 'Englishmen'; then at the natives of the setting, 'Frenchmen'. Once again our hypothesis is falsified as the list continues, moving away again through Europeans to the entirely alien 'Turks'. Still, humanity is clearly present at last, in large numbers, and the inhuman 'shadow' of the title has changed to the human 'shade'.

The third paragraph ranges over the same hot landscape as the first, but this time it is a peopled landcape. It is still indeterminate – and painful: 'The universal stare made the eyes ache' (anybody's eyes). The link with the first paragraph is made by the repetition of 'stare'. The transition is gradual, beginning with 'Italian', a human concept linking with and limiting the survey of world population in the second paragraph. The roads do not merely stare in an unfocused manner but are 'deep in dust', a phrase which puts us in the position of a traveller upon them. The vines, too, are now seen as part of human habitation, 'overhanging wayside cottages'. And the roads are perceived fully from a human point of view, as 'monotonous . . . avenues . . . without shade'. Other travellers besides ourselves are upon the road – horses, carts and drivers; and there are labourers in the fields.

The fourth paragraph moves us abruptly (by using passive verbs: 'were all closed and drawn') from outside in the sun to inside trying to avoid the sun. We are now clearly in the city and at human eye- and ear-level. It is worth noting here that we move from the total silence of the first two paragraphs (broken only by the suggestion of legendary noise with the mention of Babel) through the quiet sounds of the third ('drowsy bells' and the chirp of the cicala) to the fully human cacophony of the end of the fourth paragraph, in which the 'rattle' of the cicala has been magnified to 'the rattling of vicious drums'. The clarity of vision, of feeling (heat and cool) and hearing is completed by the remaining senses – 'a fact to be strongly smelt and tasted' – as the last sentence catches us up and with a swift variation on the opening sentence place and time are made clear: 'Marseilles . . . lay broiling in the sun one day'. The point of view is fixed and, senses alert, we are ready for the story to unfold.

Another facet of the lack of person in the opening paragraphs is created by that feature of Dickens's style pointed out by a number of critics. That is the application of words which are normally used of inanimate objects to animate beings and vice versa. In the first paragraph people ('strangers') are merely objects of the verb 'stare', while houses, walls and streets 'stare' and the vines (or grapes) 'wink'. The leaves of the vine are 'faint'. And at the end of the third paragraph the air seems to be 'panting'.

There is a further disconcerting lack of focus in that many of the key verbs are reciprocal: everything stares at everything else. In the opening sentence we are further confused by the verb 'burn', which is both transitive and intransitive – is Marseilles burning by spontaneous combustion or is the sun burning it?

If purposeful activity is characteristic of human beings, the inhuman stillness of the early part of the passage is partly created by the lack of transitive verbs.[1] There are many intransitive verbs ('stare', 'droop', 'wink', 'rise', 'soften') and stative passives ('were stared out of countenance', 'it was a little relieved', 'everything was oppressed'). Where there is an active transitive verb, it is negated ('*no* wind to make a ripple'; 'the point which the pure sea would *not* pass'; 'the . . . pool, with which it *never* mixed'; 'a sea *too* intensely blue to be looked at', 'the hot air *barely* moved their faint leaves'). When animate beings enter the scene, the verbs remain intransitive (horses creep, people are dozing, spitting and begging, lounging and lying). The above examples are not exhaustive, but the only exceptions to the intransitive verbs, stative passives and negated active verbs applied to things and people alike are extremely significant: 'Hindoos . . . sought the shade' in the second paragraph, and this meaning is picked up and expanded in the fourth – 'to plunge into a fiery river, and swim for life to the nearest strip of shade'.

Before examining the significance of these exceptions, there are further disconcerting contradictions to be noted. One is that a number of sentences begin with a promise of activity only to peter out in a loss of focus (e.g. 'A *blazing* sun upon a *fierce* August day . . .') or in a negative (e.g. 'These did occasionally wink *a little*, as the hot air *barely* moved their faint leaves', 'The line of demarcation . . . with which it *never* mixed'). Another odd effect is that the repetition of words and structures, far from being cumulative, seems to wash away all meaning, leaving an impression of impotent violence. This is most true of 'stare', but also of 'far away', and 'so did' in the third paragraph. This deliberate obliteration of meaning is reinforced by the repetition of the word 'white' (the negation of colour), the yoking of 'blue' and 'black', and the recurrence of the words 'everything' and 'universal'. This lack of differentiation ('Where everybody's somebody, then no one's anybody,' as Gilbert truly says in a different context) gives a sense of unreality to the whole scene. This feeling is maintained in the fourth, more focused paragraph by 'dreamily dotted with winking lamps, dreamily peopled with ugly old shadows'.

As the syntax and vocabulary defeat one's expectations, so does the symbolism. Since the villainous prison turns out to be unremittingly dark and sordid, one expects the world outside to be pleasant by contrast. In fact, as we have seen, the first paragraph depicts an intolerable and inhuman landscape. Since the land is so unbearable, perhaps the sea will offer a smiling contrast, but it transpires that it is 'too intensely blue to be looked at'. More perturbing, the harbour, a traditional symbol of safety, is an 'abominable pool', where ships blister at their moorings. If the landscape without people is intolerable, humanity in the shape of 'exhausted labourers' and 'ugly old shadows' offers no comfort. If the silence is insupportable, the 'jangling of discordant church bells, and rattling of vicious drums' is harder to bear. If the 'white-hot arrow' of sunlight is to be avoided, the churches with their 'ugly old shadows piously dozing, spitting, and begging' offer a comfortless alternative.

It is, in fact, a passage whose dissonant polarities create an arid world which is, both literally and symbolically, identical to that created by different means in the last book of *The Waste Land*. The exceptions to the frustration of focus referred to earlier make this clear. At the end of the second paragraph the narrowing focus is suddenly reversed and the reader finds himself face to face with 'a sea too intensely blue to be looked at, and a sky of purple, set with one great flaming jewel of fire'. Purple and jewels are the attributes of majesty, and the king here can only be God. This is not part of Christian iconography only – 'hapless Semele' was consumed by fire when she dared to gaze upon the Godhead. And this is the harsh and terrible God of the Old Testament, ruling a world in which 'a line of demarcation' is drawn between 'the pure sea' and 'the abominable pool', which never mix – the damned are left to their fate. The 'builders of Babel' and 'the interminable plain' (with its city) as well as the word 'abominable' all suggest the Old Testament. In this pitiless world humanity seeks to escape from the sun and swims 'for life to the nearest strip of shade'.

We see here how the macrostructure of the entire novel is adumbrated in the microstructure of these opening paragraphs. The feeling of frustration generated here is the dominant mood of the narrative (painfully reflected, for instance, in the chapters 'Nobody's Weakness', 'Nobody's Rival', 'Nobody's State of Mind' which describes Arthur Clennam's unrequited love, or in the brilliant absurdity of his futile struggles with the Circumlocution Office). The dissonant symbolism of sea and harbour, sun and shadow is articulated into the feelings of characters which seem always out of phase: Little Dorrit and her father, Arthur Clennam and Flora Finching, and the most painful scene of all between William Dorrit and John Chivery in chapter 18 of part II, for example. The scene of unreality sketched in here is continued in the depiction of the empty world of fashion and Society, the fortunes of Mr Merdle, Affery's hallucinations and Mr Dorrit's castles in the air. The roads which lead nowhere become real roads which take the Dorrits and the Meagles on their pointless wanderings. Above all, the full significance of the major image of prisons which human beings make for themselves and others is foreshadowed in the flight of humanity from the sun ('Human kind cannot bear very much reality').

Here is the final part of the novel:

And they were married, with the sun shining on them through the painted figure of Our Saviour on the window. And they went into the very room where Little Dorrit had slumbered after her party, to sign the Marriage Register. And there, Mr Pancks (destined to be chief clerk to Doyce and Clennam, and afterwards partner in the house), sinking the Incendiary in the peaceful friend, looked in at the door to see it done, with Flora gallantly supported on one arm and Maggy on the other, and a back-ground of John Chivery and father, and other turnkeys, who had run round for the moment, deserting the parent Marshalsea for its happy child. Nor had Flora the least signs of seclusion upon her, notwithstanding her recent declaration; but on the contrary was wonderfully smart, and enjoyed the ceremonies mightily, though in a fluttered way.

Little Dorrit's old friend held the inkstand as she signed her name, and the clerk paused in taking off the good clergyman's surplice, and all the witnesses looked on with special interest. 'For, you see,' said Little Dorrit's old friend, 'this young lady is one of our curiosities, and has come now to the third volume of our Registers. Her birth is in what I call the first volume; she lay asleep on this very floor, with her pretty head on what I call the second volume; and she's now a-writing her little name as a bride, in what I call the third volume.'

They all gave place when the signing was done, and Little Dorrit and her husband walked out of the church alone. They paused for a moment on the steps of the portico, looking at the fresh perspective of the street in the autumn morning sun's bright rays, and then went down.

Went down into a modest life of usefulness and happiness. Went down to give a mother's care, in the fullness of time, to Fanny's neglected children no less than to their own, and to leave that lady going into Society for ever and a day. Went down to give a tender nurse and friend to Tip for some few years, who was never vexed by the great exactions he made of her in return for the riches he might have given her if he had ever had them, and who lovingly closed his eyes upon the Marshalsea and all its blighted fruits. They went quietly down into the roaring streets, inseparable and blessed; and as they passed along in sunshine and in shade, the noisy and the eager, and the arrogant and the froward and the vain, fretted, and chafed, and made their usual uproar.

This is a moment of reconciliation. *Little Dorrit* is a painful book, relieved only occasionally by comedy, but it ends in marriage – that is, in consummation and renewal. Little Dorrit is married from the Marshalsea in the presence of the turnkeys, who have 'deserted the parent Marshalsea for its happy child'. So past and present are in harmony – the room where the register is signed reminds us of Little Dorrit's 'party', where she passed unscathed through the extremes of poverty and sordidness. And the complement of love, which is death, is also suggested: Little Dorrit's birth is recorded in the first volume, her marriage in the third, and she lay her head on the second volume, which is the Burial Register. Arthur is middle-aged already and the sun's rays, though bright, are those of autumn. Tip's wasted life was to last only 'some few years' before he 'lovingly closed his eyes upon the Marshalsea and all its blighted fruits'. This cannot mean that he died in the Marshalsea; it must mean that figuratively he never left it. It is a way of reminding us of the dominant image of the novel right at the end. The 'blighted fruits' remind us perhaps of the dusty grapes of the opening, which have been expanded into the distorted lives of so many of the characters. The breakdown of meaning expressed again by a failure of deixis in the opening passage is picked up in the summary of Tip's and Fanny's future careers. Fanny is embarked on an initiation which contradictorily has no end (*going into* Society *for ever and a day*). The futility of Tip's attachment to wealth is embodied in the unfulfilled conditionals: 'the riches he might have given her if he had ever had them'.

The last sentence of *Little Dorrit* is one of the most moving and beautiful endings in English literature and, as it is not a fragile beauty to be destroyed by analysis, I will attempt to begin to account for its effectiveness. In large part it is derived from what has gone before. The main force, however, comes from the accumulation of adjectives for erring humanity. They suggest immense activity but are without their complements, which might indicate that something had been achieved (noisy in what? eager for what? vain of what?). The active but intransitive verbs 'fretted and chafed' suggest the same meaningless activity. Above all, the accumulation of 'ands' in this last sentence, first coupling then tripling, indicates mere conjunction without meaning. Those quiet characters, Little Dorrit and Arthur Clennam, disappear into the 'roaring streets' and are not likely to have much effect on the rest of us. It is not the irremediable wickedness of Rigaud which, on the whole, makes for frustration and waste, but being 'noisy, eager, arrogant, froward and vain', adjectives which we must all subscribe to. The last phrase, 'their usual uproar', brings us back to the dissonant unfocused world of the beginning of the novel, created by similar syntax and semantics, the world which is the normal state of man.

Note: Chapter 2

1 See Halliday (1971). Also the chapter by Kennedy in this volume [Ed.].

Suggestions for Further Work: Chapter 2

1 Find out for yourself how deixis works. Take a report from a newspaper and substitute 'a' for 'the' or 'the' for 'a' and see what changes result. Try altering the 'orientational' features of the language so that (a) the writer seems subjectively bound up with what he is describing, (b) the writer is impersonal and distant from his points of reference. What elements of language have you had to change and why?
2 Try writing a description or account of your actions in getting up in the morning using only parts of your body or inanimate 'things' as the subjects of your sentences. What effects result from this? Repeat the exercise using only intransitive verbs.
3 Compare the function of deixis here with that employed by Hemingway in 'Cat in the Rain'. See Ron Carter's discussion of this in this volume. How is the meaning of the respective passages altered? In what ways are some similarities discernible?
4 The kinds of patterns of transitivity discerned here might usefully be set against those described in the chapters by Chris Kennedy and Walter Nash. In terms of what is described here of 'animacy' relations (that is, inanimate objects having animate verbs and vice versa), have a look at the opening paragraphs of Joseph Conrad's novel *The Secret Agent* and explore whether similar patterns of meaning are set up or not. Apply what Mary Mason says to chapter 3 of *Little Dorrit*, which describes Arthur Clennam's 'view' of London. How applicable is it? Or to passages such as this later in the same novel?

> It was now summertime; a grey, hot, dusty evening. They rode to the top of Oxford Street, and there alighting, dived in among the great streets of melancholy stateliness, and the little streets that try to be as stately and succeed in being more melancholy, of which there is a labyrinth near Park Lane. Wilderness of corner houses, with barbarous old porticoes and appurtenances, horrors that came into existence under some wrong-headed person in some wrong-headed time, still demanding the blind admiration of all ensuing generations and determined to do so until they tumbled down; frowned upon the twilight. Parasite little tenements, with the cramp in their whole frame, from the dwarf-hills in the mews, made the evening doleful. Rickety dwellings of undoubted fashion, but

of a capacity to hold nothing comfortably except a dismal smell, looked like the last result of the great mansions breeding in-and-in; and, where their little supplementary bows and balconies were supported on thin iron columns, seemed to be scroufously resting upon crutches. Here and there a Hatchment, with the whole science of Heraldry in it, loomed down upon the street, like an Archbishop discoursing on Vanity. The shops, few in number, made no show, for popular opinion was as nothing to them.

5   As far as the deictic function of tense is concerned, attempt an opening to a story by either adopting an 'unconventional' tense or constantly varying time of occurrence for the events you depict. How far have you produced something similar in meaning to the opening to *Little Dorrit*? Consider the various kinds of distancing effect brought about by the adoption of a wholly *present* tense for a narrative. Useful examples of this for textual examination are Michael Frayn, *A Very Private Life*; Muriel Spark, *The Driver's Seat*; and Malcolm Bradbury, *The History Man*.

6   Lastly, on the question of the function of various types of negative formation in English, it may be useful to compare the opening paragraph of E. M. Forster's *A Passage to India* with the one analysed here.

Except for the Marabar Caves – and they are twenty miles off – the city of Chandrapore presents nothing extraordinary. Edged rather than washed by the river Ganges, it trails for a couple of miles along the bank, scarcely distinguishable from the rubbish it deposits so freely. There are no bathing steps on the river front, as the Ganges happens not to be holy here; indeed there is no river front, and bazaars shut out the wide and shifting panorama of the stream. The streets are mean, the temples ineffective, and though a few fine houses exist they are hidden away in gardens or down alleys whose filth deters all but the invited guest. Chandrapore was never large or beautiful, but two hundred years ago it lay on the road between Upper India, then imperial, and the sea, and the fine houses date from that period. The zest for decoration stopped in the eighteenth century, nor was it ever democratic. There is no painting and scarcely any carving in the bazaars. The very wood seems made of mud, the inhabitants of mud moving. So abased, so monotonous is everything that meets the eye, that when the Ganges comes down it might be expected to wash the excrescence back into the soil. Houses do fall, people are drowned and left rotting, but the general outline of the town persists, swelling here, shrinking there, like some low but indestructible form of life.

References: Chapter 2

Halliday, M. A. K. (1971), 'Linguistic function and literary style', in Chatman, S. (ed.), *Literary Style: A Symposium* (London: OUP), pp. 330–65; repr. in Halliday, M. A. K. (1973), *Explorations in the Functions of Language* (London: Edward Arnold), pp. 103–43.

Introduction to Chapter 3

Henry Widdowson's study of Shakespeare's play focuses on one specific and interesting characteristic feature of Othello's dramatic speech; the fact that he can be seen to refer to himself both as the first-person 'I', and, more surprisingly, often as the third-person 'he' (or equivalent noun phrases). Two main points are made from this useful observation. First, it is suggested that, in this way, Othello refuses to face a stable reality of himself, frequently representing himself, to self and others, in a falsely exaggerated favourable light. Secondly, Widdowson shows that since these references to himself in the third person lead Othello to a confused image of self, and a false identification with others, then it follows that references to genuine third-person others, made by Iago in interaction with Othello, are easily understood by Othello as being references to himself. A detailed examination and discussion of the crucial Act III, scene iii, where Iago so easily persuades Othello of Desdemona's supposed infidelity, shows how Iago is given dialogue which reveals him exploiting his knowledge of Othello's use of language as it relates to his inner state of mind.

Although it is analysis at the level of discourse rather than syntax which reveals most about the nature of linguistic interaction, and therefore has most to offer when applied to the analysis of drama dialogue (see Burton, 1980: bibliography), this chapter shows how analysis of certain central syntactic categories overlaps with that of discourse and is a clear and helpful demonstration of valuable practical stylistic techniques in this area.

3 Othello in Person

H. G. WIDDOWSON

Of Shakespeare's four great tragic figures, two take a good deal of persuasion to act, and two act precipitately without sufficient circum-spection. Hamlet and Macbeth, the first pair, are brooders and dream-ers, inclined to introspection and prone to visions of the supernatural world. Lear and Othello, on the other hand, are men of action and only reflect when reflection is forced upon them. The tragedy of the dream-ers comes about when they are put in a position which requires action. The tragedy of the men of action comes about when they are called upon to pause and use their powers of reason and imagination. What we see in all of them, I think, is the conflict between the virtues of practical action and imaginative thought, whose combination is sup-posed to represent the ideal quality of Renaissance man. All of Shakespeare's four tragedies deal in cases where this combination fails.

In this paper I want to consider how this failure comes about in *Othello*. Of all the characters I have mentioned, Othello is in many ways the most problematic. He appears to approximate most closely to the Renaissance ideal: he is, on the one hand, a soldier, an adventurer, a man of action; and, on the other hand, he is a romantic lover who uses language in the way of an imaginative man. It is the poet not the soldier in him that beguiles Desdemona of her tears, and the gift is effective enough to be mistaken for witchcraft. Othello himself denies this gift when in the very act of using it:

> Rude am I in my speech
> And little blest with the set phrase of peace.
> (I, iii, 81–2)[1]

But this image of the blunt simple soldier will not do. In speech after speech the poet is proclaimed. Why, then, does Othello say this? He says it, I suggest, because there is in him a fundamental, and fatal, division between what he is and what he believes he is. Consistently throughout the play Othello confuses first-person self with third-person others, so that he is prone to represent himself favourably as a third-person figure, as in the lines quoted above, and conversely to take what is said about others as applying to himself. And it is because everything is subjected to this paranoiac process that Othello is so easily deceived.

The lines quoted above are an example early in the play of Othello saying something about himself which is plainly untrue. Another and more striking example occurs in the last speech he utters before his death:

> . . . then must you speak
> Of one that lov'd not wisely, but too well:
> Of one not easily jealous, but being wrought,
> Perplex'd in the extreme. . . .
>   (V, ii, 344–7)

Not easily jealous, indeed! It takes Iago a bare half-hour's traffic of the stage to convince him of his wife's infidelity. Characteristically, what Othello does here is to create a favourable third-person image of himself. He presents his own obituary of a man of honour and noble feeling, a man 'more sinned against than sinning'. There is no expression of regret for his recent cold-blooded murder, no recognition that he may have been to blame, no acknowledgement of guilt. The contrast with Desdemona's last speech is complete. Her last thought is to remove the blame from her husband and take it upon herself. His last thought is to remove the blame from himself and to protect his reputation. 'One that lov'd not wisely, but too well': the description fits Desdemona, but not Othello. Although 'like the base Indian' he may 'throw a pearl away richer than all this tribe', he takes care to retain what Iago refers to as 'the immediate jewel of our souls', to ensure that his death leaves his good name intact. Thus, even to the end he refuses to face the reality of himself. For he *is* easily jealous, and Iago is able to deceive him because he so easily deceives himself.

So Othello's character realises the theme of the play as a whole: the lack of correspondence between reputation and reality (a theme on which each of the major Shakespeare tragedies is a variation). The whole of the first Act, which contributes little or nothing to the plot, establishes this theme through the deception of Brabantio in his daughter. It is then played out by Iago and Othello each projecting a false image of himself to the world. But there is, of course, a crucial difference: Iago deceives others but not himself. He well knows the difference between the first-person self and a third-person projection of self. Othello, on the other hand, does not. He cannot distinguish between them: first and third persons are confused in his character.

This becomes clear, I believe, by a careful consideration of pronoun use and discourse structure of the crucial conversion scene: Act III, scene 3. In a discussion of this scene, Malcolm Coulthard points out how Iago uses the assumption associated with asking questions to suggest to Othello that he is concealing something from him. Thus, by an avoidance of normal question–answer interaction, Iago gives the impression that he has information which he is reluctant to disclose. Coulthard's thesis (1977: 173) is this:

> I want to suggest that Iago rouses Othello's suspicion by a sequence of unanswered questions, not simply because the questions are unanswered but because they are avoided apparently, but in fact deliberately, clumsily, which suggests to Othello that Iago is concealing something.

This does, indeed, seem to be the way in which Iago makes Othello suspect that he is concealing something, but it does not explain the arousal of Othello's *jealousy*. Why is Othello such an easy prey to what is after all a fairly obvious device? Why does the conviction of his wife's adultery take such rapid root in his mind? The reason, I think, is that Iago plays upon Othello's inability to sort out semblance from reality and upon his concomitant tendency to confuse first- and third-person reference. Sensitive as he is to his own image, Othello is disposed by nature to jealousy before Iago begins his intrigue. And Iago is expert at exploiting the failings of his fellow men for his own purposes, as witness his use of Roderigo's credulousness and Cassio's weak head for drink.

As Coulthard demonstrates, Iago's first tactic in this central scene is to suggest to Othello that he has something on his mind that he is reluctant to impart, something concerning Cassio and Desdemona. But he is then required to say what it is as Othello confronts him with a direct request for information:

> I prithee, speak to me as to thy thinkings,
> As thou doest ruminate, and give the worst of thought
> The worst of word.
> (III, iii, 135–7)

Coulthard says (1977: 177)

> Iago is able to build on the foundations of his suspicious question-avoiding and gradually becomes more specific in his accusations until he can warn
>
> > Look to your wife, observe her well with Cassio
> > (III, iii, 201)

But how does Iago build on the success of this tactic? What happens in the intervening sixty lines or so? I suggest that, having by means of this first tactic engaged his opponent, Iago by a series of feints forces Othello to take the initiative when at a disadvantage and so to reveal his weakness. Once Othello's defence is down, Iago is ready with the fatal thrust. Let us now consider how this is done.

Iago's tactics here are, essentially, to advance by personal statement and to retreat by generalisation, engaging Othello by reference to their actual first- and second-person selves and then disengaging by reference to third-person situations. Thus, in response to Othello's request that he reveal his thoughts (cited above) Iago engages him personally:

> Good my lord, pardon me;
> Though I am bound to every act of duty,
> I am not bound to that all slaves are free to;
> Utter my thoughts? Why, say they are vile and false. . . .   (140)

And then he disengages by shifting into an impersonal generalisation:

> As where's that palace, whereinto foul things
> Sometimes intrude not? Who has a breast so pure,
> But some uncleanly apprehensions
> Keep leets and law-days, and in session sit
> With meditations lawful?   (145)

Othello is drawn to reason with Iago on this level of general detachment, making reference not to his own self but to a third-person entity – 'thy friend':

> Thou dost conspire against thy friend, Iago,
> If thou but thinkest him wrong'd, and makest his ear
> A stranger to thy thoughts.

Othello is not yet personally engaged, as he would have been had his speech run as follows:

> Thou dost conspire against me, honest Iago,
> If thou but thinkest me wrong'd, and makest my ear
> A stranger to thy thoughts.

Iago's next move is to shift into the personal key. Having stepped away, as it were, he now advances:

> I do beseech you
> Though I perchance am vicious in my guess,
> (As I confess it is my nature's plague   (150)
> To spy into abuses, and oft my jealousy
> Shapes faults that are not). . . .

The parenthetic confession arrests the completion of what we expect to be a personal statement, perhaps at last a revelation of his thoughts, but then Iago steps back once more into third-person reference:

> I entreat you then,
> From one that so imperfectly conjects,
> You'ld take no notice, nor build yourself a trouble
> Out of his[2] scattering and unsure observance. ...   (155)

This pass corresponds exactly to that of Othello's which precedes it: in both cases there is ambiguity in that the third-person references, 'thy friend', 'his ear' and 'one', and 'his scattering and unsure observance', can be understood as having first-person implication in this context. Neither Iago nor Othello is committing himself at this stage of the contest. But now Iago makes a direct personal move:

> It were not for your quiet, nor your good,
> Nor for my manhood, honesty, or wisdom,
> To let you know my thoughts.

And Othello engages immediately:

> Zounds!

And Iago's reaction is then to disengage once more as he again shifts into the generalisation of proverbial statement:

> Good name in man and woman, dear my lord,
> Is the immediate jewel of their souls;   (160)
> Who steals my purse, steals trash, 'tis something, nothing,
> 'Twas mine, 'tis his, and has been slave to thousands:
> But he that filches from me my good name
> Robs me of that which not enriches him,
> But makes me poor indeed.   (165)

Although this has the character of a general apophthegm (and would apparently have been recognised as such by the audience), we should note the subtle intrusion of a personal element.[3] As I pointed out, the third-person references in previous speeches by Othello and Iago can be understood as having first-person implication. In this speech, Iago uses first-person reference in a generalised third-person sense. There is a shift of perspective from third-person reference in the first line here ('man and woman') to first-person reference in the lines that follow, in which the very repetition of the pronouns suggests personal involvement and serves to blur the distinction between the experience of self and the observation of others, between first- and third-person reality.

Othello's reaction to this speech engages Iago at the personal level and in the following exchange the pronouns take on their conventional value:

Othello:	By heaven, I'll know thy thought.
Iago:	You cannot, if my heart were in your hand,
	Nor shall not, whilst 'tis in my custody.
Othello:	Ha![4]

Iago's refusal to reveal his thoughts is now direct, and it challenges Othello's authority. Having thus come to close quarters, Iago then rapidly disengages and retreats once more into generalisation before Othello can take the initiative. But now, from this safe distance, he shifts the direction of attack. He now no longer speaks about reputation and by implication the damage he may do to the good name of Cassio by his revelations. He now for the first time mentions jealousy and associates it with Othello (he has already mentioned it in association with himself), and the generalisations which follow, therefore, although by definition general in reference, are represented as having relevance to Othello's case in particular. At the same time, Iago expresses his own emotional involvement by the use of exclamation.

> O, beware, jealousy;
> It is the green-ey'd monster, which doth mock   (170)
> That meat it feeds on. That cuckold lives in bliss,
> Who, certain of his fate, loves not his wronger:
> But, O, what damned minutes tells he o'er
> Who dotes, yet doubts, suspects, yet strongly loves.

Whereas previously we had first-person pronouns used with third-person implication, we now have third-person pronouns used with second-person implication. And Othello reacts to the relevance and not to the reference: he recognises at once the particular application of Iago's remarks to his own case:

> O misery!   (175)

It is not clear whether this remark is intended as an expression of personal distress or as a sympathetic comment on the cuckold's plight in general. Most commentators appear to prefer the latter, but it seems to me that the former is more consistent with Othello's character; and presently I will give other reasons for preferring it. At all events, under either interpretation Othello is clearly identifying with the cuckold and expressing a sense of personal involvement. In both cases, then, there is a convergence of first- and third-person realities.

Iago has now drawn Othello into exposing himself. In his next speech, he first keeps his distance by detached generalisation and then once more introduces a note of personal involvement by his last exclamation:

Poor and content is rich, and rich enough,
But riches, fineless, is as poor as winter
To him that ever fears he shall be poor:
Good God, the souls of all my tribe define
From jealousy!   (180)

In these exchanges, then, we see Iago as an astute tactician manipulating his opponent by the subtle shifting from detachment to involvement, from the general to the particular, from the third-person observed reality to that of first-person experience, deliberately fusing these distinctions by the skilful deployment of pronominal reference. The effect of this tactic is to establish in Othello a state of mind to which he is by character inclined anyway: one in which the distinction between the first-person self and the conception of self as a third person become confused. Othello is thus manoeuvred into a psychological position particularly conducive to his own self-exposure; and in which any move he makes will leave him open to attack. Having drawn him into this position, Iago at last allows him to take the initiative, and Othello produces his first speech of any real substance.

Perhaps the first thing to notice about this speech is that it sounds like soliloquy: Othello does not really engage in an interaction with Iago at all, but with himself. He begins by a series of questions:

Why, why is this?   (180)
Think'st thou I'ld make a life of jealousy?
To follow still the changes of the moon
With fresh suspicions?

We have here four points of possible interaction; four points, that is, where it would be possible for Othello to shift the onus of response on to Iago, for the asking of a question bestows both right and obligation on the interlocutor, and so can be used to gain tactical advantage. But Othello makes no such use of his questions. We can get some idea of how Othello could have proceeded by interposing possible responses at these points of interaction in the following way:

Othello:	Why? (i.e. Why do you say this?)
(Iago:	Well, I think one should guard against jealousy)
Othello:	Why is this? (i.e. What has this got to do with me?)
(Iago:	Everybody is a likely prey of jealousy)
Othello:	Think'st thou I'ld make a life of jealousy?
(Iago:	Well, no, I suppose not, but. . . .)
Othello:	To follow still the changes of the moon with fresh suspicions?
(Iago:	Well, I was only thinking that. . . .)
Othello:	No; to be once in doubt is once to be resolved.

If Othello were to clarify his puzzlement about Iago's meaning along these lines, using the authority of his rank (as he well knows how to do), then it is easy to see how Iago could be reduced to mumbling ineffectiveness. But Othello never does take the initiative in this way. Having posed these questions, he then provides his own answer:

> No, to be once in doubt,
> Is once to be resolved. . . .

This sounds decisive enough, and one might expect that the speech would end on this note of finality. But no. Othello goes on to deny his own decisiveness by revealing the very state of mind he seems so determined to avoid. There is again a shift from the presentation of self as a third-person figure to an expression of the feelings of the first-person self. The speech continues in this way:

> exchange me for a goat,
> When I shall turn the business of my soul   (185)
> To such exsufflicate and blown surmises,
> Matching thy inference. . . .

Bravely spoken. The third-person appearances are kept up, but only just. Othello, like the Player Queen in Hamlet, 'doth protest too much', as if straining to sustain the image he wishes to project. Iago, we must imagine, looks on and waits for Othello's first-person self to appear. As it does in the lines that follow:

> 'tis not to make me jealous,
> To say my wife is fair, feeds well, loves company,
> Is free of speech, sings, plays, and dances well. . . .

Here again we must note the ambiguity of the first-person pronouns. On the one hand, they can be interpreted as having third-person value, and in this case Othello's remarks represent a generalisation comparable to Iago's earlier speeches (e.g. 'Who steals *my* purse steals trash . . . *my* good name . . . robs *me* of that'). After all, Iago has made no mention of Desdemona's beauty or her behaviour. On the other hand, these pronouns could refer to Othello's own particular situation, and in this case the speech expresses his own awareness of those qualities in his wife which might cause him to be jealous. If this is so, he is not reporting what others say but what he says to himself. This ambiguity, which, as we have seen, recurs as a persistent feature throughout this exchange, moves us once more to the personal level of actual experience.

Then follows an odd single statement which sounds like a confused attempt to maintain a general third-person level of discourse:

> Where virtue is, these are more virtuous. . . .   (190)

And then Othello moves quite unambiguously on to the personal level; and the first-person pronouns assume their more customary first-person value:

> Nor from mine own weak merits will I draw
> The smallest fear, or doubt of her revolt,
> For she had eyes, and chose me.

Othello reveals his doubts more clearly in this last line here, perhaps, than anywhere else. For in the first Act of the play it is made clear that Desdemona chose Othello not because of her eyes but in spite of them. Brabantio is amazed that his daughter should behave so unnaturally as

> To fall in love with what she fear'd to look on!
> (I, iii, 98)

But, as Othello himself explains, Desdemona did not fall in love with what she saw but with unseen qualities of character. As she puts it:

> I saw Othello's visage in his mind,
> And to his honours and his valiant parts
> Did I my soul and fortunes consecrate.
> (I, iii, 252–4)

So this remark of Othello's –

> For she had eyes, and chose me.

– although intended as a statement of assurance, is really an expression of doubt. It sounds, indeed, like a recollection of Brabantio's disbelief and an echo of his parting words of warning:

> Look to her, Moor, if thou hast eyes to see:
> She has deceived her father, and may thee.
> (I, iii, 292–3)

As we might expect, Iago notes the significance of the echo and characteristically exploits it to his advantage in the speech which follows. For the time has now come for him to strike. He has drawn Othello to reveal his thoughts by the very tactics he uses to conceal his own. We can, I think, now interpret Othello's earlier exclamation, 'O misery!', as a genuine *cri de cœur* as he recognises the relevance of Iago's general third-person description to his own particular first-person condition:

> But, O! what damned minutes tells he o'er
> Who dotes, yet doubts; suspects yet strongly loves!

Having enticed Othello into exposing himself, then, Iago moves in for the kill. There are no more feints and evasions: the approach is direct.

> I am glad of it, for now I shall have reason
> To show the love and duty that I bear you
> With franker spirit: therefore, as I am bound
> Receive it from me: I speak not yet of proof. . . .   (200)

Taking care not to drop his guard ('I speak not yet of proof'), Iago delivers his decisive blow, and he does so by the use of words referring to visual perception which, as it were, amplify the resonance of Othello's earlier remark which seems so clearly to sound his inner anxiety:

> *Look* to your wife, *observe* her well with Cassio;
> Wear your *eye* thus, not jealous nor secure.
> I would not have your free and noble nature
> Out of self-bounty be abused, *look* to't:
> I know our country disposition well;   (205)
> In Venice they do let God *see* the pranks
> They dare not *show* their husbands; their best conscience
> Is not to leave undone, but keep unknown.

We must note again how first- and third-person worlds, experience and observation converge: Desdemona is now directly associated with the adulterous wives of Venice and Othello with their cuckolded husbands, and Iago makes this quite explicit in his next speech, as he strikes again at his now helpless adversary:

> *Othello:*   Dost thou say so?
> *Iago:*   She did deceive her father, marrying you;   (210)
>   And when she seem'd to shake and fear your looks,
>   She lov'd them most.
> *Othello:*   And so she did.
> *Iago:*   Why, go to then,
>   She that so young could give out such a seeming,
>   To seel her father's eyes up, close as oak,
>   He thought 'twas witchcraft. . . .   (215)

I have tried to show how, in this crucial scene, Iago's tactics are to create a confusion of first- and third-person worlds which is a reflection of Othello's own mental disposition. Such a confusion, therefore, provides the conditions in which Othello will reveal his own weakness, the inner uncertainty and doubt that he customarily conceals by the projection of a third-person image. In his final speech, Othello talks about being 'perplex'd in the extreme'. I have here tried to adduce linguistic evidence to indicate that this perplexity is inherent in Othello's character and that Iago's achievement is to project it into the world of actual events so that it becomes a force of self-destruction.

Notes: Chapter 3

1 Line references are to the Arden edition, edited by M. R. Ridley.
2 *his* is the Folio reading. The Arden edition, following the Quartos, has *my*.
3 It is interesting to compare the contemporary version of this saw as quoted in the Arden edition:

> a slanderer is worse than any thief, because a good name is better than all the goods in the world . . . and a thief may restore that again which he hath taken away, but a slanderer cannot give a man his good name which he hath taken from him. . . .

This is quite unambiguously general and impersonal.
4 This, again, is from the Folio. The Quarto, which the Arden edition follows, has no exclamation at this point.

Suggestions for Further Work: Chapter 3

1 Compare the sly allusiveness of Iago's conversational moves in the extract examined here from *Othello* with the scene in *Troilus and Cressida*, III, iii, 37–242, where Ulysses tries to persuade Achilles to rejoin the campaign by moving from third-person propositions to personal-pronoun address and thus subtly and indirectly planting suggestions in Achilles' mind.
2 R. D. Laing and A. Esterson, in *Sanity, Madness and the Family* (1970), have examined the question of adults repeatedly talking about their children in the third person, despite the physical presence of those children at the conversation. Take one of their case-studies and, explaining this feature of syntax in relation to both the adults and the child, write a short series of exchanges yourself in order to explore precisely how confused images of self can emerge. Apply the fruits of your study to a discussion of the character of Mr Duffy in the short story by James Joyce, 'A Painful Case', in *Dubliners* where he is initially described as follows:

> He had an odd autobiographical habit which led him to compose in his mind from time to time a short sentence about himself containing a subject in the third person, and a predicate in the past tense.

Examine the dialogue in G. B. Shaw's *Pygmalion* and Harold Pinter's *The Birthday Party* for similar characteristics.
3 Readers should not forget the significance of the overtones carried by 'thou' and 'you' in plays in Shakespeare's time. A useful analysis of the use Shakespeare makes of this in his portrayal of the relationship between

Celia and Rosamund in *As You Like It* is made by Angus McIntosh (McIntosh and Halliday, 1966). Further rich areas for analysis are Act I, sc. i, of *King Lear* – in particular, the exchange between Lear and Kent and in the conversations between Lear and the Fool. Why does the Fool refer continually to third-person examples in his replies to Lear? (But see the subsequent shift from 'thou' to 'you' in II, iv.) The chapter by Gillian Alexander in this book also provides many points of reference for extension and further exploration.

4   Consult the essay on *Othello* in Coulthard (1977) referred to in this chapter. In that essay the main point is that, even if a speaker is wholly innocent in intent, if he behaves oddly in terms of a conversationalist's expectations, then his co-conversationalist will interpret this behaviour in a strong way. Coulthard's analysis of taken-for-granted assumptions about conversation likewise shows Iago to be a skilful manipulator of conversational assumptions. He further goes on to examine how the tragedy is compounded in Othello's later confrontation with the *innocent* Desdemona. For all three characters, conversational skills, or lack of them, are destiny. Coulthard's essay is one in *discourse analysis*, and is not specifically analytical of syntactic categories, but it is a useful example of how literary texts can be illuminated by analysis from within different levels of language organisation. For the more advanced student his discussion is a useful supplement and point of comparison with Widdowson's chapter.

References: Chapter 3

Burton, D. (1980), *Dialogue and Discourse* (London: Routledge & Kegan Paul).

Coulthard, M. (1977), *An Introduction to Discourse Analysis* (London: Longman).

Laing, R. D. and Esterson, A. (1970), *Sanity, Madness and the Family* (Harmondsworth, Penguin).

McIntosh, A. and Halliday, M. A. K. (1966), *Patterns of Language: Papers in General Descriptive and Applied Linguistics* (London: Longman).

Introduction to Chapter 4

By using the term 'literary linguistic stylistics' Mick Short advocates the need for linguists writing stylistic analysis to be alert to defined literary concerns. In this his argument follows that of Crystal (1972) cited in the Introduction to this volume. Although he criticises the failure of literary critics to understand some of the principal aims and methods of linguistics, his 'general strategy will be literary'. He holds explicitly the view that 'linguistics is only likely to be of service to literary criticism if it follows its general aims and strategies'.

The chapter then goes on to demonstrate the value of practical stylistic analysis in confirming and overtly attesting 'impressions of T. S. Eliot's style in "Prelude I" '. He shows how intuitions concerning the 'bittyness' and unrelatedness of the style can be validated by reference to particular syntactic operations. The detailed and relevant linguistic analysis Mick Short provides makes for considerable accuracy and clarity of presentation.

4 'Prelude I' to a Literary Linguistic Stylistics

M. H. SHORT

The purpose of this chapter is twofold: first, to make a number of general observations on the use of stylistics in literary criticism and, secondly, to use those observations as the basis for an analysis of the first of T. S. Eliot's 'Preludes'. It will be suggested that much of the discussion over stylistics and the related topic of objectivity in literary criticism has been fogged by misunderstandings by both literary critics and linguists. These misunderstandings have promoted a polarisation of attitudes such that either side in the debate often seems to be prepared to reject the other out of hand. I would like to suggest that criticism can benefit from a fusion of 'literary' and 'linguistic' method. The general approach adopted here is that of using linguistic stylistic analysis as a means of supporting a literary or interpretative thesis. The version of the text discussed is on page 23 of T. S. Eliot's *Collected Poems 1909–1962* (London: Faber, 1963). During the analysis I will refer to the section concerned as a 'poem'. I do this knowing full well that the text in question is only part of a larger poem. But such an expedient avoids the introduction of laborious circumlocutions.

The debate as to the relevance of linguistic stylistics to literary studies has been in progress for some time now. The fullest presentation is probably the debate between Roger Fowler and F. W. Bateson in *Essays in Criticism*.[1] Participants in the discussion have tended to move to extremes, declaring either that linguistics has nothing to offer or that it possesses a kind of objectivity which literary criticism cannot have. For example, F. W. Bateson's comments are meant to show the irrelevance of linguistics to criticism. In an illustrative analysis of Ezra Pound's poem 'Spring . . . /Too long . . . /Gongula . . .' he says:

> The poem's internal grammatical relationships cannot in fact be determined. In English 'Gongula' may be either the subject, the object, or the person addressed. . . . In this poem therefore the word order *has* to be ungrammatical. . . .

This shows a remarkable ignorance of the procedures of descriptive linguistics. He implies that the linguist would be forced to assign the word in question to one of the categories he mentions. But this is not so. The linguist recognises the existence of indeterminate cases like these (witness the use of the Z element in the analysis below), and says that this indeterminacy may well have a particular stylistic effect, as it does in the poem by Pound. In other words, the linguist and literary critic appear to be saying the same thing. This suggests that part of the problem in the debate on linguistic stylistics is an ignorance on the part of some literary critics as to the aims and methods of linguistics.[2] Similarly, some linguists appear to have little awareness of what is needed to make a good literary argument. They often produce linguistic detail which is irrelevant to the purpose, and assume that their categories will always give the information required. The following analysis will be performed from a standpoint somewhere between these two extremes. Much of the information used in the discussion will be linguistic, but purely 'literary' points will be made as well. The general strategy will be literary. An overall interpretation of the poem will be given, and this interpretation will be backed up by more detailed analysis. Thus, linguistic detail is used only where it is relevant for the purposes of the argument. It is not implied that all linguistic data must be relevant; nor is it suggested that linguistic points are more objective than literary ones.[3] No detailed work has been done on this latter topic, and it would be presumptuous to produce unchecked assertions to one side or the other. Linguistics is only likely to be of service to literary criticism if it follows its general aims and strategies.

Before discussing 'Prelude I' I will present a sentence and clause analysis of the poem, along with an outline of its rhyme scheme. All this is outlined in Table 4.1.

The method of grammatical analysis is of the rank-scale type and follows particularly J. McH. Sinclair.[4] The following abbreviations are used: F = Free clause, S = Subject, P = Predicator, A = Adjunct, C = Complement, Z = a nominal group in a construction which has no Predicator; as S, C and A are usually defined in terms of the Predicator, these terms are inappropriate. Thus, it can be seen, for example, that sentence 1 consists of a Free clause, which is in turn composed of a Subject, a Predicator and two Adjuncts.

Briefly, a rank-scale grammar breaks sentences down into clauses, clauses into phrases, and so on. Two main types of clause are used, the Free type, which is similar to the main clause in traditional grammar, and the Bound clause, which is roughly equivalent to the traditional subordinate clause. As the grammar is descriptive, not prescriptive, there is no stricture that a clause must contain a finite verb; assignment to classes is largely in terms of function. Thus, sentence 2 is analysed as a Free clause even though it has no verb. Clauses which have a delimiting function inside noun phrases are said to be rankshifted, as they do not operate at the usual level of structure for the clause (thus,

Table 4.1 *The Rhyme Scheme and a Sentence and Clause Analysis of Prelude I*

	Rhyme Scheme	Sentence and Clause Analysis	
The winter evening settles down	A		
		F(SPAA)	Sentence 1
With smell of steaks in passageways.	B		
Six o'clock.	C	F(Z)	Sentence 2
The burnt-out ends of smoky days.	B	F(Z)	Sentence 3
And now a gusty shower wraps	D		
The grimy scraps	D		
		F(AASPCAC)	
Of withered leaves about your feet	E		
And newspapers from vacant lots;	F		
			Sentence 4
The showers beat	E		
		F(SPA)	
On broken blinds and chimney-pots,	F		
And at the corner of the street	E		
		F(AASP)	
A lonely cab-horse steams and stamps.	G		
And then the lighting of the lamps.	G	F(AAZ)	Sentence 5

'the man I met last week' is the Subject of the sentence 'the man I met last week is ill' and 'I met last week' is a rankshifted clause delimiting 'man'). The constituents of clauses are defined mainly in terms of the Predicator or verbal group. The complement of the sentence is the noun phrase which characteristically comes after the Predicator and is roughly equivalent to both traditional complement and direct object. The Adjunct comprises the remaining elements of clause structure and so includes adverbs, prepositional phrases, words which link clauses together and the like. Adjuncts are generally much more mobile than the other constituents which make up clauses. It can now be seen that the clause which constitutes sentence 1 is analysed as follows: *The winter evening* (S) *settles* (P) *down* (A) *with smell of steaks in passageways* (A).

The first of Eliot's 'Preludes' is the description of a winter evening in a town. It is essentially a mood poem. It creates an atmosphere of decay, lack of care, and darkness, challenged only by the last line, which is set apart typographically from the rest of the poem. The general style can be described as simple and bitty.[5] Eliot gives short descriptions of a number of different things, which, at first sight, seem to be unrelated.

The bittyness and simplicity of the style can be related to a number of structural features. The rhyme scheme is not very regular, consisting of non-rhyming lines, alternate rhymes and couplets. Three of the fourteen lines are very short, consisting of three words each. The sentence distribution is irregular: there are three one-line sentences, one of two lines, and one of eight lines. Only the long sentence has more than one clause, and there are no Bound or rankshifted clauses at all in the poem. This simplicity and irregularity is also reflected at clause level. The poem contains three Z constructions, two of which act as sentences. There is little evidence of 'poetic' constructions, no inversion of S and P, no '-eth' endings to words, very little arrest,[6] and so on. All these features help to back up a general comment often made on Eliot's poetry, that it is not 'poetic', that it uses everyday language and situations. The objects used to evoke the winter evening are not traditionally poetic: grimy scraps, withered leaves, broken blinds and chimney-pots.

Every clause has a different topic, and there are no obvious relations between them. The linking device of anaphora is totally absent in the poem. The lack of Bound clauses, which usually provide some sort of comment on the Free clause that they are bound to, also reflects this disjointedness. The extra or extending elements in clauses are not predicted situationally in any way by the elements which precede them. There is no immediate reason for the *smell of steaks* to be in *passageways*, or for *chimney-pots* to be linked with *blinds* for example. The Free clauses in sentence 4 have no inherent relation to each other, yet grouping them together in one sentence suggests a strong connection. In this light, the construction of the first of the three clauses is interesting. I have analysed it as a three-line clause with two Complements, *The grimy scraps of withered leaves* and *newspapers from vacant lots*. But one could argue that line 8 was a separate Free clause. It is an extension; *wraps* predicts a Complement, already supplied, and also another completing element in the form of a preposition or an Adjunct, thus giving constructions like 'wrap up', 'wrap round' or, in this case, 'wrap about your feet'. Both these predictions are thus satisfied before the occurrence of *And newspapers from vacant lots*. It would have been a much more obviously integral part of the clause if it had been inserted immediately after the first Complement. This, and the fact that it has a line to itself, adds to the disjointedness of the poem. The relative autonomy of the clauses in the poem is reinforced phonologically by the use of local alliterative effects within the clause. This can be seen in *a gusty shower wraps/The grimy scraps, The showers beat/On broken blinds and chimney-pots, steams and stamps* and *the lighting of the lamps.*

The last main feature involved in giving the poem its random bitty style is the nature of the inter-clausal and inter-sentential connectives. The only item which acts as a clause-linker is *And at the corner of the street* (11). There are two inter-sentential connectives, *And now* (5) and *And then* (13). All three items are prominent because of their line-initial position; and they all begin with *And*. But in each case the Adjunct following *And* produces a complete change in the time- or place-focus. This switch is underlined by the fact that there is no carry-over of Subject. The difference in effect can be seen by comparing the following sentences:

(1) We drove into town, and went to the cinema.
(2) We drove into town, and then we went to the cinema.
(3) We drove into town, and then George went to the cinema.

So far we have a large amount of evidence to support the poem's bitty style. But to provide a substantial proof one would also have to show that the poem contained no unifying features. This in fact is not the case, as one would expect, because the thirteen lines under discussion are a complete section of a poem. If all the seemingly random observations are to be seen as a poetic text, these observations must be related in some way. This object is partly achieved by the obvious fact that the lines are presented as a piece of poetry on a printed page. But the presentation of something *as* a poem is not enough for it to *be* a poem.

The major unifying factor in the poem is its rhyme system. We have noted earlier that the rhyme scheme is by no means regular. But the fact that two lines rhyme implies a link of parallelism or contrast between them. The poem could be seen as having two rhyme-scheme stanzas, marked by the two couplets. But such a division is not supported by the spatial arrangement of the poem, and is immediately seen to be at odds with the syntax. Couplets tend to unify the two lines involved, but the second one in this poem consists of two separate sentences which are on different topics and are separated from each other by a gap. The first rhyming couplet occurs at the beginning of sentence 4. Again, the syntax plays against the rhyme, this time because the structural unit of the clause concerned does not coincide with the rhyme unit. The second half of the couplet also contains only the first part of a Complement phrase, which is completed by the following line.

This feature of rhyme unification can be seen throughout the poem. By rhyming lines which at first have no obvious connection Eliot forces us to look for one, so that cooking and burning are seen to be related, for example, and the smells attached to them are focused on *smoky days*. Lines 5 and 6 have similar elements in that showers, like scraps, are small and irregular. The *newspapers from vacant lots* are linked with *broken blinds and chimney-pots* because they are all associated with decay and lack of care (it is interesting in this respect that the landscape contains no people – even the cab-horse is *lonely*). Moreover, the newspapers are linked with *grimy scraps* and hence the dirty associations of the first part of the poem because they are both Complements to the rhyming Predicator *wraps*. The showers also act as a unifying factor because they act on the blinds and chimney-pots as well as on the leaves and newspapers.

Thus, the main function the rhyme scheme is seen to fulfil is that of helping to link what at first appear to be random observations into an area of association. Common elements and roles link the lexical elements in a chain-like manner to give a general impression of loneliness (*vacant lots, lonely cab-horse*), closing darkness and dirtiness (*winter evening, burnt-out ends of smoky days, grimy scraps*), and decay (*burnt-out ends, scraps, withered leaves, broken blinds and chimney-pots*).

The only part of the preliminary critical statement that has not been examined is the question of the last line, which to some extent interrupts the tenor of the foregoing description. The fact that it is somewhat unlike the rest of the poem is marked by its physical separation from the main body. Its claim to distinction is mainly in terms of vocabulary, in that two of the three lexically full words in the line are concerned with light (*lighting, lamps*), which thus reinforce one another (the other word with pretensions to lexical fullness is *then*). This contrasts with the grubbiness and darkness of the preceding lines. The contrast is brought out by the parallelism of the couplet rhyme. But the contrasting feature of the last line should not be regarded as a reversal of attitude or as a cure-all. As already shown, the use of the connecting *And then* suggests that the lighting of the lamps is on the same level as the other 'actions' in the poem. Moreover, in the larger context of the poem as a whole, the line has to be seen as a linking device with the following prelude. And it is apparent that the movement on from the first of the preludes to the others is not to be regarded as an improvement. The other sections are no lighter in tone, and the circular movement of the whole, ending up with evening again 'emphasizes the attitude of the poem, portraying the dreary cycle in which evening is simply a prelude to night, night to morning and another day, and day to evening and another night again'.[7]

It can be seen that the foregoing analysis does not rely solely on linguistic evidence. It would surely be too heavy a stricture on stylistics that it should confine itself in this way. An imagist critic would hardly be expected to talk only of images. What is important is that the analyst uses the most detailed and accurate types of description that he has at his disposal. No surprising, new interpretation is offered here. A look at critical history shows that literary critics are by no means short of ingenuity. Instead, this analysis is a plea for detailed and relevant evidence of various types for a particular point of view. This can be achieved by a preliminary general statement followed by detailed analysis as shown above. The advantages are accuracy and clarity of presentation (a factor strangely absent in the debate over 'objectivity' in literary criticism), and that general characteristic of literary critical analysis of showing that superficially unconnected (and often previously unseen) points can all be related in a particular overall analysis. Linguistic stylistics is more likely to be of help to literary criticism if it adopts some of its general strategies.

Notes: Chapter 4

1   See (i) 'Argument II: literature and linguistics', *Essays in Criticism*, vol. XVII (1967), pp. 322–47; and (ii) 'Argument II (continued): language and literature', *Essays in Criticism*, vol. XVIII (1968), pp. 164–82. (See also the Introduction to this volume, Section II.)
2   There is also, I think, a partial but genuine difference in viewpoint between the two disciplines. Literary analysis is often primarily concerned with providing interpretations or judgements as to a work's style, whereas linguistic stylistics is concerned mainly with showing the mechanisms which underlie that work's meaning or style. One would expect to see evidence of both viewpoints in good criticism or good stylistics; it is the difference in emphasis which is the distinguishing factor.
3   Non-linguistic points can be unquestionably true – for example, statements of the form 'X did Y' in a novel. Facts of this sort are often used in literary analysis to support particular interpretations.
4   See Sinclair (1972).
5   The sense in which the word 'bitty' is used here is defined in *Webster's Third New International Dictionary*: 'bit-ty made up of bits: SCRAPPY; also: containing particular matter'.
6   See Sinclair (1966: 70–4). Grammatical arrest occurs where an element delays the onset of an item already predicted. Thus, 'ponderously' in 'he moved ponderously to the door' is an arresting element. Conversely, in the sentence 'he moved to the door ponderously', the same word is an *extra* or *extending* element. The clause would still be grammatically well formed if it was omitted. See also the chapter by Sinclair in this volume.
7   See Nicholson (1958).

Suggestions for Further Work: Chapter 4

1   The most obvious starting-points for further work are other examples of 'imagist' or 'modernist' poetry or, in a more general sense, poetry which produces particular effects as a result of syntactic patterns which do not quite relate coherently or logically to each other. Examples which might be felt to be especially close in form to 'Prelude I' are: Louis MacNeice, 'The

Dowser'; Wallace Stevens, 'Gray Stones and Gray Pigeons'; W. H. Auden, 'The Wanderer'; William Empson, 'Aubade'; W. B. Yeats, 'The Stare's Nest by My Window' from *Meditations in Time of Civil War*; and T. S. Eliot, 'Rhapsody on a Windy Night'. What are the different effects produced in these poems by the syntactic structures the poet employs? In what ways are they similar to 'Prelude I'? Examine the unifying role of rhythm and metre in 'Prelude I'. Is it the same as in the other poems? What is the part played by rhyme or its absence? 'Rhapsody on a Windy Night' is discussed fully in Traugott and Pratt (1980), pp. 24–9.

2 Compare this text with poems which produce a sense of unrelatedness and disorientation by other than syntactic means. For example, Eliot's own 'Sweeney among the Nightingales' lacks a certain cohesion in its lexis and patterns of discourse. What kinds of effect are produced by this? Are they different from the feelings produced by 'Prelude I'? If so, why? If not, why not? For further examples along these lines, see: John Crowe Ransome, 'Janet Waking'; W. H. Auden, 'The Capital', 'Mundus et Infans', 'Oxford'; Philip Larkin, 'Toads', 'A Study of Reading Habits', 'Sad Steps', 'Poetry of Departures'.

3 Undertake a syntactic analysis of poems that are much more deviant and 'bitty' in terms of the elements of *clause structure* than Eliot's 'Prelude I'. Useful examples by Eliot might be 'Marina' or the opening section of *Little Gidding*. Other examples could include many of the poems of G. M. Hopkins, Dylan Thomas or e. e. cummings. Are the same kind of effects produced? If so, why? If not, why not?

4 Using Mick Short's analysis, write a poem by filling in the elements of sentence structure with lexical choices of your own. That is, use Eliot's poem as a model at SPCAZ elements in grammar. Write an essay analysing your choices. Pay particular attention to the effect of these structures on your choices. What kind of constraints did you experience in your composition? Examine the relationship between your subject-matter and the linguistic form in which it has been constructed. What other elements of form in poetry contribute to the establishment of meanings and effects?

References: Chapter 4

Crystal, D. (1972), 'Objective and subjective in stylistic analysis', in Kachru, B. and Stahlke, H. (eds), *Current Trends in Stylistics* (Edmonton, Alberta: Linguistic Research Inc.), pp. 103–13.

Nicholson, J. (1958), 'Musical form and the Preludes', in Braybrooke, N. (ed.), *Eliot: A Symposium for His Seventieth Birthday* (London: Hart-Davis), pp. 110–12.

Sinclair, J. McH. (1966), 'Taking a poem to pieces', in Fowler, R. (ed.), *Essays on Style and Language* (London: Routledge & Kegan Paul), pp. 68–81.

Sinclair, J. McH. (1972), *A Course in Spoken English: Grammar* (London: OUP).

Traugott, E. C. and Pratt, M. L. (1980), *Linguistics for Students of Literature* (New York: Harcourt Brace Jovanovich).

Introduction to Chapter 5

This chapter is about *practical stylistics* and explores the ways in which a close analysis of features of language can show how some key literary meanings in the story are made. In the story 'Cat in the Rain' by Ernest Hemingway there are subtle shifts in the emotional attitudes of the characters, and these shifts can be associated with changes in the structure of the nominal groups used to describe them and the setting in which the events of the story take place. This grammatical structure, together with changes in the kinds of verb used and a device known as 'free indirect speech', embody, it is argued, crucial features of the viewpoint from which the story is read and contribute to its ambiguity. An examination of changes in linguistic patterning across the text leads Carter to propose that a basic interpretation of the story is that it deals with the frustration of expectations.

5 Style and Interpretation in Hemingway's 'Cat in the Rain'

RONALD CARTER

There were only two Americans stopping at the hotel. They did not know
any of the people they passed on the stairs on their way to and from their
room. Their room was on the second floor facing the sea. It also faced
the public garden and the war monument. There were big palms and
05 green benches in the public garden. In the good weather there was
always an artist with his easel. Artists liked the way the palms grew and
the bright colours of the hotels facing the gardens and the sea. Italians
came from a long way off to look up at the war monument. It was made of
bronze and glistened in the rain. It was raining. The rain dripped from the
10 palm trees. Water stood in pools on the gravel paths. The sea broke in a
long line in the rain and slipped back down the beach to come up and
break again in a long line in the rain. The motor-cars were gone from the
square by the war monument. Across the square in the doorway of the
café a waiter stood looking out at the empty square.
15   The American wife stood at the window looking out. Outside right
under their window a cat was crouched under one of the dripping green
tables. The cat was trying to make herself so compact that she would not
be dripped on.
       'I'm going down to get that kitty,' the American wife said.
20   'I'll do it,' her husband offered from the bed.
       'No, I'll get it. The poor kitty out trying to keep dry under a table.'
       The husband went on reading, lying propped up with the two pillows at
the foot of the bed.
       'Don't get wet,' he said.
25   The wife went downstairs and the hotel owner stood up and bowed to
her as she passed the office. His desk was at the far end of the office. He
was an old man and very tall.
       'Il piove,' the wife said. She liked the hotel-keeper.
       'Si, si, Signora, brutto tempo. It is very bad weather.'
30   He stood behind his desk in the far end of the dim room. The wife liked
him. She liked the deadly serious way he received any complaints. She
liked his dignity. She liked the way he wanted to serve her. She liked the
way he felt about being a hotel-keeper. She liked his old, heavy face and
big hands.
35   Liking him she opened the door and looked out. It was raining harder.
A man in a rubber cape was crossing the empty square to the café. The
cat would be around to the right. Perhaps she could go along under the

eaves. As she stood in the doorway an umbrella opened behind her. It
was the maid who looked after their room.

40   'You must not get wet,' she smiled, speaking Italian. Of course, the
hotel-keeper had sent her.

   With the maid holding the umbrella over her, she walked along the
gravel path until she was under their window. The table was there,
washed bright green in the rain, but the cat was gone. She was suddenly

45 disappointed. The maid looked up at her.

   'Ha perduto qualque cosa, Signora?'

   'There was a cat,' said the American girl.

   'A cat?'

   'Si, il gatto.'

50   'A cat?' the maid laughed. 'A cat in the rain?'

   'Yes,' she said, 'under the table.' Then, 'Oh, I wanted it so much. I
wanted a kitty.'

   When she talked English the maid's face tightened.

   'Come, Signora,' she said. 'We must get back inside. You will be wet.'

55   'I suppose so,' said the American girl.

   They went back along the gravel path and passed in the door. The
maid stayed outside to close the umbrella. As the American girl passed
the office, the padrone bowed from his desk. Something felt very small
and tight inside the girl. The padrone made her feel very small and at the

60 same time really important. She had a momentary feeling of being of
supreme importance. She went on up the stairs. She opened the door of
the room. George was on the bed, reading.

   'Did you get the cat?' he asked, putting the book down.

   'It was gone.'

65   'Wonder where it went to?' he said, resting his eyes from reading.
She sat down on the bed.

   'I wanted it so much,' she said. 'I don't know why I wanted it so much. I
wanted that poor kitty. It isn't any fun to be a poor kitty out in the rain.'
George was reading again.

70   She went over and sat in front of the mirror of the dressing-table,
looking at herself with the hand glass. She studied her profile, first one
side and then the other. Then she studied the back of her head and her
neck.

   'Don't you think it would be a good idea if I let my hair grow out?' she

75 asked, looking at her profile again.

   George looked up and saw the back of her neck, clipped close like a
boy's.

   'I like it the way it is.'

   'I get so tired of it,' she said. 'I get so tired of looking like a boy.'

80   George shifted his position in the bed. He hadn't looked away from her
since she started to speak.

   'You look pretty darn nice,' he said.

   She laid the mirror down on the dresser and went over to the window
and looked out. It was getting dark.

85   'I want to pull my hair back tight and smooth and make a big knot at the
back that I can feel,' she said. 'I want to have a kitty to sit on my lap and
purr when I stroke her.'

'Yeah?' George said from the bed.

'And I want to eat at a table with my own silver and I want candles. And
90 I want it to be spring and I want to brush my hair out in front of a mirror
and I want a kitty and I want some new clothes.'

'Oh, shut up and get something to read,' George said. He was reading
again.

His wife was looking out of the window. It was quite dark now and still
95 raining in the palm trees.

'Anyway, I want a cat,' she said. 'I want a cat. I want a cat now. If I can't
have long hair or any fun, I can have a cat.'

George was not listening. He was reading his book. His wife looked
out of the window where the light had come on in the square.
100 Someone knocked at the door.

'Avanti,' George said. He looked up from his book.

In the doorway stood the maid. She held a big tortoise-shell cat
pressed tight against her and swung down against her body.

'Excuse me,' she said, 'the padrone asked me to bring this for the
105 Signora.'

I shall begin this chapter by making a number of observations about
some effects produced by this short text. The observations correspond
to the main intuitions I have felt in reading and rereading the story a
number of times. Needless to say, my intuitions may be different from
those of others, and, therefore, what I want to investigate here will be
limited by and to those intuitions. I then go on to suggest some
questions relevant to an interpretation of the story which those same
intuitions give rise to. The central core of the chapter is taken up by a
linguistic examination of those parts of the text which seem most
prominently to produce the effects I have noticed. The 'hidden'
assumption in all this is that some linguistic analysis of a literary text is
essential if something other than a merely intuitive or impressionistic
account of the story is to be given.

I have three main intuitions about the story:

(1) The style is very simple and straightforward but it produces complex
effects. I am left with a feeling of uncertainty and ambiguity at the end.
(2) The story is 'about' some kind of rift in the relationship between the two
Americans. Without ever mentioning the word or related words
Hemingway conveys a feeling of 'the American wife's' *frustration*.
(3) The 'cat' of the title is somehow made to stand for something else. For
want of a better word, I might say that it is symbolic.

Perhaps it will be thought that only intuition (1) has anything to do
with the way in which the language of 'Cat in the Rain' is patterned. I
hope to demonstrate that (2) and (3) are to a large extent conditioned
by linguistic patterning. In any case, I certainly do not feel I can
account for them by reference only to singularly literary co-ordinates
such as 'theme', 'symbolism', 'plot', or 'character'.

In the course of my analysis I shall be referring to a number of different features of the text's linguistic structure. Among these are: the role of modal verbs in the story; cohesion, and cohesion by repetition; the function of a narrative device which has come to be termed 'free indirect speech'. Above all, I want to try to show that a primary locus for stylistic effects in 'Cat in the Rain' is to be found in the structure of nominal groups and in the links between them. (Put simply, a nominal group can be defined as those features which are in a relationship with *nouns*.) These linguistic features may be conveniently divided into three main areas for exploration:

I   Nominal Group Structure
II Verbal Structures and Free Indirect Speech
III Cohesion, Repetition and Ambiguity.

The features are selected because they are particularly striking and because they seem, in varying degrees, to be responsible for the effects I have outlined.

I Nominal Group Structure

Most critical writing about Hemingway's 'style' tends to converge on a limited range of adjectives by which it is characterised. 'Clipped', 'laconic', 'bare', 'colourless', 'simple' appear to be among the most frequent. Perhaps the most striking aspect of this 'simple style' can be found in the opening paragraph of our text (lines 1–14).

I am struck here above all by a preponderance of the definite article. 'The' occurs twenty-seven times in that relatively short paragraph. It occurs, too, in nominal groups where there is little between the definite article and the noun (what can be termed minimal modification of the headword) and in groups where there is little which follows or further defines the noun to which the definite article points (termed qualification of the headword). Take, for example, a sentence such as the following which I have invented for purposes of comparison and contrast:

```
A   d       e        e         e       h      e                  h
    The vivacious young American woman with deep, penetrating eyes
        └──────── m ────────┘        └─────── q ──────────┘
        d     e   e            d     e     h
    stood at the half-open door of the dilapidated hotel.
        m                         m
```

The nominal groups contain definite articles (*d*), headwords (*h*), epithets (*e*), noun-modifiers (*n*) and structures which modify (*m*) and qualify (q) those same headwords.[1] Compare these with what are typical structures in the paragraph in question:

B   *d*   *h*   *d*   *n*   *h*
   (i) The rain dropped from the palm trees.

        d   *h*   *d*   *h*   *d*   *n*   *h*
  (ii) The motor-cars were gone from the square by the war-monument

               e   *h*   *e*   *h*   *d*   *n*   *h*
 (iii) There were big palms and green benches in the public garden

One structure in particular – that of definite article (d) and headword (h) – is largely repeated in other nominal groups:

the hotel	*dh*
the beach	*dh*
the café	*dh*
the square	*dh*
the empty square	*deh*
the hotels facing the gardens	*dh/dh/dh*

$$\underbrace{\text{facing the gardens}}_{q} \qquad q$$

and the sea
$\underbrace{\phantom{\text{and the sea}}}_{q}$

I am not, of course, saying that sentence A is in itself necessarily 'normal', but the comparison does allow us to draw some conclusions about the 'style' being used. The kind of structures in B allow a description to emerge where objects or things appear without any particular characteristics. It is as 'bare' as the square is 'empty'. But isolating the nominal group structures in this way does not explain all the effects produced in this opening paragraph.

    Looking back at the nominal groups in Section B above produces an impression of what might be termed 'familiarity'. It is a familiarity which comes in a way from knowing what is referred to. Particularly in encountering 'the hotel', 'the room facing the sea', 'the beach', 'the bright colours of the hotels facing the gardens and the sea', the 'palms . . . in the public garden' I feel I am faced with a typical scene – one I might find on picture postcards or read about in a not dissimilar 'style' in numerous travel brochures. In other words, I somehow do not need to be told more than the writer reveals because, given these props, I, as it were, supply or fill in the details myself. It is as if Hemingway is saying that such a setting is something that we all know so well. It needs no elaboration. In a related way, we might reasonably be expected to infer that this is the type of hotel typical Americans abroad would stay at. Given this opening paragraph, the reader might be forgiven for expecting that a description of a typical or stereotyped relationship between 'the American wife' and 'her husband' will follow. In any case, the paragraph gives a good example of the complex range of effects which can be brought about by this apparently simple style. I shall be returning to the 'language' of this paragraph several times in the course of the chapter.

It is interesting to explore further how both nominal group structure and definite-article usage, in particular, are patterned across the whole text. Basically, our observations for the first paragraph hold for the remaining paragraphs. For example, some representative 'structures' are as follows: the umbrella; the cat; the door; the gravel path; the maid; the hotel-keeper; the office; the doorway; the book; the padrone; the signora; the dressing table; the hand-glass – though it should be noted that the repetition of items is not quite so concentrated after the first paragraph. But there is still no marked deviation from the 'simple style' and the particular effects established in that significant opening.

This is not to say that there are no variations on the norm created by the text. In fact, where they do occur, variations are all the more foregrounded. For example:

She liked his old, heavy face and big hands.
a cat
a big, tortoise-shell cat . . . swung down against her body
cat in the rain

Here we have the greatest degrees of modification in the text applied to a description of the hotel-keeper and the cat respectively. We also notice the indefinite article used in relation to what is elsewhere predominantly *the* cat; connected with 'cat', too, is the title where the noun has no definite article in front of it.

In fact, not only are the hotel-keeper and the cat brought into some degree of prominence, but with attention focused on nominal groups stylistic patterns are also noticeable with reference to the other main 'subjects' of the story:

The Wife	*The Cat*	*The Husband*
the American wife (l.15)	cat (in the rain)	her husband (l.25)
the wife (l.28)	the cat (l.17)	the husband (l.28)
the American girl (l.47)	the kitty (l.21)	George (l.73)
his wife (l.94)	a big tortoise-shell cat (l.102)	

In particular, we might note that George – the name of the husband – recurs unaltered from the middle to the end of the story.

Discussion of the kind of meanings elicited by such patterns and variations in nominal group structure must await corresponding analysis of other structures, but some preliminary deductions can be recorded at this stage:

(1) Contact with the 'kitty' seems to equate with the wife being referred to as a 'girl'. In the hotel room she is 'the wife' or 'the American wife'.
(2) The husband remains unaffected. By contrast, the wife, who at the end is referred to as *his* wife, remains nameless throughout. There is a clear contrast in the identities they are given.
(3) The tortoise-shell cat may not be identical with the 'kitty' the woman was searching for. In any case, the cat seems both definite and indefinite.
(4) The 'setting' for the story is made to seem a familiar and expected one.

II Verbal Structures and Free Indirect Speech

In this section I want to explore a number of observations relevant to verbal group organisation in this text, and to see what significance might be attached to them. I also want to draw attention to what I see as a relationship between verbal group structure and viewpoint in the story. I hope to show that analysis of such features allows some further support for intuitions concerning the nature of the relationship between the husband and wife and the 'ambiguity' of the whole text.

It is noticeable how, in this story, a limited range of verbs are employed in a relatively limited range of structures. The main pattern for most verbal groups in the text is as follows:

> The wife *went* downstairs and the hotel owner *stood up* and *bowed* to her as she *passed* the office. His desk *was* at the far end of the office. He *was* an old man and very tall.

That is, a sentence contains either one (usually) or more than one (occasionally) main verb in either simple past or past progressive tense (e.g. 'was reading'). It is a feature which contributes to our impression of the simplicity of the story's style. They are also the basic and expected tenses for conveying narrative action. But what are we to make of those structures which draw attention to themselves by deviation from this expected pattern?

The presence of both auxiliary or modal verbs which add a different 'colouring' to the basic structure and/or switches in tense should be of some communicative import in the process of the story. Take the following stretch of text, for example:

> C Liking him she opened the door and looked out. It was raining harder. A man in a rubber cape was crossing the empty square to the café. The cat would be around to the right. Perhaps she could go along under the eaves. As she stood in the doorway an umbrella opened behind her. It was the maid who looked after their room.

'You must not get wet,' she smiled, speaking Italian. Of course, the hotel-keeper had sent her.

This is the first time modal verbs occur in the text. We have 'could', 'would', 'must' – and a switch in *tense*, 'had sent'. Their occurrence, I would argue, coincides with a moment of excitement in the story, aroused by the woman's nearness to the cat she is seeking and by the kindness shown her by the hotel-keeper (see lines 25–34). As a result, this passage stands out from the otherwise flat and repetitive narrative. In fact, the 'wife' in the story becomes, as it were, 'associated' with modal verbs in contrast to her husband, whose actions and talk remain very much on the same plane:

D 'Anyway, I want a cat', she said. 'I want a cat. I want a cat now. If I can't have long hair or any fun, I can have a cat.'
   George was not listening. He was reading his book.

We can also note near the end of the story an important switch to the present tense in 'I want a cat' from 'I wanted that poor kitty' and observe a corresponding shift from reference to a particular kitty she had looked for to an expression which is both more general and indefinite. But, most of all, I am struck in passage C by the fact that the emotional contours of the wife's 'state' are rendered by a stylistic device known as 'free indirect speech'. It is a feature which works largely to confirm and extend what has already been said about verbal group organisation.

At this juncture some explanation of the notion of 'free indirect speech' is needed. Consider the following three sentences:

(1) He stopped and said to himself: 'Is that the car I saw here yesterday?' – DIRECT SPEECH
(2) He stopped and asked himself if that was the car he had seen there the day before – INDIRECT SPEECH
(3) He stopped. Was that the car he had seen yesterday? – FREE INDIRECT SPEECH

As the term indicates, free indirect speech finds itself somewhere between direct and indirect speech. In literary terms this puts it between an author's reproduction of a character's actual dialogue or speech and a (reported) account of what a character has said. With a free indirect speech, or FIS, a kind of fusion takes place between authorial and character viewpoint in which the shape and texture of the character's voice can be preserved without any loss of the narrator's objective interpretation of events. Pascal (1977), in an extensive study of this narrative device, has aptly termed it 'the dual voice'. In passage C the locutions

Perhaps she could go along under the eaves.
The cat would be around to the right.
Of course, the hotel-keeper had sent her.

are examples of FIS and mark a point in the text – the only point, it should be added – where there is a momentary identification of viewpoint in both Hemingway, as narrator, and 'the American wife'.

The convergence of FIS and a foregrounded concentration of modal verbs marks this as a moment of particular significance in the story. It also reveals this to be a not wholly objective narrative presentation. However 'colourless' or 'neutral' is the style overall, Hemingway seems to allow a merging of his point of view with that of his protagonist. It may not be coincidental that immediately subsequent to passage C the 'American wife' is transformed into 'the American girl'. After that, a more objective narrative mode prevails, but the FIS 'fusion' enables us to conclude that *viewpoint* may be a significant contributory factor in any interpretation of this ambiguous and open-ended text. Do we sympathise with the woman and her plight? To what extent is the rift in the relationship attributable to the husband's failure to 'orient' himself to her needs? Or is her longing too vague and indefinite to evoke sympathy? The presence of 'free indirect speech' here seems to tip the scales slightly towards some identification with the 'American *girl*'.

At all events, we should not be in a position to approach answers to the questions raised above *without* the evidence available from a linguistic examination of aspects of nominal and verbal group structure. In the remaining section of the article I hope to draw together the points raised thus far and pay some attention to features in both nominal and verbal groups in the text which have been omitted. The main features come under the headings of *cohesion* and *repetition*. (The term 'cohesion' is used to describe those features of language which provide links and connections between sentences.) I then proceed to attempt to establish a basis for interpretation of 'Cat in the Rain'.

III Cohesion, Repetition and Ambiguity

The first aspect of cohesion with which I wish to deal concerns the nature of the suprasentential organisation in the opening paragraph. Here I shall return to those definite articles. Firstly, however, a brief digression is needed.

Basically, in English, 'the' can fulfil a number of functions. These can be approximately demarcated as follows:

(1) *The* school is worth supporting.

(2)   *The* moon is covered by clouds.
(3)   It was raining. *The* rain was cold.

Put simply: (1) is *exophoric*; that is, if it has not been mentioned previously in the text, it refers outwards to information or knowledge which listeners or readers can be presumed to share; (2) is *homophoric* and similarly outward-pointing, but the referent is in such cases singular and unique; (3) is *anaphoric* in that it points backwards to information which has already preceded. In each case, 'the' works to establish co-ordinates within and across sentences so that, in particular, when they are linked, the links are cohesive. It can be noted here, too, that verbal repetition can work similarly in establishing the cohesive texture of a passage.

On this basis we might usefully ask, what are the effects produced by cohesion in this stretch of text from the middle of the first paragraph:

E   In the good weather there was always an artist with his easel. Artists liked the way the palms grew and the bright colours of the hotels facing the gardens and the sea. Italians came from a long way off to look up at the war monument. It was made of bronze and glistened in the rain. It was raining. The rain dripped from the palm trees.

This passage contains definite articles occurring anaphorically (the rain; the palm trees) and as a result of verbal repetition (rain; palms; artists); a number of items, too, have already been established previously in the text by exophoric reference (the hotel; the sea; the gardens). What we seem to have, therefore, is a passage which is especially cohesive and harmonious. These inter-sentential cohesive effects operate to strengthen and reinforce expectations. It is achieved by quite simple and conventional means. But, again, I want to suggest that a number of quite complex literary effects are brought about by this patterning. In fact, I want to suggest that a major effect is, paradoxically, that expectations are *deflated* as well as confirmed. How exactly is this done? One main way in which it is done is for lexical items in the nominal groups to be repeated verbatim. Where reference to 'the hotel', 'the square', 'the palm trees', 'the war monument' recurs, we expect, I think, that there will be variation in the way cohesive links are established. For example, they could be substituted by a pronoun, be further modified or qualified or be replaced by a synonym or hyponym.[2] But nothing changes. There is cohesive fit, but the discourse does not actually go anywhere.

Another example of this 'deflation' is provided by the sentence:

The sea broke in a long line in the rain and slipped back down the beach to come up and break again in a long line in the rain.

The sentence is symmetrical, but it does not, once again, go anywhere. The effect of rhythmic devices and of verbal repetition is to enact a circularity of sameness and repetition. 'Expectations' are fulfilled and yet somehow not fulfilled. Similarly, in passage E (above), the positioning of words, tense and sentence structure combine with 'cohesive' devices to reinforce further the deflation or reversal of expectations. In the first sentence, expectations of 'good weather' are set up, along with a 'romantic' picture of artists and bright colours. The reference to the war monument which 'glistened in the rain' tends to be read as 'whenever it rained'. The glistening seems lexically connected, too, with the bright colours. The sentence which follows, 'It was raining', deflates these expectations. We suddenly realise the artists and the good weather are absent.

Cohesive organisation in the opening paragraph may, then, be concluded to have quite particular effects. On the one hand, exophoric references make us establish a familiar and stereotypical world. On another level, the same familiarity is reinforced by repetition; the repetition works to make it all seem somehow *too* familiar.

This paragraph is 'deflationary', then, for a number of reasons. We expect repeated items to be further modified or qualified in some way. But they are not. Things are also 'deflationary' because the features bringing colour and life to the scene are characterised by their absence but are described almost as if they were present. The pattern is one of familiarity leading to over-familiarity and stereotype and of expectation leading to the frustration of expectation. And it is created in the very linguistic texture of the paragraph.[3]

Conclusion

I shall now attempt to draw some of the results of our linguistic examination into the basis of an interpretation of the story, though we must remember that I have throughout been working from a limited number of intuitions about the text and that it is to these that, for better or for worse, we should now return.

(1) 'Simple' Style and Ambiguity
(2) The Marital Rift
(3) The Significance of the Cat in the Story

The simplicity of the 'style' of this text does not point to a simple or straightforward interpretation. Complex effects – chief among these are a sense of expectation and 'deflation', emotional heightening and a *development* of the subjects' identity across the *process* of the text – are achieved using some very basic linguistic patterning. A sense of deflation and of stereotypicality, especially in the first paragraph (which acts as a *backcloth* for the story), is produced by a particular nominal group structure and a number of basic cohesive devices.

Slight, but significant, shifts in awareness are also communicated by shifts among words or from one word to its lexical collocate or partner. In the case of something like 'cat', such shifts, though achieved by the simplest of means, cannot be without significance. In fact, we need to return here to questions raised in Section I such as: Is the cat the same as the 'kitty'? Why does the 'woman' undergo some metamorphosis in the course of the text from 'wife' to 'girl', and so on? And finally, we should remember that Hemingway's *neutral* style does not prevent authorial intrusion. Free indirect speech, again achieved by the simplest of means, allows an identification with a character to occur. It gives the subtlest of orientations to an otherwise objective and indeterminate narrative.

That the 'core' of the story is a rift in the relationship between the husband and the wife is made clear on a number of levels. But in drawing the threads of linguistic analysis together into the basis of some kind of interpretation of the story, I would argue that a dominant impression we are left with is that of the stereotyped nature of the relationship between the American wife and the American husband. The stereotypicality and familiarity of it all seems a basic part of Hemingway's purpose – particularly at the opening of the story. Within this pattern we are made, albeit only marginally, to identify with the needs of the wife. She is clearly searching for some means of escape from this routine scene. She seems to want a new identity. The hotel-keeper is ostensibly more sympathetic than her husband. The search for the kitty serves to rejuvenate her and to break the dull and repetitive frame in which she is trapped.

But what does the cat symbolise? How do we account for what the linguistic details of the text highlighted elsewhere suggest? That is, that the cat is not the same as the 'kitty' the wife is looking for. For, after all, if it is not what she is looking for, this may lead to a deflation of the wife's expectations. The linguistic texture of the story would lead us to conclude that the 'kitty' is not the same as the cat described at the end:

In the doorway stood the maid. She held a big tortoise-shell cat pressed tight against her and swung down against her body.

Though some appeal would have to be made to informants to substantiate my impressions in some inter-subjectively valid terms, I do not see a correlation here between 'cat' and 'kitty'. To me, this is a grotesque outcome to the kind of associations aroused in me by the word 'kitty'.

We must acknowledge, of course, that the wife's reaction is withheld from us and as a result an essentially indeterminate outcome to the narrative is preserved. But, recalling what we have analysed within the language of the story as a main pattern of expectation→frustration of expectation, it may not be too much of an assertion to say that an interpretation of the story in these terms is possible.

The hotel-keeper remains a hotel-keeper and is fixed within the strictly denotative role he is assigned by the linguistic representation 'the hotel-keeper'. If he doesn't supply the *right* cat, perhaps he is not quite a 'third party' but, like a 'model' hotel-keeper, simply attempting to placate the foibles of his hotel guests. Similarly, George remains George. Immovable, passive and the American husband. His wife's search hardly affects him.

In this situation the American wife evokes our sympathy (and the narrator's), but as the story progresses we are, as it were, moved towards a conclusion. As her desire for *a* cat becomes more and more indefinite, and as she becomes more desperate, we might conclude that the cat represents something in her experience which cannot be fulfilled – something which is present but is characterised here by its absence (like the artists and other 'features' of the opening paragraph). The cat begins by being something specific and ends up as a general symbol; simply

Cat in the Rain

It is neither definite nor indefinite.[4] It might be ultimately that the indeterminacy I have felt in connection with the story stems not so much from the possibility of dual interpretation at the end, or from symbolic ambiguities surrounding 'cat', but from this intuition of expectations unfulfilled and leading only back to the same place.

As far as interpretation via linguistics is concerned, I would claim that the analysis undertaken appropriately substantiates my original intuitions and that I would want to use this analysis as the *basis* for any further work on the text. Certainly, it enables me to incline towards a particular interpretation in a relatively systematic and objective way. I use the word 'incline' advisedly and in recognition that interpretation is to a considerable extent an individual matter. But language is a shared property and should, therefore, when analysed, provide a common basis for the release of meanings. Whether this can be said of the analysis here of 'Cat in the Rain', I cannot be the judge.

Acknowledgements

I am especially grateful to Margaret Berry, Walter Nash and Michael Stubbs for their comments on a first draft of this paper. I have adopted many of their suggestions in this final version.

Notes: Chapter 5

1   For fuller definition and description of the nominal group organisation, see Berry (1975: ch. 5) and Sinclair (1972: ch. 3).
2   See, for example, the kind of changes which result from experimenting with different cohesive links ('Suggestions for Further Work', II, ii, below).
3   And this is not to exclude the presence of semantic oppositions in the paragraph such as public garden (peace) v. *war* monument. One 'state' is quickly counteracted by its contrary.
4   In fact, articleless singular headwords are unusual in modern English. One of the uses to which they are put is in captions to pictures or sculptures. Is Hemingway suggesting here that his story is analogous to the 'frozen action' of a picture, that is, activity within a frame which does not go anywhere? See discussion by Widdowson (1975: 108–15) of a not unrelated feature of Roethke's poem 'Child on Top of a Greenhouse'.

Suggestions for Further Work: Chapter 5

I   Nominal Group Structure

The *basic* structure of nominal groups in English consists, as we have seen, of five main elements. They may be demonstrated again in the following sentence:

```
    d       e       n       h
All the  attractive  stone  fireplaces
designed by Nash in the deep-gray shades of
    q
the seventeenth century  are on show in the exhibition.
    q
```

(i)   Rewrite the opening paragraph to 'Cat in the Rain' making full use of as many elements of the nominal group as possible. Discuss any changes in communicative effects which you feel may have been brought about.
(ii) Examine the main differences in nominal group organisation and communicative intent between the opening to 'Cat in the Rain' and this extract from the opening chapters of Iris Murdoch's *An Unofficial Rose*:

> The drawing-room was a long room with three big windows hollowed and upholstered with shabby chintz window-seats. Beside the front porch, it also had the view of the beach-fringed lawn. The lines of roses were out of sight now below the hill and between the towering beeches there was only visible the blue and white swiftly moving sky which before a brisk north-west wind was descending across the pallid chequered Marsh in the direction of Dungeness and the twenty miles distant sea. The room, which apart from Randall's bedroom was the only 'serious' room in the house, was pleasant enough, its panelling a faded green, its furniture of a battered elegance, old miscellaneous 'finds' in lesser antique shops. The thick fawn carpet

was scattered with a dim glow of threadbare rugs, which although 'if perfect' would be treasures, were now almost impossibly, manifestly, imperfect. A huge rosewood bookcase held the family library: rarely disturbed now since the younger Peronetts were not great readers.

(iii)   Rewrite the above paragraph employing the nominal group structures as used in 'Cat in the Rain' (e.g. use an absolute minimum of items at q). What changes occur?

II   Cohesion and the Nominal Group

(i)   Rewrite the paragraph from *An Unofficial Rose* using the kind of cohesive devices employed in 'Cat in the Rain'. Make particular use of verbatim repetition. Is it possible to produce a similar effect of boredom and stasis?

(ii)   Try writing out a few sentences from 'Cat in the Rain', linking them up in different ways. For example:

(*a*)   Their room was on the second floor facing the sea, public garden and war monument.

(*b*)   It was raining so that it dripped from the palm trees and stood in pools on the gravel paths.

(*c*)   It also faced the public garden and the war monument. There were big palms and green benches in that richly aromatic and carefully cultivated sanctuary.

(*d*)   Across the square in the doorway of the café a waiter stood looking out at the dully shining pavements and cobbles.

What changes are produced as a result of these different types of cohesion? Compare the effects with the cohesion by repetition employed by Hemingway.

III   Deixis

The and *a* are often referred to as deictic determiners. Explore some of their functions in 'Cat in the Rain' by:

(i)   Substituting *the* cat for *a* cat in the last ten paragraphs. How is the ambiguity of the ending affected?

(ii)   Rewrite the opening paragraph substituting *a* for *the* where it makes sense to do so. Discuss some of the specific and non-specific uses to which *the* and *a* can be put in English.

(iii)   Alter the title to (*a*) A Cat in the Rain, (*b*) The Cat in the Rain, (*c*) Cats in the Rain. What happens to the way we read the story?

IV   Free Indirect Speech

(i)   Examine this passage from chapter 16 of Jane Austen's *Mansfield Park*. Point out examples of FIS and discuss what seems to you to be the author's purpose in employing this narrative device.

He went; but there was no reading, no China, no composure for Fanny. He had told her the most extraordinary, the most inconceivable, the most unwelcome news; and she could think of nothing else. To be acting! After all his objections – objections so just and so public! After all that she had heard him say, and seen him look, and known him to be feeling. Could it be possible? Edmund so inconsistent! Was he not deceiving himself? Was he not wrong? Alas! it was all Miss Crawford's doing. She had seen her influence in every speech, and was miserable. The doubts and alarms as to her own conduct, which had previously distressed her, and which had all slept while she listened to him, were become of little consequence now. This deeper anxiety swallowed them up. Things should take their course; she cared not how it ended. Her cousins might attack, but could hardly tease her. She was beyond their reach; and if at last obliged to yield – no matter – it was all misery *now*.

References: Chapter 5

Berry, M. (1975), *Introduction to Systemic Linguistics*, Vol. I (London: Batsford).
Sinclair, J. McH. (1972), *A Course in Spoken English: Grammar* (London: OUP).
Widdowson, H. G. (1975), *Stylistics and the Teaching of Literature* (London: Longman).

Introduction to Chapter 6

Chris Kennedy's chapter summarises simply and clearly aspects of Halliday's work on clause types and their constituent functions and relationships in terms of the following:

(1) clause types as (a) actions
  (b) mental processes (perception, reaction cognition, verbalisation)
  (c) relations (attributive, equative);
(2) constituents of transitivity relations as
  (a) processes
  (b) participants (actors, goals, results, beneficiaries, instruments)
  (c) circumstantial features.

He follows this with an extended discussion of these same features in a less obvious case – the passage dealing with the murder of Verloc in Conrad's *The Secret Agent*. One important point being made here is that stylistic analysis need not be directed towards foregrounded examples of linguistic 'deviance', but can be used successfully in elucidating features and meanings in *any* text – however much the use of the language there may seem to be unremarkable prior to linguistic analysis.

The work on Conrad is followed by a discussion of a James Joyce story from the collection *Dubliners* entitled 'Two Gallants'. The representation of the two main characters in that story is analysed first in terms of the features drawn from Halliday and already discussed, and secondly in terms of the different statuses of the two men as indicated by their differing uses of address terms and question and answer, and also in relation to the lexis associated with the description of each man. In this way, Chris Kennedy shows how Halliday's overriding notion of the three main functions of language (the ideational, the interpersonal and the textual), which he introduces at the beginning of his explanatory opening to the whole chapter, can *all* be examined in a text, in order to articulate the contributory factors to a reader's interpretation of the events and participants in the microcosm of that text.

6 Systemic Grammar and its Use in Literary Analysis

CHRIS KENNEDY

This chapter will first review certain aspects of the grammatical system developed by Halliday and describe how he proposes to apply his system to the literary analysis of texts. Two main texts will then be analysed in an attempt to explore the usefulness of this approach to stylistics.

Halliday sees language in terms of three functions which, though distinct in the sense that they can be isolated and listed, act together to produce a passage of discourse. These three functions are (1) the ideational, (2) the interpersonal, and (3) the textual (Halliday, 1970). The ideational function is concerned with cognitive meaning, the interpersonal with describing the relations between persons (hence questions and answers, positive and negative forms, are part of this function), and the textual is concerned with the process enabling the speaker or writer to construct texts as a logical sequence of units.

In his writings on language functions, Halliday has chosen to discuss one of the possible options available within the ideational function, the transitivity function, to illustrate how stylistics may be able to profit from the application of a grammatical model to the analysis of a literary text. The transitivity function is composed of three elements:

(a) the process, represented by the verb,
(b) the participants, the roles of persons and objects,
(c) circumstantial functions, in English typically the adverbials of time, place and manner.

Thus in the sentence

(1) John painted the house

the *process* is represented by the verb form 'painted' and the participant functions by the actor 'John' and the goal 'the house'. Where the 'goal' comes into existence as a result of the process, it is referred to as the object of result. For example, in (2) 'poem' is the object of result since it comes into existence as a result of the process of composing:

(2)   He composed a poem.

A further participant function is that of beneficiary, who may be either the recipient of an object, 'John' in (3), or of a service, 'the baby' in (4):

(3)   He's given John a present.
(4)   She's knitted the baby a cardigan.

Although at first sight it may appear that the term 'actor' is simply a newly coined term for what in traditional terms is called the 'grammatical subject', this is not in fact the case, since in the examples (5)–(7) 'John' is actor in all three sentences, but grammatical subject only in (5):

(5)   John attacked the referee.
(6)   The referee was attacked by John.
(7)   John's attacking of the referee. . . .

A final participant role is that of instrument, which is distinguished from 'actor' by virtue of the fact that it is inanimate. Thus, in

(8)   The ball broke the window.

'ball' may be regarded as instrument. However, if we consider two transformations of (8):

(9)   The window was broken by the ball.
(10)   The window was broken with the ball.

we see that the addition of 'with' and 'by' to the sentences appears to change their meaning. By using 'with' in (10) the implication is that the window was broken deliberately. On the other hand, there seems to be no such implication of intent to break the window in (9) where 'by' is used. A further distinction must therefore be drawn between the role of instrument ('with the ball'), indicating that the process described was deliberate, and that of force ('by the ball'), where the meaning is neutral in the sense that the process is not regarded as a deliberate action.

Roles may therefore be summarised as (a) actor, (b) goal or object of result, (c) beneficiary or recipient, and (d) instrument of force. It may be that certain verbs are always associated with certain participant roles, even though the roles do not necessarily have to be expressed. Thus, the verb 'hit' has three participant roles associated with it, actor, goal and instrument, as in

(11)   The boy hit the animal with a stick.

Although the goal must be stated in English with the verb 'hit', the 'instrumental' role may or may not be expressed, depending on the context and information structure of the discourse of which the sentence is a part. The sentence

(12)   The boy hit the animal.

is therefore acceptable and, since the instrumental role is optionally expressed, the verb 'hit' is classified as *inherently* instrumental, in the same way as 'give' and 'lend' are *inherently* benefactive.

In dealing with clause types, Halliday distinguishes three main types, those of action, mental process, and relation. The mental-process verbs are further divided into verbs of perception, reaction, cognition and verbalisation, all of which, rather than having actor and goal as participant roles, have processor and phenomenon:

(13)   He saw his sister (person)
           the purpose (abstraction)
           the Trooping of the Colour (event)
           the jewel (object)

In (13) 'he' is the processor, 'saw' the process, and the items within the brackets different types of phenomena. Relational clauses are those in which the process describes or states a relation between two roles. Thus

(14)   He's a musician (attributive type)
(15)   Mr Smith is the secretary (equative type)

are examples of this type of clause. Halliday also classifies action clauses and mental-process clauses in terms of what he calls the ergative function. He defines this function in terms of an affected participant which is the one inherent role associated with action clauses, and which is the goal in a transitive and the actor in an intransitive clause:

(16)   He fell.
(17)   The dog frightens me.

In (16) 'he' is the affected participant; in (17) it is 'me', with 'the dog' classified as the 'causer' of the process.

I now want to consider how certain features of grammar can provide insights into the literary effects of a description of an event in a novel and how the same features can inform the theme of a short story taken as a whole. What I also hope to show is that Halliday's approach can be used with texts which are not obviously deviant in the sense that at first sight the language patterns form part of 'standard' English. If it is shown that Halliday's system can be used for analysis of a much broader range of texts to bring out the significance of passages and the author's intention by revealing a semantically motivated pattern of language functions, then this will prove a valuable approach to textual analysis.

The first passage I wish to discuss is taken from Joseph Conrad's *The Secret Agent*, and the particular scene I have analysed is the murder of Mr Verloc by his wife. The event comes at the end of a chapter describing Mrs Verloc's reaction to the news that her brother Stevie is dead and that Mr Verloc, as she sees it, caused his death. There are some interesting literary effects produced here. They relate in particular to the central characters of Mr and Mrs Verloc, and the passage is thus a seminal one in the novel. Most prominent are my intuitions of Verloc's submissiveness and that Mrs Verloc is somehow not really responsible for what she does although this is nowhere stated explicitly by Conrad. I propose to look first at the verbs describing the murder and the events leading up to it.

She started forward at once, as if she were still a loyal woman bound to that man by an unbroken contract. Her right hand skimmed lightly the end of the table, and when she had passed on towards the sofa the carving knife had vanished without the slightest sound from the side of the dish. Mr Verloc heard the creaky plank in the floor, and was content. He waited. Mrs Verloc was coming. As if a homeless soul of Stevie had flown for shelter straight to the breast of his sister, guardian and protector, the resemblance of her face with that of her brother grew at every step, even to the droop of the lower lip, even to the slight divergence of the eyes. But Mr Verloc did not see that. He was lying on his back and staring upwards. He saw partly on the ceiling and partly on the wall the moving shadow of an arm with a clenched hand holding a carving knife. It flickered up and down. Its movements were leisurely. They were leisurely enough for Mr Verloc to recognize the limb and the weapon.

They were leisurely enough for him to take in the full meaning of the portent, and to taste the flavour of death rising in his gorge. His wife had gone raving mad – murdering mad. They were leisurely enough for the first paralysing effect of this discovery to pass away before a resolute determination to come out victorious from the ghastly struggle with that armed lunatic. They were leisurely enough for Mr Verloc to elaborate a plan of defence, involving a dash behind the table, and the felling of the woman to the ground with a heavy wooden chair. But they were not leisurely enough to allow Mr Verloc the time to move either hand or foot. The knife was already planted in his breast. It met no resistance on its way. Hazard has such accuracies. Into that plunging blow, delivered over the side of the couch, Mrs Verloc had put all the inheritance of her immemorial and obscure descent, the simple ferocity of the age of caverns, and the unbalanced nervous fury of the age of bar-rooms. Mr Verloc, the secret agent, turning slightly on his side with the force of the blow, expired without stirring a limb, in the muttered sound of the word 'Don't' by way of protest.

There are thirteen verbs referring to Mr Verloc as a participant in the role of actor. Of these thirteen, eight are verbs describing a mental process – in particular, that of perception. Of the remaining verbs with Verloc as actor, all except one are intransitive, that is, they are used without a goal, and are passive in the sense that the processes are not initiated by Verloc, who is the affected participant not the causer. Thus, the verbs express processes over which Verloc does not exercise any control and in which he plays a submissive role. For example,

   (i) 'he was content' (because he hears the plank creaking, indicating that Mrs Verloc is coming over to him)
  (ii) 'he waited' (for Mrs Verloc)
 (iii) 'he expired' (his death is caused by Mrs Verloc's attack).

There are only three verbs describing Verloc's actions. All three are non-finite; one an infinitive, and two participial phrases, the participant not being explicitly expressed:

        (a) '. . . the time to move either hand or foot'
        (b) '. . . turning slightly on his side'
        (c) '. . . without stirring a limb'.

Notice that the potential of these processes (two of them goal-directed, (a) and (c)) to indicate deliberate action on the part of Verloc is not realised. In (b) Verloc does not turn himself on his side, but the movement is caused by the force of the blow delivered by Mrs Verloc. In (a) and (c) the goals are parts of the body and refer back to the actor (Verloc) and, thus, we are not aware of an action extending beyond that of the participant; indeed, the goals 'limb' and 'hand or foot' could be omitted with little change in meaning. The effect of the action is negated since in reality Verloc had no time to move before he was killed by his wife, and so the verbs actually tend to add to the overall impression of Verloc's impassivity.

If we look at the transitive verbs of mental process, we find that the phenomena and the processes are:

  (i) 'elaborate a plan'
       'taste the flavour of death'
       'take in the full meaning of the portent'
 (ii) 'hear the creaky plank'
       'not see that' (referring to Mrs Verloc's resemblance to Stevie)
       (see) 'the moving shadow of an arm'
       'recognise the limb and the weapon'

Both groups have Verloc as the processor. In group (i) the verbs of recognition and reaction are followed by (not unusual) abstract and metaphorical phenomena. However, the second group of verbs of perception are interesting in that the phenomena emphasise Verloc's role as a passive observer of an act he can do nothing to prevent. Mrs Verloc's actions and her husband's perception of them are described only indirectly (Mr Verloc never sees his wife, but makes connections between certain sounds and sights and her physical presence). He hears a plank creak and infers that she is coming towards him. He does not see the knife, the hand and the arm, but sees a shadow which he recognises as a limb and a weapon which he further identifies as an arm and a knife.

To summarise, the verbs with Verloc as actor are either mental-process verbs or intransitive with no goals, and none has Verloc as causer or initiator of the action. Verloc cannot control the situation and act in it, but is the passive observer of his own death, unable to influence the course of events. He sees and understands what is about to happen but does not have the time to transfer his thoughts on defence into action.

If we turn to the description of Mrs Verloc's actions, we notice that when she is the actor in a clause the verbs are intransitive verbs of action. Her actions are described without a goal; there is movement but no explicit goal mentioned, as though she is not fully in control of the situation. There seems to be no connection between her physical actions and the mental processes involved, as if she is driven by a force which she is unable to bring under control. This feeling that she is unaware of her actions is strengthened when we notice that explicit reference to Mrs Verloc as actor and causer is avoided in the transitive verbs of action which describe the steps leading up to the murder. Parts of the body take on the role of actor or the actor is replaced by an instrument. For example, we read:

(i) 'her right hand skimmed lightly the end of the table'
(ii) 'she passed on'
(iii) 'the carving knife had vanished'.

Obviously Mrs Verloc has taken the knife, but this is not stated in those terms. We have the pattern

(i) actor, causer (part of body) + process (action + instrument), affected (the table)
(ii) actor (she) + process (action)
(iii) instrument, affected (knife) + process (supervention)

In (i) the actor is not Mrs Verloc but her hand. This is followed by (ii) in which Mrs Verloc's actions are described, but notice a simple intransitive verb of movement is used with no goal, and in (iii) 'the knife' is used with a 'supervention' verb, (see chart p. 199), a verb describing a change which can be observed or which affects the actor but over which he has no control. We are not told 'Mrs Verloc took the knife', nor even 'her hand took the knife', but 'her hand skimmed . . . the table . . . the knife had vanished . . .'.

The reader is left to make the connection between the two actions, and this has the effect of 'distancing' Mrs Verloc from her own actions. It is as though her hand has a force of its own, detached from Mrs Verloc's mental processes. We are told the fact that the knife vanished but not the cause of its disappearance.

This impression of detachment, of someone who is not responsible for her actions, is strengthened by further examples of the avoidance of clauses with Mrs Verloc as actor. It has already been pointed out above that her movement towards her husband is signalled by a sound (the creaking plank) and that the references to Mrs Verloc are indirect; thus Verloc sees 'an arm with a clenched hand holding a carving knife', 'the limb and the weapon', which are seen not as physical objects but in the form of shadows. Notice, too, the use of the passive transformation, not 'she planted the knife', 'she delivered the blow', but 'the knife was . . . planted' and 'the blow [was] delivered', where the reference to the actor or causer (Mrs Verloc) is removed, and the instrument becomes the grammatical subject. The only specific reference to Mrs Verloc as actor in a transitive verb of action is after she has dealt the blow:

> Into that plunging blow . . . Mrs Verloc had put all the inheritance of her . . . descent, the simple ferocity . . . the unbalanced nervous fury. . . .

Here the goals are abstract concepts, not physical objects, the meanings of which serve to underline her disturbed mental state.

If we turn to an aspect of the inter-personal functions, that of mood, we notice that almost all the clauses are in the form of positive statements describing the events and thoughts of the two actors. There are four instances of negation in one form or another:

(i) But Mr Verloc did *not* see that.
(ii) But they were *not* leisurely enough to allow Mr Verloc the time to move. . . .
(iii) It met *no* resistance on its way.
(iv) Mr Verloc . . . expired *without* stirring . . . in the muttered sound of the word '*Don't*'. . . .

All four instances refer to Mr Verloc's inability to act to prevent his death. Moreover, the incomplete negative imperative 'Don't' contrasts with Verloc's positive imperative 'Come here' which precipitated the murder. The two imperatives, the one a command, the other a weak protest, form a frame round the events. It is interesting to note that the only 'action' Verloc is able to take before it is too late is this 'muttered sound'. The negative sentences (i) and (ii) are the only ones introduced by the conjunction 'but' and they play a significant part in the overall structure of the passage. Sentence (i) follows the description of the growing physical resemblance between Stevie and Mrs Verloc, which, had Mr Verloc noticed it, might have saved his life – hence the force of the 'but' and the negative.

Sentence (ii) is the last in a series of five, all with the same form, the difference in the last of the series being the addition of 'but' and 'not'. The series of repetitions is as follows:

They [the movements of the shadow] were leisurely enough
  (i)   for Mr Verloc to recognise the limb and the weapon . . .
  (ii) for him to take in the full meaning of the portent . . .
  (iii) [for him] to taste the flavour of death . . .
  (iv) for the first paralysing effect of this discovery to pass away . . .
  (v)   for Mr Verloc to elaborate a plan of defence . . .
  (vi) *But* they were not leisurely enough to allow Mr Verloc the time to move either hand or foot.

The force of the 'But' and the 'not', together with the previous repetition of the sentences, again serves to emphasise the fact that Verloc has time to see and think but not to *act*. His mental reactions to the situation are itemised (i)–(v), but his inability to take action is expressed in the one sentence (vi) which contrasts syntactically with the previous five sentences in the addition of 'But' and 'not'.

Figure 6.1 summarises the significant patterns which the analysis has revealed.

What we have seen from the analysis of the preceding passage is that, by selecting certain options available within certain functions, especially, in this case, the transitivity functions, the roles of participants in a situation may be defined, and an understanding of the reasons for their actions may be arrived at. It would be of interest to see whether such a pattern as came to light in the passage from Conrad is ever sustained throughout a novel as a whole, rather than just in a short passage. Although it is outside the scope of this chapter to attempt the analysis of a novel, I should like to analyse a short story with a view to discovering whether any pattern of options is present and, if so, whether the pattern is significant. The short story as a literary form is ideally suited to such an analysis since it is complete in itself, and a short-story writer has to achieve his ends as concisely and economically as possible. We might therefore expect that he would choose to highlight certain linguistic patterns in order to achieve a certain effect or to reveal particular facts about the participants in the story.

The story concerned is taken from the collection of short stories by James Joyce entitled *Dubliners*, and is called 'Two Gallants'.[1] The two

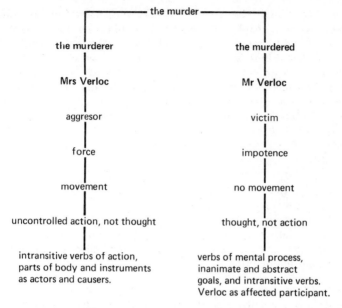

Figure 6.1 *Transitivity functions.*

'gallants' are Corley and Lenehan on their way to a rendezvous Corley has arranged with his latest woman admirer. The aim is that at the end of the evening the woman may be persuaded to give Corley money, which both men need, in return for his favours. The story presents a picture of two different characters, Lenehan and Corley, and the intention of the analysis is to see whether the considerable differences between the two men, of which we become aware as the story progresses, are communicated to the reader by the use of certain language patterning.

Taking the transitivity functions first, and counting the number of sentences in the story in which Lenehan and Corley are participants, there are approximately three times as many sentences with Lenehan as participant as there are with Corley (165 to 53, approximately, excluding dialogue). This is perhaps not surprising since Corley and Lenehan appear as participants together for the first half of the story, but then Corley meets the woman and they spend the evening together, leaving Lenehan, who is the sole participant in the rest of the story, until shortly before the end when he meets Corley once more. It might be argued it would be expected that a greater proportion of sentences with Lenehan as participant would be found. What is significant, however, is that, although this is the case, the reader is aware throughout the story that Lenehan does not in fact play an 'active' role, and is the 'passive' observer of events which Corley initiates. Although only one-third of the sentences have Corley as participant, it is Corley who is the leader and controller of events. This is obvious if we look at the story's content, since it is Corley who arranges the meeting with the woman, who obtains the money, and who already has experience of such manoeuvring. This difference between the two men is thus revealed by the action itself, but running through the whole story are certain linguistic patterns which confirm these impressions.

Firstly, of the 72 verbs of action with Lenehan as participant, two-thirds (47) are intransitive, that is, used without a goal. This contrasts with an equal distribution of transitive and intransitive verbs of action with Corley as participant. The fact that there are so many intransitive verbs of action is particularly evident during Lenehan's aimless walk round the town while waiting for Corley. A further point is the number of relational clauses serving simply to describe Lenehan's appearance rather than his actions. Again there is a contrast between the number of relational clauses describing Lenehan (20) and those describing Corley (9). These relational clauses tell us more of Lenehan's character, his appearance or his physical state, but they provide a 'static' description in the sense that they do not show us Lenehan acting.

But perhaps the most interesting pattern to emerge is the number of verbs of perception with Lenehan as implicit participant, twenty in all, and five times the number used with Corley as participant (only 4). In these four sentences, Corley is the actor:

(i)   He stared straight before him.
(ii) He gazed at the . . . moon.
(iii) Corley glanced . . . at his friend.
(iv) Corley stared before him.

For Corley, 'staring before him' seems part of his character – he looks at someone or something only if provoked in some way. This emphasises the description of Corley as a man who acts and who is not distracted from his actions by what is happening around him. His environment does not interest him unless women are involved. It is significant, therefore, that the processes in (ii) and (iii) are indirectly concerned with the subject of women. He gazes at the moon while thinking of a past sexual adventure and glances at his friend when he thinks Lenehan is taking too keen an interest in his (Corley's) woman.

As we have already noted, the verbs of perception with Lenehan as participant are twenty in number and consist of a variety of different verbs: 'glance', 'peer', 'watch', 'search', 'observe', 'make a scrutiny of', 'note', 'take note of', 'see', 'behold', etc. The impression this gives the reader is therefore of a man who observes situations but remains outside them and is unable to act within them. This impression is reinforced since in seven clauses Lenehan is not the actor, but 'his eyes'; for example: 'his eyes noted her body', 'his eyes glanced towards his face'. If the sentences had had Lenehan as actor ('he noted' and 'he glanced'), we would have been more aware of Lenehan's actions. As it is, with 'his eyes' as actors or, rather, processors, we are made aware of a lack of physical involvement and deliberate action on the part of Lenehan – his eyes reflect mental rather than physical processes. We notice this avoidance of mention of Lenehan as actor in 'his gaze was fixed... on the moon' which contrasts with the sentence describing the same process but referring to Corley: 'he gazed at the moon', where Corley is the actor and the process becomes a verb of action rather than perception. What emerges, then, is the picture of Lenehan as a passive character and Corley as an active, more determined individual who gets what he wants. This situation is, as noted above, reflected in the use of a part of the body, namely 'eyes', to describe Lenehan's actions. If we look at the parts of the body used as actors or, more appropriately, instruments, in the case of Corley we notice that both 'body' and 'head' occur. For example:

(1) His head was large.
(2) Corley swung his head.
(3) ... swaying his head.
(4) he watched Corley's head.
(5) Corley's ... head calmed him.

Notice, too:

(6) When he wished to gaze after someone, it was necessary for him to move his body from the hips.
(7) Corley's stride acknowledged the compliment.
(8) The swing of his burly body made his friend. ...
(9) His bulk, his pace, had something of the conqueror in them.
(10) His broad figure hid hers.

The repetition of 'head' suggests a physical presence which is also suggested by sentences (6)–(10). In sentences (7)–(10) parts of the body or expressions suggestive of physical attributes are used as actors ('stride', 'swing of his burly body', 'bulk', 'broad figure') where 'he' or 'Corley' would more normally be used. We would expect a human actor to be used with 'acknowledge', but in sentence (7) 'stride' is used instead. Corley's reaction to Lenehan's compliment is not expressed verbally as we might expect but physically. Similarly sentence (6) suggests that looking at someone is a process involving the whole body; compare this process with 'his [Lenehan's] bright small eyes searched his [Corley's] face', with the emphasis on 'bright small eyes' as actor in the clause. This difference between the two men, the one being a passive observer, the other an active initiator, is a significant factor in the personal relationships between the two friends. Essentially the relationship is based on a powerful/powerless dichotomy, expressed in the story in terms of leader/led, or master/servant, Corley being the former, Lenehan the latter.

Throughout the story, Lenehan maintains a deliberately servile position towards Corley. At the beginning there are references to Lenehan's reaction to Corley's 'long monologue' about a former mistress which are interesting in actor/process terms:

(1)   Lenehan wore an amused listening face.
(2)   The narrative made . . . waves of expression break forth over his face.
(3)   Jets of . . . laughter followed one another.
(4)   . . . waves of expression had passed over [his face].

In (1) the effect of using 'wore' in a metaphoric sense and describing Lenehan's face as 'amused' and 'listening' rather than directly expressing the feelings of Lenehan himself (e.g. 'he was amused') is to cause the reader to question the genuineness of Lenehan's reactions to Corley's monologue. Similarly examples (2), (3) and (4), avoiding explicit reference to Lenehan as actor, tend to dissociate him from the action, so that the result is a description of the act of laughter rather than someone (i.e. Lenehan) laughing. The laughter is artificially created for Corley's benefit, and is part of the systematic flattery Lenehan uses.

The power relationships between the two men are revealed if we examine the text in terms of the textual functions, in this case that of dialogue, and the inter-personal functions of mood, the occurrence of question-and-answer forms, statements, commands, etc., within the dialogue. A dialogue implies the presence of two people, the roles changing from speaker to listener, listener to speaker. However, it is evident from the analysis that Lenehan has the role of listener, Corley that of speaker, and this pattern reflects the passive/active contrast discussed above. In terms of quantity, Corley speaks more than Lenehan – 50 utterances to Lenehan's 28. All except 7 of the 50 utterances spoken by Corley are descriptive statements or answers to Lenehan's questions. The actors in Corley's utterances are predominantly 'I' or 'she'. There are 30 instances of 'I', 16 of 'she'. That is to say, Corley talks about himself for the majority of the time and, if this is not the case, then he is talking about a woman, either one he has known or the woman he is going to meet that evening. Even when he is not talking about himself, then, he is talking about someone intimately concerned with his actions, and in this sense it can be maintained that his concern is totally with himself, not with others. The actor in Lenehan's utterances, however, is predominantly 'you', that is, Corley.

Lenehan uses 'I' only eight times, and never with a verb of action but with verbs of cognition ('know') or those expressing uncertainty ('I suppose you'll be able to pull it off?'). Lenehan's attention, then, is centred not on himself but entirely on Corley.

This is illustrated when we consider the function of mood as applied to Lenehan's speech. Corley only asks one question, and his speech consists of statements. What is significant about Lenehan's speech is the number of questions he asks Corley. Now, a series of questions and answers tends to set up a relationship between questioner and answerer which is one of superior/inferior contrast depending on a system of power relationships. If it is the superior who is the questioner, the answerer is being tested in some way, whereas if the questioner is addressing a superior, then he is either requesting authoritative confirmation or asking for information he does not possess from someone who does possess that information and, indeed, has the power to withhold it. In this story, it is Lenehan who is in the position of the inferior questioner, addressing a superior, Corley. The questions Lenehan asks are of these types. First, they serve to show Corley that Lenehan is interested in what he is saying, and as such they are a form of flattery. Secondly, they express Lenehan's anxiety about the meeting between Corley and the woman, and are an appeal for reassurance that the plan will succeed. (Notice, incidentally, that Corley, in his replies to these questions, shows no such signs of anxiety or fear of failure.) Thirdly, at the end of the story, Lenehan wishes to find out whether Corley did obtain any money. Lenehan asks four times, but Corley gives no verbal reply. Ten further utterances spoken by Lenehan (five exclamations and five statements) consist of flattering remarks referring to Corley's success with women, and a further three express Lenehan's agreement with something Corley has said. Lenehan specifically avoids confrontation with Corley and adopts a servile position, in contrast to Corley, who succeeds in maintaining a superior position – for example, not stopping or replying when Lenehan calls out to him after his meeting with the woman. It is significant that Lenehan's earlier request, 'let's have a look at her', is interpreted by Corley as a potential attack on his 'property', the woman, and he counters it with the only question he asks in the story, which is in fact a veiled threat: 'Are you trying to get inside me?' It is the only time Corley actually addresses Lenehan using the form 'you'.

Lenehan, therefore, through a skilful use of his speech flatters Corley, agrees with him, and asks him questions, primarily to reassure himself of the success of the venture. Corley reacts favourably to the flattery but sometimes resents Lenehan's questioning since he himself never foresees any problems in getting the money. Corley twice reacts angrily to Lenehan's questioning, once as mentioned above in connection with the woman, and once when he tires of Lenehan's anxious questions. He holds himself in a superior position, sometimes not answering Lenehan's questions and never calling Lenehan by name. Lenehan, on the other hand, addresses Corley by his first name six times, both as an act of deference and to establish and maintain contact with him.

This difference between the two men is also described in physical terms. If we examine the lexis in relation to the physical appearance of Corley and his actions, we find (1) 'burly', 'broad figure', 'bulk' and (2) 'solid sound of his boots', 'easy pace', 'long stride', 'saunter'. The first set of words denotes physical mass, the second slowness and deliberation associated with mass. In the case of Lenehan, the lexis denotes the opposite, lightness and speed. Thus, we find 'light steps', 'swift scrutiny', 'softly padded feet', 'nimbly', 'quickly', 'step lightly', 'light skips', 'skip'. The contrast is neatly demonstrated in the sentence 'The swing of his burly body made his friend execute a few light skips from the path to the roadway and back again,' where the cause/effect relationship is expressed in terms of the contrast between 'burly body' and 'light skips'.

What the analysis has shown is that the three functions, the ideational, inter-personal and the textual, combine to create a picture of two different personalities: the one, Corley, an active initiator with a strong physical presence, essentially an independent force tolerating the friendship of Lenehan; the other, Lenehan, a passive observer of the situation, lacking the confidence of Corley and skill in dealing with women as a means of obtaining money, and therefore needing Corley's friendship and support, which he can retain only by resort to flattery and servility. A summary is given below:

	Lenehan Observer/Listener	Corley Actor/Speaker
(1)	Intransitive verbs of action	Intransitive/transitive verbs of action – no predominant pattern
(2)	Relational clauses	Few relational clauses
(3)	Verbs of perception	Few verbs of perception
(4)	'Eyes' as actors	'head', 'body' as participants
(5) (a)	Few utterances	Produces more utterances
(b)	Questions/flattery agreement	Statements
(c)	'you' as actor	'I', 'she' as actors

I hope to have shown that, by using certain elements of systemic grammar, patterns can be isolated from a text which will provide an objective linguistic basis for interpreting a work. In the examples drawn from Conrad and Joyce, two characters were shown acting and thinking in certain individual ways which were reflected in the different linguistic options chosen by the writers to describe those thoughts and actions.

Note: Chapter 6

1   James Joyce, *Dubliners* (Harmondsworth: Penguin, 1961), pp. 47–58.

Suggestions for Further Work: Chapter 6

1   Take a passage of prose and rewrite it so that, instead of individual
    characters doing things (like seeing, stroking, hitting, etc.), parts of their
    bodies are given as performing their actions. For example, 'her eyes
    watched him', 'his hand hit the table'. What different effects are created by
    doing this? Why might an author want to create these different effects? For
    comparison see the following passage from James Joyce's *A Portrait of the
    Artist as a Young Man*, where the hero is making a first visit to a prostitute.

> As he stood silent in the middle of the room she came over to him and
> embraced him gaily and gravely. Her round arms held him firmly to her
> and he, seeing her face lifted to him in serious calm and feeling the warm
> calm rise and fall of her breast, all but burst into hysterical weeping.
> Tears of joy and relief shone in his delighted eyes and his lips parted
> though they would not speak.
>   She passed her tinkling hand through his hair, calling him a little
> rascal.
>   – Give me a kiss, she said.
>   His lips would not bend to kiss her. He wanted to be held firmly in her
> arms, to be caressed slowly, slowly, slowly. In her arms he felt that he
> had suddenly become strong and fearless and sure of himself. But his
> lips would not bend to kiss her.

   For further examination of a related passage from Sylvia Plath's *The Bell
   Jar*, see the chapter by Deirdre Burton in this volume.

2   Examine the following extract from William Golding's *Pincher Martin* in
    terms of different transitivity relations. What particular literary effects is
    Golding attempting to produce? The question might be explored further
    by systematically rearranging the actors and the processes involved and
    examining the functions of the changes that are made.

> His mouth was clever. It opened and shut for the air and against the
> water. His body understood too. Every now and then it would clench its
> stomach into a hard knot and sea water would burst out over his tongue.
> He began to be frightened again – not with animal panic but with deep
> fear of death in isolation and long drawn out. The snarl came back but
> now it had a face to use and air for the throat. There was something
> meaningful behind the snarl which would not waste the air on noises.
> There was a purpose which had not yet had time and experience to
> discover how relentless it was. It could not use the mechanism for
> regular breathing but it took air in gulps between the moments of burial.
>   He began to think in gulps as he swallowed the air. He remembered
> his hands again and there they were in the darkness, far away. He
> brought them in and began to fumble at the hard stuff of his oilskin. The

button hurt and would hardly be persuaded to go through the hole. He slipped the loop off the toggle of his duffle. Lying with little movement of his body he found that the sea ignored him, treated him as a glass figure of a sailor or as a log that was almost ready to sink but would last a few moments yet. The air was regularly in attendance between the passage of the swells.

Other passages rich for investigation include: the opening to Albert Camus' *The Outsider*; scenes in Muriel Spark's *The Comforters*, after the typewriter has mysteriously started typing out the story of the novel 'by itself'; Nathaniel West's *Miss Lonelyhearts*; many other passages from the Joyce novel given above – after Confession, the illness at school, the Christmas-dinner scene. However, any passage chosen at random can be studied in these terms, and all will reveal some interesting facts about the relationship between the syntax used and the readers' interpretations of the text.

Poems are also interesting to study in this way. Again, there are poems which are notably rich in their exploitation of these features, like Donne's 'A Nocturnal upon St Lucy's Day' and Auden's Song XII ('Stop all the clocks, cut off the telephone'), but many poems will yield useful insights when analysed in this way.

3   Compare Kennedy's analysis of 'Two Gallants' with a similar, systematic analysis of one or more other stories in *Dubliners*. Is Joyce consistent in his use of language, when seen in these Hallidayan terms? What conclusions do you draw about the stylistic relations between different stories in the volume? A particularly useful example for comparison is the story 'A Painful Case'.

4   A useful article by Halliday which applies particular grammatical categories (especially those of transitivity) in an analysis of extracts from a literary text (William Golding's *The Inheritors*) is 'Linguistic function and literary style' (Halliday, 1971). Use the strategies and analytical categories employed by Halliday to analyse prose work which, like Lok in *The Inheritors*, include characters whose consciousness of the world around them is clearly meant to be different from our own – either more limited or strangely extra-perceptive. Examine the *linguistic* means by which this is achieved in the presentation of some of the following examples: Benjy in Faulkner's *The Sound and the Fury* (see Cluysenaar (1976: 90–2) – and for further discussion of the passage from *The Secret Agent* above); the various inmates in B. S. Johnson's *House Mother Normal*; the dog with a human brain in Olaf Stapledon's *Sirius*; the dying Mrs Hunter in Patrick White's *The Eye of the Storm*; the robots in Isaac Asimov's *I, Robot* and *The Rest of the Robots*.

5   Write a story, or a description that might be part of a story, from the point of view of a participant with a different consciousness. This might be, perhaps, from the point of view of a child – fringe participant to an adult drama – or a visiting Martian trying to make sense of an alien world. See, for example, Craig Raine's volume of poetry *A Martian Sends a Postcard Home* (OUP, 1979). Try to incorporate techniques learned from analytical studies. Be specific about what sorts of linguistic devices are going to be useful here. What problems do you run into?

6 Write a three-paragraph review of a film you have seen recently. Confine each paragraph to one main clause type as outlined in Chris Kennedy's chapter (action, mental process, relation). What is the most appropriate order for the paragraphs? Why? Which aspects of your review go with which main clause type?

7 Examine other texts in terms of their sentence types in the dialogue and the characters who use them. An interesting example is Hemingway's 'Indian Camp' – a story from the collection *In Our Time*. Here is the dialogue from the end of the story:

> 'Do ladies always have such a hard time having babies?' Nick asked.
> 'No, that was very, very exceptional.'
> 'Why did he kill himself, Daddy?'
> 'I don't know, Nick. He couldn't stand things, I guess.'
> 'Do many men kill themselves, Daddy?'
> 'Not very many, Nick.'
> 'Do many women?'
> 'Hardly ever.'
> 'Don't they ever?'
> 'Oh yes. They do sometimes.'
> 'Daddy?'
> 'Yes.'
> 'Where did Uncle George go?'
> 'He'll turn up all right.'
> 'Is dying hard, Daddy?'
> 'No, I think it's pretty easy, Nick. It all depends.'

Compare this final conversation with features of the characters' conversations throughout the story. What is the effect of these textual features?

Examples for comparison or further exploration would include dialogue in Joseph Heller's *Catch 22* and *Good as Gold*; the prose passages for Becket and the four knights in T. S. Eliot's *Murder in the Cathedral*; the question-and-answer sequence at the opening to Tom Stoppard's *Rosencrantz and Guildenstern Are Dead*.

Or write a dialogue as part of a possible piece of prose fiction and distribute sentence types between the characters talking, so as to reinforce whatever it is they are talking about, with reference to information you would like a reader to have in terms of subordinate and dominant relationships between them. How subtly can you do this? What else needs to be taken into account?

References: Chapter 6

Cluysenaar, A. (1976), *Introduction to Literary Stylistics* (London: Batsford).

Halliday, M. A. K. (1970), 'Language structure and language function', in J. Lyons (ed.), *New Horizons in Linguistics* (Harmondsworth: Penguin).

Halliday, M. A. K. (1971), 'Linguistic function and linguistic style', in Chatman, S. (ed.), *Literary Style: A Symposium* (London: OUP), pp. 330–65; repr. in Halliday, M. A. K. (1973), *Explorations in the Functions of Language* (London: Edward Arnold), pp. 103–43.

Introduction to Chapter 7

Walter Nash's chapter may be divided into two parts. The first is a practical analysis of a text in terms of its distinctive linguistic features. The passage is seen to enact locally the kind of meanings which may be said to be those distributed across the whole story 'Odour of Chrysanthemums'. Chief among these is a sense of alienation. In his discussion of the items of language deployed to establish this sense, Walter Nash discerns the functions of deixis, changes in articles, transitivity, placement of adjunct, passivisation and particular verb-types to be especially significant.

The second part of the chapter is broadly theoretical. Here Walter Nash discusses the particular procedures he has adopted for stylistic analysis. He discerns three main elements in this: 'an intuitive response to the text'; 'a search for textual pattern'; 'an identification of the linguistic/stylistic patterning that supports intuition and demonstrates the patterning'. Discerning textual pattern or 'structure' is not at all straightforward, and to do this is also not necessarily a wholly linguistic procedure. Yet we do not want to have to analyse every word of the text before that pattern can be released. In his division of the text into 'planes of articulation' and 'planes of informa-tion' such as 'setting and perspective', 'the actors' and 'the environment', Walter Nash shows how a frame can be provided which grows from a perception of the struc-ture of the text. Such a frame provides a specific focus for the analysis of this text but, as demonstrated in the suggestions for further work, it can be productively applied to other texts, too.

7 On a Passage from Lawrence's 'Odour of Chrysanthemums'

WALTER NASH

I A Sample Text

Intuitive response to D. H. Lawrence's classic story 'Odour of Chrysanthemums' suggests that its theme might be defined in the one word *alienation*. A woman is alienated from her husband, and this is the major issue; but it includes or is contingent upon other alienations – family relationships are strained, a housewife is uneasy among her neighbours, man is a mere tenant in his industrial environment. These paradigmatic variants of the general theme are explored cumulatively in a series of episodes any one of which would provide a representative stylistic sample.

One such sample text, perfectly defined and self-contained, occurs shortly after the beginning of the narrative. The following notes take into account the general patterning of the text as a narrative framework, the structuring of its content, and the relevance of stylistic device to structural intention. My metalanguage, except where other-wise indicated (and apart from *ad hoc* terms) is based on Quirk *et al.* (1972). The text is that of the Penguin (1968) edition of *The Prussian Officer and Other Stories*. Lines are numbered for convenience of subsequent reference:

```
 1    The engine whistled as it came into the wide bay of
 2  railway lines beside the colliery, where rows of trucks
 3  stood in harbour.
 4    Miners, single, trailing and in groups, passed like
 5  shadows diverging home. At the edge of the ribbed
 6  level of sidings squats a low cottage, three steps down
 7  from the cinder track. A large bony vine clutched at
 8  the house, as if to claw down the tiled roof. Round
 9  the bricked yard grew a few wintry primroses. Beyond,
10  the long garden sloped down to a bush-covered brook
11  course. There were some twiggy apple-trees, winter-
```

12 crack trees, and ragged cabbages. Beside the path
13 hung dishevelled pink chrysanthemums, like pink cloths
14 hung on bushes. A woman came stooping out of the
15 felt-covered fowl-house, then drew herself erect,
16 having brushed some bits from her white apron.
17   She was a tall woman of imperious mien, handsome,
18 with definite black eyebrows. Her smooth black hair
19 was parted exactly. For a few moments she stood
20 steadily watching the miners as they passed along the
21 railway; then she turned towards the brook course.
22 Her face was calm and set, her mouth was closed with
23 disillusionment. After a moment she called:
24   'John!' There was no answer. She waited, and
25 then said distinctly:
26   'Where are you?'
27   'Here!' replied a child's sulky voice from among
28 the bushes. The woman looked piercingly through the
29 dusk.
30   'Are you at that brook?' she asked sternly.
31   For answer the child showed himself before the
32 raspberry-canes that rose like whips. He was a
33 small, sturdy boy of five. He stood quite still,
34 defiantly.
35   'Oh!' said the mother, conciliated. 'I thought
36 you were down at that wet brook – and you remember
37 what I told you—'
38   The boy did not move or answer.
39   'Come, come on in,' she said more gently, 'it's
40 getting dark. There's your grandfather's engine
41 coming down the line!'
42   The lad advanced slowly, with resentful, taciturn
43 movement. He was dressed in trousers and waistcoat
44 of cloth that was too thick and hard for the size of
45 the garments. They were evidently cut down from a
46 man's clothes.
47   As they went towards the house he tore at the
48 ragged wisps of chrysanthemums and dropped the petals
49 in handfuls along the path.
50   'Don't do that – it does look nasty,' said his
51 mother. He refrained, and she, suddenly pitiful,
52 broke off a twig with three or four wan flowers and
53 held them against her face. When mother and son
54 reached the yard her hand hesitated, and instead of
55 laying the flower aside, she pushed it in her apron-
56 band. The mother and son stood at the foot of the
57 three steps looking across the bay of lines at the
58 passing home of the miners. The trundle of the small
59 train was imminent. Suddenly the engine loomed past
60 the house and came to a stop opposite the gate.

II Setting: Symmetry and Perspective

An eminent feature of this passage is the symmetry of its scenic arrangement; it begins and ends with the lively bustle of the little engine and the silent, shadowy 'passing' of the miners. The engine appears first in 1, the miners following in 4–5, while at the end of the text the miners reappear in 58 and the engine in 59. The inversion (*engine–miners/miners–engine*) seems to suggest that industry has the first and last word; machines have greater vitality than human beings. (The engine is of course mentioned at one other point – in 40–1 – but the reference is made in direct speech, and is not an element in the general pattern of scenic description.)

Within this frame other symmetries are incorporated. Thus, in 6 the cottage 'squats' *three steps down from the cinder track*, while in 56–7 a woman and a boy (two of the inhabitants of the cottage) are seen standing *at the foot of the three steps*. There is another striking example of symmetrical recursion in the *dishevelled pink chrysanthemums* of 13–14, which reappear as *the ragged wisps of chrysanthemums* in 48. These two phrases occur at almost exactly correspondent points in relationship to the beginning and end of the text. By line 14, indeed, the scene is set, and we return to it, after the presentation of the actors, in 47ff. Its elements, and their placing in the text, may be recapitulated thus: *engine* (1) – *miners* (4–5) – *steps* (6) – *chrysanthemums* (13–14)/ /*chrysanthemums* (48) – *steps* (57) – *miners* (58) – *engine* (59).

The layout plots a simple scheme of movement, from the railway line to the house to the garden, where the central encounter between the woman and the boy takes place, and so from the garden back to the house and the railway line; a tour in the course of which attention is carefully drawn to the chrysanthemums that figure in the title and symbolise the theme of the narrative. Throughout the text, shifts in perspective are marked by the occurrence of constructions (mainly adjuncts) indicating a position or direction. Some place adjuncts – for example, *past the house* (59), *opposite the gate* (60) – look forward to another scene, but the majority relate to the staging of the current action: *At the edge of the ribbed level of sidings* (5), *Round the bricked yard* (8), *Beyond* (9), *Beside the path* (12), *towards the brook course* (21), *before the raspberry canes* (31), *towards the house* (47), *at the foot of the three steps* (56).

The position of these elements in their respective sentences is of some relevance to the structure of the text as a whole. The first four of the quoted instances make a well-defined group; as their typography indicates, each of them occurs at the beginning of a sentence. The second paragraph, in which these examples occur, is in effect a set of stage directions – a register in which the 'fronted' place adjunct is not uncommon. There is, however, a further stylistic point. The effect of this positioning is to create a powerful end-focus on the scenic elements in the sentences concerned – for example, on the *low cottage, the few wintry primroses, the dishevelled pink chrysanthemums*. The adjuncts thus point to features of landscape which constitute not only a background imagery but also a source of feeling, in that they condition the reader's responses to the text.

In the remaining examples the place adjuncts have receded to a post-verbal position where as a rule they merely specify the location or direction of a movement on the part of one or other of the actors. The focus is now on people, on humanity depressed and struggling, rather than on the vegetation that so compellingly symbolises the depression and the struggle. The place adjuncts lose something of their dynamic importance and become mere labels of position. In one instance (*and dropped the petals in handfuls along the path*, 48–9) this softening of emphasis is particularly noticeable; the place adjunct *along the path* occurs after, and is in a sense subordinate to, the process adjunct *in handfuls*. The latter is involved in the emotive energy of *tore at* and *dropped* in a way that the former is not. These differences in the positioning and semantic implication of the place adjuncts are by no means fortuitous. They are symptomatic of a deliberate shift of emphasis, further discussed below, from environmental colouring to human response.

III   The Development of the Scene: Phases and Modes of Narrative

The scene develops through passages of description and direct speech which intermesh, gradually constructing the pattern of relationships between the human figures and their environment. Though they are not typographically signposted, it is possible to discern the phases of development with some degree of certainty. The text appears to be constructed on the following frame:

Phase

I	*from:*	The engine whistled as it came into the wide bay of railway lines beside the colliery, where rows of trucks stood in harbour. (1–3)
	to:	Beside the path hung dishevelled pink chrysanthemums, like pink cloths hung on bushes. (12–14)
II	*from:*	A woman came stooping out of the felt-covered fowl-house. . . . (14–15)
	to:	Her face was calm and set, her mouth was closed with disillusionment. (22–3)
III	*from:*	After a moment she called: (23)
	to:	They were evidently cut down from a man's clothes. (45–6)
IV	*from:*	As they went towards the house he tore at the ragged wisps of chrysanthemums. . . . (47–8)

to: Suddenly the engine loomed past the house and came to a stop opposite the gate. (59–60)

Of these phases, I and II present a clear descriptive unity; in I an environment is described, while II shifts to a description of the woman. Phase IV begins as Phase I ends, with an allusion to the chrysanthemums, and returns to 'environmental' description; thus, in formal marking and in content it, too, is fairly well defined. Only Phase III is irregular, not so obviously devoted to a single purpose (e.g. describing a background or a personality), shifting back and forth between speech and description, leaving unanswered certain questions of character and behaviour. In this very lack of closure it is the vital centre of the text, a seed of narration rather than a descriptive ground.

In the shifts from phase to phase, the mode of narration alters in relationship to the content. A rough account of these changes is presented in the following table:

Phase	Lines	Mode	Content
I	1–14	Description	An environment
II	14–16, 17–23	Description	A woman placed in the environment: her relationship to it by implication discordant
III	24–6	Direct speech, with some descriptive intrusions	The woman and a child in confrontation
IV	47–60	Descriptions, with one brief intrusion of direct speech	Woman and child together confronting the environment.

This requires some amplificatory comment. Phase II consists in effect of two separate passages of description (11–14, 15–21), in the first of which the woman makes a 'dynamic' entry into the scene, while in the second she holds something of a 'static' pose. This shift is reflected in stylistic details to be discussed presently. Another feature which is necessarily overlooked in the tabular account is the role, in Phase III, of what are called 'descriptive intrusions' (31–4, 38, 42–6). It is in fact through these, and not through speech, that the boy is presented. He speaks only one word; otherwise it is the woman whose voice is heard in this bleak setting, and whose character is reflected in the reporting tags or style adjuncts – *said distinctly* (25), *asked sternly* (30), *said more gently* (39).

The salient point of this development is the involvement of the human figures with each other and with their shiftily animated surroundings. (By 'human figures' I mean of course the woman and the boy; the miners are neutralised figures, mere shadows in the dusk of industry.) The environment has a suppressive power which is hinted at in the figurative language of Phase I (e.g. *clutched at the house*, *as if to claw down the tiled roof*, 7–8), and which is quite strongly established for the reader by the time he reaches Phase IV. In the responses of the woman towards her surroundings we sense both antagonism and a helpless resignation; while the boy appears as the victim of an anxious parental concern that expresses itself in fruitlessly punitive gestures (cf. *raspberry canes that rose like whips* (32), where the environmental detail indirectly suggests the threat of punishment for disobedience). Woman and boy alike are engaged in a struggle to exert an individual will, against each other and against the conditions that overwhelm them.

IV   The Actors: (i) Identity and Relationship

The relationship of the two actors is ingeniously plotted in the grammar and lexis of Phases II and III. A series of minor shifts in syntax or vocabulary brings the characters closer to each other and also to the reader; by almost insensible degrees they are 'established' for him as figures with an identity – not yet complete, not yet so fully realised that they are actually mentioned by name, but certain enough for them to be accepted as textual acquaintances, as 'the woman and the boy in our story'.

In 14 *a woman* (note the indefinite article) is introduced; in 17 she is described quite fully as *a tall woman of imperious mien*, etc.; in 28 she is *the woman*; in 35 her role is specified and she is *the mother*; in 50 there is a further change of determiner – *his mother* – fully establishing her relationship to the boy.

The son first appears as a disembodied voice (*a child's sulky voice*, 27) and then as *the child* in 31. In 33 a descriptive phrase specifies his sex and age – he is *a small sturdy boy of five*. At his next appearance, in 38, he is *the boy*, a designation that shifts to a 'warmer' synonym in 42, with *the lad*. The establishment of the actors as a pair, or corporate unit, conforms to the general pattern of movement from general to particular identity; thus *mother and son* in 53 is followed by *the mother and son* in 56.

The tactics of establishment are remarkably consistent. Determiners (*a*, *the*, *his*) lead from an unmarked or 'inchoate' preliminary identification (e.g. *a woman*) towards the firmer base of an anaphoric reference (e.g. *the woman*), or yet further towards the endophoric allusion that makes the textual connection between one figure and another (e.g. *his mother*). Synonymic and hyponymic variants (*child*, *boy*, *lad*, *son*; *woman*, *mother*) are also of obvious importance in the progressive familiarising of the two characters. We may note further how in two places an expanded description of the actor (*a tall woman of imperious mien*, etc., 17, *a small sturdy boy of five*, 33) is the precursor of the anaphoric reference with definite article + noun denoting sex and age (*the woman*, 28, *the boy*, 38). The process of identification can be summarised thus:

A   *The Woman*

	Designation	Comment
(i)	A woman, 14	Indefinite article: preliminary, 'inchoate' identification
(ii)	a tall woman of imperious mien, handsome, with definite black eyebrows, 17	Indefinite article: pre- and elaborate post-modification; figure described
(iii)	the woman, 28	Definite article: figure now 'anaphorically based' in the text
(iv)	the mother, 35	Definite article: hyponymic variation of noun: the woman's social role textually established
(v)	his mother, 50	Shift of determiner to possessive pronoun: connection with other figure textually established

B   *The Boy*

	Designation	Comment
(i)	a child's sulky voice, 27	Pre-modifying genitive makes preliminary identification; denotes age, not sex
(ii)	the child, 31	Definite article: anaphoric reference gives figure some base in text, but sex still unspecified
(iii)	a small sturdy boy of five, 33	Indefinite article: pre- and post-modification: age and sex specified
(iv)	the boy, 38	Definite article: figure now 'anaphorically based' in text
(v)	the lad, 42	Definite article: synonymic variation; warmer, more intimate response suggested, the reader's sympathy invited – cf. the effect of pathos in the description of trousers and waistcoat 'cut down from a man's clothes'

C   *Woman and Boy Together*

	Designation	Comment
(i)	mother and son, 53	No determiner: preliminary identification of the corporate unit: further hyponymic shift (to *son*), in line with already established shift (see A (iv)) to *mother*

(ii) the mother and son, 56	Definite article: anaphoric reference gives textual underscoring to the relationship

As a footnote to this analysis of identities and relationships in the text, it may be added that a further relationship is introduced in the woman's remark, *There's your grandfather's engine coming down the line!* (41–2). This has a twofold function. It makes a point of intersection between what we see of the environment and what we learn about the actors – we might say that the outer, descriptive phases I and IV here briefly intrude upon the inner phase III. Secondly, it establishes a point of connection with the next episode (Penguin, pp. 206–7), in which the engine-driver/grandfather is seen in conversation – or, rather, confrontation – with his daughter.

V The Actors: (ii) the Woman

As well as establishing the woman's social position, the text provides a number of effective indices to her character. A feature of obvious importance is the alternation of modifier and adjunct as carriers of evaluative description: *tall, imperious, handsome, definite, smooth, calm, set/exactly, steadily, piercingly, sternly*.

The adjuncts are particularly noteworthy, in that they relate or 'interlock' presentations of three different aspects of her being – physical appearance, activity, and manner of speech. Thus, the manner adjunct in *her smooth black hair was parted exactly* (18–19) defines an appearance or, to use a distinctive and convenient term, a *pose*; in *the woman looked piercingly* (28) the adjunct qualifies an *activity*; while in *she asked sternly* (30) a style adjunct denotes her manner of speech.

Pose, activity and speech-style are the three elements by means of which her nature is intimated to the reader, and in 17–23, a passage of extended description, these elements appear to be arranged in a patterned scheme, punctuated by time adjuncts (*for a few moments, then, after a moment*). The scheme may be summarised: Pose – TA – Activity – TA – Activity – Pose – TA – Speech. The elements of the pattern are diversely weighted, however, as a reading of the passage will show:

> She was a tall woman of imperious mien, handsome, with definite black eyebrows. Her smooth black hair was parted exactly (POSE). For a few moments (TA) she stood steadily watching the miners as they passed along the railway (ACTIVITY); then (TA) she turned towards the brook course (ACTIVITY). Her face was calm and set, her mouth was closed with disillusionment (POSE). After a moment (TA) she called (SPEECH):

Throughout the text generally, her 'activities' present a point of stylistic interest. There is some contrasting of transitive and intransitive patterning; more precisely, there is a contrasting of operative and static processes. At her first appearance, in 11–14 (the first part of Phase II), the woman is an agent with some volitional and operative power over her own person and the things around her (cf. *drew herself erect, having brushed some bits from her apron*, 15). In the remainder of Phase II, and throughout Phase III, however, all effective activity withers, and the agent makes no impress on her surroundings. Such phases as *she stood steadily watching, she said distinctly, the woman looked piercingly, she asked sternly* denote no activity more positive than looking and speaking.

This recession into 'inoperativeness' is introduced by a sequence of 'pose' elements (see above). The clauses presenting these are, as one might expect, structures in which the verb is a mere copula (*was*) and the subject is in most cases a noun denoting a part of the body (*hair, face, mouth*). She becomes for a time a face, a voice, a *mien* – nothing more. It is only in the passage's last phase that the will to goal-directed activity is reasserted (*broke off a twig with three or four wan flowers and laid them against her face*, 52–3, *she pushed it in her apronband*, 55–6).

She is characterised by one fine stylistic touch in Phase IV, where instead of 'she hesitated' we read *her hand hesitated* (54). There is a shift of initiating agency from the whole person to a part, the hand, which is treated as though it had an independent will. This device expresses in a very telling way her division against herself, her alternations of voluntary act and involuntary response, and her reluctance to admit any feeling of tenderness about her marriage. It betrays a vulnerability which we might not suspect in *a tall woman of imperious mien . . . with definite black eyebrows*.

VI The Actors: (iii) the Boy

The boy is not so intensively portrayed, and yet the presentation of this secondary figure is carefully structured. There are analogies between his introduction into the text and that of the woman. Of her, it is observed that she *drew herself erect, having brushed some bits from her white apron* (15–16), and then, in immediate continuation, *She was a tall woman of imperious mien* (17). Subsequently it is stated of her son that *the child showed himself before the raspberry canes that rose like whips* (31–2) and that *He was a small, sturdy boy of five* (32–3). Here are obvious parallels between the reflexive constructions (*drew herself erect, showed himself*) and between the descriptive statements (*She was a tall woman of imperious mien, He was a small, sturdy boy of five*). There is, moreover, a subtler functional parallel between the participial clause *having brushed some bits* etc. (16) and the place adjunct *before the raspberry canes* etc. (31–2). Each of these in its own way projects a character: the woman's active and precise, the child's passive before the intimation of punishment.

He is presented through alternations of 'pose' and 'activity'. The 'activity' is at first merely existential (*He stood quite still*, 33, *The boy did not move*, 38), yielding to movement (*the lad advanced slowly*, 42) and then to suddenly positive (and destructive) action (*he tore at the ragged wisps of chrysanthemums*, 47–8). Thus, although he says practically nothing, he gradually emerges as an active 'wilful' personality – a development which, indeed, makes something of a counterpoise to the mother's recession from stern admonition into conciliation, gentleness and pitiful hesitancy. The earlier stages of his emergence are marked by the strategic use of manner adjuncts (*defiantly*, 34, *with resentful, taciturn movement*, 42) as well as by the modifier (*sulky*, 27) that characterises his one utterance. The description of his clothing in 43–6 – the most extended 'pose' – is important in constituting a transition between the earlier, 'passive', and the later, 'active', stage of presentation. The actor is endowed – literally *invested* – with a presence.

VII The Environment

It is an essential feature of the text that the environment should not be a mere background, but should seem to be informed with a covert and in some respects hostile animation. The human actors encounter the dispiriting shapes of non-human presences.

The first phase of the text is largely devoted to the establishment of a sense of the environment as a psychic shadow-partner to the human world – and here the descriptive modifier is a pervasive device: *the ribbed level* (5–6), *a large bony vine* (7), *ragged cabbages* (12), *dishevelled pink chrysanthemums* (13). There is a shadowy anthropomorphism in these constructions, a suggestion of the skeleton (*ribbed, bony*), of poor clothing (*ragged*), of neglected appearance (*dishevelled*). The environment lives a depressed and impoverished existence, like its occupants. A feeling of resignation is implicit in the very sentence-structure – e.g. in the 'existential' sentence *There were some twiggy apple-trees*, etc. (11) and in the sentences with 'fronted' place adjuncts and intransitive verbs (*grew, hung*) which suggest 'state' rather than 'event' (see Leech, 1971: 5). Only in one powerful instance (*A large bony vine clutched at the house*, etc., 7) do sentence-structure and verb-type project a sense of agency and volition.

A skilful feature of the style here is that the constructions quoted above, with their shifted, metaphor-making collocations, are set among other premodified noun-phrases where there is little or no metaphoric intent, e.g. *a low cottage* (6), *the bricked yard* (9), *a few wintry primroses* (9), *the long garden* (10), *a bush-covered brook course* (10), *some twiggy apple-trees* (11), *the felt-covered fowl-house* (15). These constructions are purely descriptive; the metaphor-bearing phrases lurk among them and in a way are natural extensions of them – there is, after all, a descriptive similarity between *bony vine* and *twiggy apple-tree*.

A related point is that the supremely symbolic chrysanthemums are also made to 'lurk' in the general hyponymy of vegetation which includes the wintry primroses, the bushes by the brook, the apple-trees, the winter-crack trees, the cabbages and, a little later in the text, the raspberry canes. At a first encounter, the chrysanthemums are seemingly no more than neglected flowers in a straggly and soured garden. If it were not for the title of the story, we might pay no particular attention to them. There is, however, a further stylistic focus upon them, a device of presentation which they share with the vine and the raspberry canes. All three items (vine, chrysanthemums, raspberry canes) are marked in the text by subordinate or complementary con-structions with *like* or *as if: as if to claw down the tiled roof* (8), *like pink cloths hung on bushes* (13–14), *like whips* (32).

In the first and last of these instances, the focus is powerfully sharp-ened by the inclusion in the construction of verbs or nouns with antagonistic or punitive connotations ('clutched', 'claw', 'whips'). There are fairly obvious reasons for this heavy stylistic underscoring. The image of the bony, clutching vine marks the beginning of a description of the cottage, the garden, and the two actors; from the outset a note of hostility and struggle is sounded. The stylistic emphasis is thus related to the general structure of the text. Similarly, the allusion to the raspberry canes makes the point that the child lives against a background of hostility; to some extent the plants symbolise the environment he has to contend with, and to some extent they express the character of his relationship with his parents. It may be noted incidentally that this is another point in the text at which there is an 'intersection' of structural elements, that is, of the description of the environment which mainly occupies the opening and closing phases of the passage, and the encounter of personalities which constitutes the central phase (cf. the allusion to the engine in 40, and my comment on this).

The initial reference to the chrysanthemums (*hung . . . like pink cloths hung on bushes*, 13–14) is not quite so emphatically under-scored; indeed, there is a gesture of ineffectuality both in the simile itself and in the apparently flaccid repetition of *hung*. The reference is marked, if we are alert to it, but not so strongly marked that we cannot be distracted by other matters. Strength of allusion is postponed until the flowers are referred to a second time, after a human encounter, when the *ragged wisps of chrysanthemums* (47–8) assume something like a personality. Common collocations of *ragged* and *wisps* – 'ragged clothes', 'wisps of hair' – suggest this to the reader and perhaps suggest also a pathetic contrast with the earlier description of the woman, whose *smooth black hair was parted exactly* (18–19).

VIII Conclusion

These notes assume as indispensable three elements (if that is the right word) of procedure: an intuitive response to the text, a search for textual pattern, and an identification of the linguistic/stylistic features that support intuition and demonstrate the patterning. The assumption is possibly commonplace and applicable to any piece of stylistic analysis, but it implies footnotes which may well be worth writing.

The first of these concerns the importance of *structure*. In the analysis of lyric poems (hitherto a major preoccupation of stylisticians) one important element of structure – the articulatory pattern, or 'frame' of the text – is manifested through the poem's metre, stanzaic scheme, and so on. In prose the discursive framework is rarely manifested in this way, and so a structural interpretation at this primary level becomes an important preliminary to further observations on the text. Without such an interpretation remarks on language and style are necessarily random and unrelated. However, it is not simply a matter of determining a structure which then provides a framework of reference for stylistic features. The case is rather that linguistic *and other* promptings suggest a structural scheme which provides points of reference for stylistic features which then amplify and confirm the scheme.

It is important to realise that the reader's intimations of the patterning of a text may be guided by clues other than linguistic. A literary text has a total power of appeal which is to be described in terms of semiotics or aesthetics, *including some aspects of linguistics*, rather than of a strictly and exclusively linguistic model. In certain respects a text may be similar to a picture, in that it has an iconographic programme (this could, indeed, be said of the Lawrence passage); or it may have something in common with music, say, in its repetitions of a *Leitmotiv*, or even with mathematics in its modelling of some principles such as that of binary alternation. All these things may be described in linguistic or quasi-linguistic terminology, but they are not in the strictest sense proper to linguistics. The point is perhaps obvious, yet it is one that linguistic stylisticians do not always readily concede.

A study of the Lawrence passage reveals the importance of two structural levels, or planes of analysis. The first of these is a *plane of articulation*, the scheme of cohesion and design in the text (described here mainly under the headings of 'setting and perspective' and 'development'); to describe this is to establish the ground upon which eminent stylistic features are mapped, and to provide for the prose text something roughly equivalent to the stanzaic or sectional scheme of a poem. The second level of structure is a *plane of information* (or possibly 'motif'), and involves the superimposition on the articulatory plane of elements of characterisation, symbolism, etc. (In the foregoing account, analysis on this plane is represented by the sections on 'the actors' and 'the environment'.) Inevitably one uses words like 'superimposition' or 'intersection' in trying to describe the relationship of the two planes, but they are misleading. 'Interlocking' or 'intermeshing' would be more satisfactory. It is necessary to understand the scheme of articulation before we can respond fully to the contained pattern; but, on the other hand, we need to have some response to the pattern of character and symbolic motif before we can properly perceive the articulatory design.

The reading of such a text is, indeed, a process of intermeshing and mutually supportive responses. Intuition (literary sensitivity, a predisposition to find patterns of meaning) is vital, but after the first impulses it does not continue to work unprompted. Further promptings come with the observation of linguistic/stylistic features which are perhaps marked by pairings, contrasts, gradations, or some other method of foregrounding. Intuition is thus strengthened or modified, and is equipped to begin the definition of structural levels in the text. The discovery of one level involves the perception of another; and meanwhile the detection of linguistic features continues, supporting or qualifying the structural interpretation, guiding the intuition to further discoveries. Figure 7.1 is an attempt to chart the process of interlinking

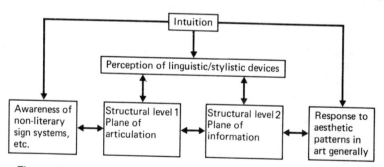

Figure 7.1 *The process of interlinking discoveries and impulses.*

discoveries and impulses. It is empirically derived from the study of one short passage and is quite certainly too simple in outline to serve as a hypothesis accounting for what happens when we attempt close reading of a piece of prose fiction. Nevertheless, it points to important elements in the reading process and may usefully draw attention to the fact that in many instances stylistic description is necessarily a complex of linguistic and extra- (or supra-) linguistic references.

Suggestions for Further Work: Chapter 7

I Exercises

1 Compare the points made in this chapter concerning the devitalisation of nature and the corresponding animation of insentient things with the analysis of the opening paragraph of Dickens's *Little Dorrit* in Mary Mason's chapter. Do you notice any similarities or any differences in the effects produced in the two passages? Apply the techniques of analysis of subject/verb relations and of adjuncts suggesting animation to this short paragraph from later in the same story, 'Odour of Chrysanthemums':

> He put his hand on the lever. The little engine strained and groaned, and the train rumbled towards the crossing. The woman again looked across the metals. Darkness was settling over the spaces of the railway and trucks; the miners, in grey sombre groups, were still passing home. The winding-engine pulsed hurriedly, with brief pauses. Elizabeth Bates looked at the dreary flow of men, then she went indoors. Her husband did not come.

What do the same techniques of analysis reveal concerning the communicative impact of this passage of description from Lawrence's *Lady Chatterley's Lover*?

> The car ploughed uphill through the long squalid straggle of Tevershall, the blackened brick dwellings, the black slate roofs glistening their sharp edges, the mud black with coal-dust, the pavements wet and black. It was as if dismalness had soaked through and through everything. The utter negation of natural beauty, the utter negation of the gladness of life, the utter absence of the instinct for shapely beauty which every bird and beast has, the utter death of the human intuitive faculty was appalling. The stacks of soap in the grocers' shops, the rhubarb and lemons in the greengrocer's! the awful hats in the milliner's! all went by ugly, ugly, ugly, followed by the plaster and gilt horror of the cinema with its wet picture announcements, 'A Woman's Love', and the new big Primitive chapel, primitive enough in its stark brick and big panes of greenish and raspberry glass in the windows. The Wesleyan chapel, higher up, was one of blackened brick and stood behind iron railings and blackened shrubs. The Congregational chapel which thought itself superior, was built of rusticated sandstone and had a steeple, but not a very high one. Just beyond were the new school buildings, expensive pink brick, and gravelled play-ground inside iron railings, all very imposing, and mixing the suggestion of a chapel and a prison. Standard Five girls were having a singing lesson, just finishing the la-me-doh-la exercises and beginning a 'sweet children's song'.

Anything more unlike song, spontaneous song, would be impossible to imagine: a strange bawling yell followed the outlines of a tune. It was not like savages: savages have subtle rhythms. It was not like animals: animals *mean* something when they yell. It was like nothing on earth, and it was called singing.

2 Walter Nash discusses the need for us to identify the textual pattern or 'structure' of a short story. Compare his division of a text into its relative 'planes' with that elucidated by Anne Cluysenaar (1976: 92–9) also in relation to a short story by Lawrence.

3 On the question of the shifting distribution of deictics across a text, particularly with reference to main characters (*the* woman, *the* boy), compare the discussion here with the points raised by Carter in his discussion of '*the* cat', '*the* American wife' and '*the* husband' in Hemingway's 'Cat in the Rain'.

4 Compare this depiction of the world of natural processes and its influence on human ways of seeing things with that undertaken in Theodore Roethke's poem 'Child on Top of a Greenhouse'. What *kinds* of verb are 'toss', 'plunge', 'billow', 'flash', 'crackle'? Are they transitive or intransitive? Do they normally belong to the kinds of subject with which they are attached in this poem? What might Roethke be saying about the nature of the child's vision and the kind of world he sees from that position? For a fuller discussion of this text with particular reference to tense in the verb see Widdowson (1975), pp. 108–15.

5 How far is it possible to extend the analysis of Free Indirect Speech made by Ron Carter in his chapter on 'Cat in the Rain' to the final pages of 'Odour of Chrysanthemums'? Here the reader encounters sequences such as the following:

> And all the while her heart was bursting with grief and pity for him. What had he suffered? What stretch of horror for this helpless man! She was rigid with agony. She had not been able to help him. He had been cruelly injured, this naked man, this other being, and she could make no reparation. There were the children – but the children belonged to life. This dead man had nothing to do with them. . . . She saw this episode of her life closed. They had denied each other in life. Now he had withdrawn. An anguish came over her. It was finished then: it had become hopeless between them long before he died. Yet he had been her husband. But how little!

What do you take to be Lawrence's main purpose in employing this narrative device at this point in the story? Return to these questions after reading the chapter by Short later in this volume.

II A Project

Not every text will lend itself to analysis precisely along the lines laid out above; nevertheless, to attempt a comparable exercise on another passage from Lawrence should make an instructive test of technique. His story 'Daughters of the Vicar' has the same general setting as 'Odour of Chrysanthemums' (the cottage by the railway line appears in both texts), and there is the same powerful emphasis on the staging of the characters.

Below is a piece of the narrative with some introductory remarks briefly relating it to its context. There follow some analytical 'projects' which, taken collectively, should reveal quite a lot about the style and structure of the passage. Finally there are one or two suggestions for extended analysis of the story.

A CONTEXT

Mr Lindley is vicar of Aldecross, a mining village in the Midlands. An alien figure among the colliers who 'have no use for him in their lives' and who are 'cheerfully contemptuous of him', he is described as 'pale' and 'neutral' and is said to have 'no particular character, having always depended on his position in society to give him position among men'. Denied his social standing and rejected by the majority of his parishioners, he now confines his ministry to 'a narrow round of cottages', one of which is tenanted by the Durants. Mrs Durant is a typically severe and disillusioned housewife, battling for respectability, and Mr Durant is that other typical figure, the drunken husband. They make up one of the couples that dance to a set of Lawrentian motifs in 'Daughters of the Vicar'. The following extract is the first, mainly descriptive, part of an episode in which the vicar pays one of his pastoral calls on the Durants.

B TEXT

1   One winter morning, when his daughter Mary was about twenty years old, Mr Lindley, a thin, unobtrusive figure in his black overcoat and his wideawake, went down into Aldecross with a packet of white papers under his arm. He was delivering the parish almanacs.

5   A rather pale, neutral man of middle age, he waited while the train thumped over the level-crossing, going up to the pit which rattled busily just along the line. A wooden-legged man hobbled to open the gate. Mr Lindley passed on. Just at his left hand, below the road and the railway, was the red roof of a cottage, showing through the bare twigs of apple

10 trees. Mr Lindley passed round the low wall, and descended the worn steps that led from the highway down to the cottage which crouched darkly and quietly away below the rumble of passing trains and the clank of coal-carts, in a quiet little underworld of its own. Snowdrops with tight-shut buds were hanging very still under the bare currant bushes.

15   The clergyman was just going to knock when he heard a clinking noise, and turning saw through the open door of a black shed just behind him an elderly woman in a black lace cap stooping among reddish big cans, pouring a very bright liquid into a tundish. There was a smell of paraffin. The woman put down her can, took the tundish and laid it on a shelf, then

20 rose with a tin bottle. Her eyes met those of the clergyman.

'Oh, is it you, Mr Lin'ley!' she said, in a complaining tone. 'Go in.'

The minister entered the house. In the hot kitchen sat a big, elderly man with a great grey beard, taking snuff. He grunted in a deep, muttering voice, telling the minister to sit down, and then took no more notice of him,

25 but stared vacantly into the fire. Mr Lindley waited.

The woman came in, the ribbons of her black lace cap, or bonnet, hanging on her shawl. She was of medium stature, everything about her

was tidy. She went up a step out of the kitchen, carrying the paraffin tin.
Feet were heard entering the room up the step. It was a little haber-
30 dashery shop, with parcels on the shelves of the walls, a big, old-
fashioned sewing machine with tailor's work lying round it, in the open
space. The woman went behind the counter, gave the child who had
entered the paraffin bottle, and took from her a jug.
  'My mother says shall yer put it down,' said the child, and she was
35 gone. The woman wrote in a book, then came into the kitchen with her
jug. The husband, a very large man, rose and brought more coal to the
already hot fire. He moved slowly and sluggishly. Already he was going
dead; being a tailor, his large form had become an encumbrance to him.
In his youth he had been a great dancer and boxer. Now he was taciturn,
40 and inert. The minister had nothing to say, so he sought for his phrases.
But John Durant took no notice, existing silent and dull.
  Mrs Durant spread the cloth. Her husband poured himself beer into a
mug, and began to smoke and drink.
  'Shall you have some?' he growled through his beard at the clergyman,
45 looking slowly from the man to the jug, capable of this one idea.
  'No, thank you,' replied Mr Lindley, though he would have liked some
beer. He must set the example in a drinking parish.
  'We need a drop to keep us going,' said Mrs Durant.
  She had rather a complaining manner. The clergyman sat on uncom-
50 fortably while she laid the table for the half-past ten lunch. Her husband
drew up to eat. She remained in her little round arm-chair by the fire.
  She was a woman who would have liked to be easy in her life, but to
whose lot had fallen a rough and turbulent family, and a slothful husband
who did not care what became of himself or anybody. So, her rather
55 good-looking square face was peevish, she had that air of having been
compelled all her life to serve unwillingly, and to control where she did not
want to control. There was about her, too, that masterful *aplomb* of a
woman who has brought up and ruled her sons: but even them she had
ruled unwillingly. She had enjoyed managing her little haberdashery
60 shop, riding in the carrier's cart to Nottingham, going through the big
warehouses to buy her goods. But the fret of managing her sons she did
not like. Only she loved her youngest boy, because he was her last, and
she saw herself free.

C PROJECTS

1 *The plane of articulation.* Can you see a design in the passage – i.e. are there
   discernible phases of development, and how would you identify them?
   How are the narrative modes of description and dialogue related to these
   phases?

2 *Setting.* Study the second paragraph of the extract (lines 5–14). Here, as in
   'Odour of Chrysanthemums', though not so fully, Lawrence suggests a
   relationship between man and his industrial environment. Identify the
   means by which this is projected. Does the description of the cottage
   present (as in the other story) a human posture?
     List the adverbial phrases in this paragraph. Is there a greater concentra-
   tion of adverbials here than elsewhere in the text and, if so, why? Note the

prepositions that head the adverbial phrases. Is there one preposition that occurs more than others? Is this stylistically related to any other feature of the text, e.g. an item of vocabulary?

List the verbs used in clauses where Mr Lindley is subject. Compare these with the verbs used in other clauses, particularly those with non-animate subjects. Has the comparison any relevance to the general description of Mr Lindley?

3   *'Stage properties'*. Three dramatic 'props' appear in the passage: the parish almanacs, the paraffin, and the jug of beer. How does Lawrence present them for the reader's comprehension? How soon, in each case, does the reader become fully aware of what the object is? From whose point of view, in each case, is the 'prop' identified? Why is the identification of the beer a more complex process than the identification of the almanacs and the paraffin? What is different about the way in which the beer (or the *jug of beer*) is identified?

Why do you suppose that Lawrence writes *'her* jug' rather than '*the* jug' in lines 35–6? Can you find, elsewhere in the passage, a pronoun that supports your supposition?

4   *Minor characters*. Two walk-on figures are included in the *dramatis personae*: the level-crossing keeper and the child who comes for the paraffin. Assuming that they are slightly more than mere exponents of local colour, what stylistic or structural purpose would you say is served by the introduction of these figures? (As far as the crossing keeper is concerned, you may have touched on this question in attempting project 2 above.)

Trace the steps by which the child is fleetingly endowed with a personality. The child is given one sentence to speak. Why should this utterance be recorded? To complete the sketch of the minor character? To fix attention on a process in the narrative? To convey a sense of community, perhaps baffling to the outsider? (*Note:* In the dialect of Nottingham, requests and polite invitations are often framed with *shall* where Standard English requires *will*: e.g. *Shall you stop at the corner? Shall you have some more meat?*)

5   *Major characters: identification*. The means by which characters are identified (i.e. as *a man, her husband, the clergyman*, etc.) may appear to be subject to casual stylistic variations, but there is often a discernible and significant pattern in the manner of denoting the emergent actors. Study the extract and note the use of the following devices to identify the participants:

    proper name
    word denoting gender or age
    word denoting social role or function
    definite and indefinite articles (or absence of these)
    possessive pronouns

6   *Major characters: description*. The following syntactic structures frame (sometimes conjointly) descriptions of the appearance or nature of the characters. References in brackets are to the appropriate paragraphs in *A Grammar of Contemporary English* (Quirk *et al.*, 1972); the same refer-

ences will serve students using *A University Grammar of English* (Quirk and Greenbaum, 1973).

> premodification (*GCE* 13.27 ff.)
> postmodification (*GCE* 13.5 ff.)
> pre- and postmodification in combination
> non-restrictive appositions (*GCE* 9.49 ff.)
> participle clauses (*GCE* 11.3, 11.35)
> intensive complementation (*GCE* 12.8 ff.)
> existential sentence (with BE) (*GCE* 14.19)
> (With HAVE) (*GCE* 14.23)
> verbs denoting style of speech
> adverbs or adverbial phrases indicating manner of behaviour or style of speech

Study the passage for examples of these, then begin to look for patterns. If we distinguish between *label*, i.e. a brief indication of age, physique or general nature, and *commentary*, i.e. an expanded description of dress, behaviour, personal history or other circumstances, would it be possible to say that some of the listed structures seem to be appropriate for labelling, others for commentary? Is there a noticeable distribution, in the passage, of 'labelling' descriptions and 'commenting' descriptions?

Take each character in turn and trace the whole pattern of identification and description, noting in particular what happens as one character 'advances' or 'recedes' in relationship to the others.

7 *Further explorations.*
   (i) We sometimes take the norms of a text for granted, when it may be important to determine and state what these norms are. Read carefully through the extract and note:
     (*a*) the clauses in which the first element – excluding conjunction, etc., is *not* the subject. (In cases of ellipsis, count the subject of the leading clause in the sequence; see *GCE* 9.21.)
     (*b*) the clauses in which the subject is *not* a personal pronoun, a name, or a noun identifying one of the three major participants.
         Interpret your findings. Is there anything significant about the location of those sentences that do not follow the norm? Note especially clauses in which the subject is inanimate but agentive (see *GCE* 7.9) and clauses in which the first element is an adverbial.
   (ii) With reference to *GCE* 3.35 and G. N. Leech (1971), *Meaning and the English Verb*, pp. 4–5, 18–22, study the extract and attempt to relate its verbs to the categories *dynamic* (or *event*) and *stative* (or *state*). In greater detail, identify *activity verbs*, *momentary verbs*, *transitional event verbs*, *process verbs*, *verbs of inert perception and cognition*, *verbs of having and being*, *verbs of bodily sensation*. Is there a predominance? A pattern? A distribution? Bear in mind your 'phasing' of the extract in Project 1.
   (iii) A routine act in the stylistic analysis of any text is to look at the distribution of transitive and intransitive complementations (*GCE* 2.7). Study our extract with this purpose in mind. Is such a distribution

reflected in the phasing of the narrative? Is there a connection, in the passage, between the concepts of transitivity and 'dynamism' (or 'event')? – e.g. do the categories of transitivity and activity always coincide? Is the combination of transitivity and event obviously associated with any of the participants in the narrative?

D THE WIDER SCOPE

The wider scope is, of course, the story as a whole; read it, taking due note of its theme (or of the interplay of psychological motifs) and of the organisation Lawrence has imposed upon it. You will see that our extract makes up about one-third of section II of the narrative. In that same section two further sub-sections are clearly discernible: one (from *This was one of the houses* . . . to '*Which is all I can afford,*' *she said*) reports the conversation at the Durants', and the other (from *Mr Lindley took his departure* . . . to *She herself was only nineteen*) describes the ensuing scene at the vicarage.

Attempt a stylistic analysis of these passages – sub-sections (ii) and (iii) of section II. Bear in mind (*a*) the dependence of each sub-section on its predecessors, e.g. in the continuity and expansion of information; (*b*) the articulation of each extract, which may be 'phased' (like the passage from 'Odour of Chrysanthemums') but which in certain cases, e.g. a protracted conversation, could be 'uniform', or static; (*c*) the patternings, distributions, norms and densities of linguistic features.

Try to relate your linguistic observations to the presentation of character and setting, to the staging of the action in movement or tableau, to the interactions of participants in the narrative, to shifts of narrative viewpoint, to the author's attempts to focus or distract the reader's attention. The features that strike you as important will not necessarily be the same as those identified in the exercises above; you are, in more than one sense of the word, 'responsible' for your own definitions.

Should you complete this task, you will have described six pages of a fifty-page story. The scope may not seem to have widened a great deal; nevertheless, there is much you will have learned about the structure of a work of art and about the language of narrative.

References: Chapter 7

Cluysenaar, A. (1976), *Introduction to Literary Stylistics* (London: Batsford).

Leech, G. N. (1971), *Meaning and the English Verb* (London: Longman).

Quirk, R., Greenbaum, S., Leech, G. and Svartvik, T. (1972), *A Grammar of Contemporary English* (London: Longman).

Quirk, R. and Greenbaum, S. (1973), *A University Grammar of English* (London: Longman).

Widdowson, H. G. (1975), *Stylistics and the Teaching of Literature* (London: Longman).

Introduction to Chapter 8

Alex Rodger's chapter is the longest and most detailed example of practical stylistics in this book. Upon initial inspection it may look daunting to the student of language and literature even though several examples of practical stylistics should have been worked through by this stage in the book. But there is nothing intrinsically difficult in Alex Rodger's account of Auden's well-known ballad; in fact, as he puts it, the linguistic details derive from reference to a good contemporary grammar of English and by appeal to a working knowledge of how certain aspects of our own native language operate. Rodger's chapter differs from others in the book in that he does not offer the basis for an interpretation by an examination of foregrounded features of language; he analyses almost every word in detail in relation to the grammatical system, poetic form and the network of meanings released by all the words in the poem in combination. His interpretation is both comprehensive and substantiated, in an attestable way, by appeal to the linguistic facts. As pointed out in the Introduction to this book, much can be learned in this chapter about the nature of language in poetry from following the close detail of a lucid linguistic examination.

8 ' "O Where Are You Going?" ': a Suggested Experiment in Classroom Stylistics

A. RODGER

The question likely to be uppermost in the minds of many who read this book is, I suspect, a frankly pragmatic and pedagogical one: can stylistics help teachers of English to achieve in their 'practical criticism' classes anything that they do not already achieve without it? Unfortunately this is a question which demands answers of two rather different kinds. One of these would be a full-scale rationale of stylistic principles and procedures, the other a practical demonstration of their relevance and value to literary education. But since no essay can hope to encompass both, and since admirable answers of the first kind have now been available for some years,[1] it seems more appropriate here to show stylistics in action with respect to some short complete work of literature. My aim in this chapter is therefore to suggest how one might adopt a stylistic approach in the classroom to a widely popular but somewhat enigmatic poem by W. H. Auden which is commonly known as ' "O Where Are You Going?" '[2]

SONG V

'O where are you going?' said reader to rider,
'That valley is fatal when furnaces burn,
Yonder's the midden whose odours will madden,
That gap is the grave where the tall return.'

5 'O do you imagine,' said fearer to farer,
'That dusk will delay on your path to the pass,
That diligent looking discover the lacking
Your footsteps feel from granite to grass?'

'O what was that bird,' said horror to hearer,
10 'Did you see that shape in the twisted trees?
Behind you swiftly the figure comes softly,
The spot on your skin is a shocking disease.'

'Out of this house' – said rider to reader,
'Yours never will' – said farer to fearer,
15   'They're looking for you' – said hearer to horror,
As he left them there, as he left them there.

Making a Start: the World within the Poem

One of the most important aspects of any poem is the implication its language may carry of some developing human situation within the world *inside* the poem itself,[3] and much of the teacher's work should be directed towards encouraging learners to reconstruct that world and make it as vividly real as possible for themselves by drawing the appropriate inferences from the linguistic details of the text. In the most general sense, Auden's poem is no exception. Nevertheless, all teachers and most learners will readily recognise that there is something very odd about the world within this poem. For there is a sense in which the bulk of post-medieval poetry – and, indeed, nearly all twentieth-century poetry – is directly relatable to the 'objective' world of public actualities. However wildly fictitious the context of address, however idiosyncratic the personal world view and language of the poet, the world within the poem is some restructured version of the external actualities among which we have to live. Carl Sandburg may surprise us by making grass address the human race in human language, but what it talks about are the brute objective facts of war and commemorative war-cemeteries.[4] ' "O Where Are You Going?" ' strikes us differently, for the world within this poem does not seem related in this fairly direct way to the world in which we live our ordinary daily lives. An appropriate opening in the classroom would therefore be to invite the group to define, in terms of their initial impressions, just what sort of world this poem does evoke for them. Here the temptation to simplify our own task as teachers by sticking a question-begging generic label ('myth', 'symbol', 'fable', 'parable' or whatever) on the poem from the start should be resisted. Quite apart from the fact that most concepts of this kind are notoriously ill-defined, all such *a priori* categorisation is pedagogically self-defeating, in that it either short-circuits or obviates completely those processes of personal discovery which should be the learner's central experience in all literary training. Students should be led to the point where, in confronting texts of varying kinds and characters, they discover the need for such terms, and so are in a sense compelled to re-invent and define them for themselves – though, as always, the teacher will have to supply the appropriate label in the end.

For this phase of the exploration the class might first be encouraged to consider the situational implications of the deictic words in the text, that is, those which have the function of 'pointing' to things, persons, etc., in the immediate environment of the speakers and their addressees.[5] These of course include the personal pronouns (*you/ your/yours* and *them*), which here refer directly to the person addressed in each quoted utterance. But for the present purpose priority should perhaps be given to the noun phrases containing demonstrative adjectives (*That valley, That gap, that bird, that shape*), which together with the adverbials of place *Yonder* and *there* all have a distancing effect that contrasts with the 'here-where-we-stand' implications of *this house*. Differing only slightly from these are the noun phrases with the definite article: *the midden, the grave, the pass, the lacking, the twisted trees, the figure, The spot on your skin*. The teacher can point out that what is common to all the noun phrases cited so far is a high degree of specificity or definiteness of reference. Those containing the definite article (with the exception of *the tall*, to which I shall revert later) are all first mentions of the things referred to, not further references to things already mentioned by any of the speakers in the poem, so these noun phrases are not textual but situational in their referential function. They imply that the things they refer to are environmental *data*, features of the 'given' situation in which the characters are at that moment speaking, and therefore immediately present or at least familiar to both speaker and addressee. On the other hand, the groups containing demonstrative adjectives are not merely definite or specific in reference: they are even more so than those with the definite article because unlike them they are *selective*, discriminating between what is relatively close to the participants in space and/or time and what is relatively distant. It may also be worth mentioning at this point that, although there are altogether eleven of these highly specific references, five selective and six non-selective, the poem ostensibly contains only a single indefinite reference to something entirely new and unidentified: *a shocking disease* (line 12).

On these grounds, the class may be led to agree (1) that the various speakers can not only clearly perceive the things they mention but know that their addressees can also perceive them, or (2) that these things are at least wholly familiar to both parties as features of a terrain well known to them, thus forming part of their shared knowledge. But students will also agree that when we first try to assemble all these into a unified setting with a realistic topography, as we do – or ought to do – when reading a novel or a short story, the individual features seem oddly assorted, and the connections among them remain mysterious and elusive for us, though they seem to be clear enough to the characters inside the poem. What sort of furnaces, for instance, are those wholly unspecified ones mentioned in line 2? What purpose do they serve, and why should the valley be a place of disaster or even death when these furnaces are alight – and, it would seem, *only* then? And what connection is there, if any, between the furnaces and the midden?

Are we to envisage a heap of industrial waste or a farmyard dunghill, and why should the odours it emits be *predictably* capable of enraging people or even driving them insane? In what sense can a gap be a grave, or vice versa? And who are *the tall* who are said, very categorically, to return to it, as if this were a wholly inevitable event? Have they been in it already? And how are all these matters connected with a route through a mountain range (line 6), someone searching for something missing (lines 7–8), a strange bird, deformed trees, an unidentified pursuer, and the physical symptoms of some horrible infection or contagion? Above all, who are the *dramatis personae* here? Why do they keep changing from one stanza to the next, and how, if at all, are they related to or connected with one another?

Systematic consideration of these questions should lead the group to two general conclusions. First, the poem at an initial reading seems to lack the sort of unity normally conferred on any sort of discourse by clear continuity of topic and by stability of addresser–addressee relationships. Clearly there is an outer stability in this respect, in so far as we are aware that Auden as impersonal narrator seems to be telling us a story of some sort. The instability is inside the world of the poem, where both speaker and addressee seem to change twice in the first three stanzas. Secondly, despite all this, the poem does seem to have some sort of unity of its own which is not readily definable in terms of any single explicit and identifiable subject-matter. Some members of the class may sense a vague connection between stanzas 1 and 2, arguing that both seem to be about people undertaking journeys, but others may object that the first seems to be a horseman while the second is clearly on foot (*the lacking*/*Your footsteps feel* . . .). On the other hand, stanzas 3 and 4 are more difficult to relate to each other and to the two that precede them. Matters of tense and time-reference become important here. The speaker in stanza 2 seems to be referring to some future or even hypothetical mountain journey planned by his addressee (. . . *will delay* . . . [*will*] *discover* . . .), whereas stanza 3 seems to imply a totally different setting, with the speaker there referring to things and happenings perceived in the immediate present. And where do the pronouncements and actions of stanza 4 take place? Who were the persons (*them*) left behind at the close of the poem, where were they left (we are only told that they were left *there*), and who was *he* who left them?

With the teacher's help it should emerge from group discussion of these questions that the first three stanzas imply various physical settings which have a vividness that endows them with a special kind of reality – a reality which is not merely 'imagined' in the sense of being fictitious but imaginary in the sense of being non-logical, fantastic, or fabulous in the technical sense of the word. The various personages, entities and actions are somehow made to hang together not by the rational connections of common sense or normal discourse structure, but by the seemingly arbitrary associations of dream or the supralogical consequentiality of a fable, fairy-tale or folk-story. Even when this has been agreed, however, the group may still find the plot-line obscure. As hinted earlier, this is perhaps most obvious in stanza 1, where the semantic relations between the main clauses and the subordinate clauses are odd. The teacher may have to direct attention to this fact rather firmly, because it will not necessarily be immediately obvious to all the students that much of the grammatically subordinate material in any normal discourse is concerned with what we might loosely define as 'the logic of circumstance', that is, the temporal, locational, causal and other conditions under which the process, event or action expressed by the main clause takes place. In this poem these relationships are peculiar, not only where the subordinate clause functions directly in the structure of the sentence as in

That valley is fatal   when furnaces burn

but also where it functions as the element postmodifying the dominant noun or headword of a complex noun-phrase, as in

. . . the midden whose odours will madden
. . . the grave where the tall return

The statement about the dangers of the valley would strike us as perfectly normal if the subsequent subordinate clause were to read *when hurricanes blow* or *when fog settles down* or *when blizzards are blowing*. In the same way, the statement about the gap would fit in with the notion of the hazards of the valley in bad weather if the defining relative clause were rewritten as *the gorge where the guides return*. Even the midden would sound less mysterious and alarming if the postmodifier of the noun were *whose smell will repel you*. Nevertheless, even if these changes were made we should still wonder why a midden should be mentioned at all in remarks about a tract of land which is dangerous in bad weather, and we wonder still more about its being mentioned in the context in which we actually find it in the poem. In itself each stanza thus lacks the kind of unity which in normal discourse arises from (1) consistency of reference to the same topics and (2) predictability of development among the propositions carried by the individual clauses. Once this is established the class will quickly point out that what is true of the clauses that constitute each single-sentence stanza is true of the four stanzas themselves. This seems to be the main source of the mystery and obscurity characterising the poem as a whole. The rapid shifts of topic within each stanza are paralleled by the equally rapid changes in characters and setting in stanzas 1–3. The shifts are abrupt and seemingly arbitrary, like the transitions in a fantasy film or a dream.

Perhaps a nightmare would be a still more appropriate analogy, since most critics seem to agree that the poem's phantasmagorical inconsequentialities are partially unified by a pervasive implication of menace.[6] We can corroborate this by asking the class to consider the vocabulary of the poem using a dictionary if necessary. It should emerge that in isolation such words as *valley*, *gap*, and *furnaces* have no inherent connotations of a sinister kind but that they acquire them here through being combined syntactically with adjectives like *fatal*, verbs like *burn* and nouns like *grave*. The same is true of *odours*, which has no necessary implication of noisome offensiveness, still less of power to induce rage or even madness. In the text of the poem, however, it takes on these values by collocating with the verb *madden* and the archaic or regional-dialect noun *midden*; and with regard to the latter, it may be worth eliciting from the class that while the latter does tend to have built-in connotations of revolting texture and smell, these are normally neutralised by the simple rural and agricultural contexts of reference to which the use of the word is commonly restricted. Both sets of connotations are revitalised and made thoroughly sinister in the context of stanza 1. The lexis of menace is rather less obtrusive in stanza 2, though an atmosphere of mystery is maintained by the elliptical and oblique manner in which the questioner expresses himself in lines 7–8. However, it reappears at its most powerful in stanza 3, in the items *horror*, *twisted trees* and *shocking disease*. Indeed, the very speech-style of the speaker in this stanza invests such intrinsically neutral words as *shape*, *figure*, *swiftly* and *softly* with contextual values of mystery and unidentified menace. This sort of scrutiny of the poem's lexical make-up should lead the group to conclude that its context-of-reference, the 'reality' represented in the poem, is not the objective reality of shared everyday experience in the world of common sense but the private, subjective reality of inner psychological tensions, anxieties and terrors.

Contexts of Address and Conventions of Genre

In attempting to define the nature of the world within the poem, the class will hardly be able to avoid some mention of its inhabitants. So far I have deliberately avoided identifying these personages more specifically, for reasons which will shortly become clear. Nevertheless, this is normally the essential point of entry to the interpretation of any poem. We should encourage learners to form the habit of thinking of poems as speech acts and of establishing whether or not the poem in hand implies any face-to-face verbal interaction between two or more human participants in the implied inner situation. Alternatively, there may be some subtler and less communicatively orthodox implication of address, as in Sandburg's 'Grass'. But in Auden's poem the answer to this question is so obvious as to be interpretatively misleading. There are clearly two planes or contexts of communication: (1) an outer context in which the poet addresses us in the role of a narrator, and (2) a series of inner contexts in which the inhabitants of the world within the poem address each other as participants in dialogues and, more specifically, as questioners and respondents in a series of interlocutory exchanges. Now, in my own classroom experiences with this poem, students have repeatedly tended to focus too exclusively on the *content* of the quoted speeches, neglecting the important implications of the narrator's own formulaic reporting clauses, all of which are modelled on the pattern 'said Addresser to Addressee'. I suspect that they have done this for three reasons. First, they have been initially puzzled by the world within the poem and have naturally tried to reconstruct it from the environmental references, all of which are contained in the Direct Speech clauses. Secondly, they have carried over into their reading of the poem habits derived from their reading of prose fiction, where the narrator's reporting clauses commonly carry little information other than the identity of the speaker and the fact that he or she has spoken. Finally, because they tend to regard unusual patterns in grammar, morphology and sound as optional extras that have no communicative value, they have ignored the prominent paradigmatic pattern which Auden as narrator has set up in his own impersonal reporting clauses. This pattern is of course located in the set of nouns used to identify the successive pairs of questioners and respondents. In failing to take it sufficiently into account for interpretative purposes, my students have missed the main clue to the poem's underlying theme, which is both the regulative principle governing the poem's aesthetic organisation as a text and its deepest significance as a message.

One way of helping students to discover this important aspect of the poem for themselves is to revert to some of the questions earlier raised about verisimilitude, but to do so from a more communicative and grammatical point of view. One might begin by returning to the problem of 'characters' and 'scenes'. How many are there of each? Ostensibly there are six different characters and at least three different settings, but some of the group may argue that there is no necessary implication of a change of scene in stanza 2. They may contend that in using the definite article in the noun phrase *the pass* the speaker in stanza 2 is alluding to a particular place which is well known both to himself and to his addressee but which is not a feature of the immediate location in which he is asking his questions. Others may then ask where these two new characters have come from and why, since nothing in the first stanza implies their presence in that setting. Again nothing should be done to suppress differences of opinion, since these are likely to induce closer attention to the peculiarities of the narrator's own usage. A few students may see possible overlaps between the inner and the outer contexts of address, taking *reader* as an ironic reference in the third person to each actual reader of the poem and *rider* (writer?) as a similar covert reference to the poet. But, if that is so, what are we to make of the other four characters? Do they, too, simply represent the reader and the poet or are we to accept them as separate persons in their own right? Certainly all six reappear in stanza 4, so all seem to be equally important in the poem. But are they connected with each other and, if so, how? Such questions as these inevitably lead to the problems posed by the final stanza, where all the speakers are the persons formerly addressed in the first three. Here some very basic grammatical questions may be needed to ensure that each speaker's utterance is correctly construed. '*Out of this house*' must be interpreted as a response to the question '*O where are you going?*' and not as an elliptical imperative of the colloquial kind ('Get out of this house!'). Similarly the reference of *Yours* in line 14 must be clearly understood to be to *Your diligent looking* in line 7 if the elliptical question in lines 7–8 is to be correctly understood and the response in line 14 properly related to it. The precise reference of the pronoun *They* in line 15 must also be established. Is this used indefinitely to refer to some anonymous and undefined social group ('They say it'll be a good summer this year') or does it refer to specific persons already mentioned as being present in one of the preceding scenes and, if so, which ones? Exactly who are the persons referred to as *he* and *them* in line 16? Once again all are likely to prove controversial questions and the teacher should suggest that the various possibilities be kept in mind for later decision based on further textual evidence.

Syntactic Parallelism and Semantic Equivalences

In the set of nouns which identify the three questioners in stanzas 1–3 the one that does not seem to fit in readily is the first, *reader*. The other two, *fearer* and *horror*, at least share a common semantic base in the notion of being afraid. Clearly, *reader* normally carries no such implications. Similarly, the addressee-nouns seem to form a semantically lop-sided set in which *hearer* is the odd man out. The first two, *rider* and *farer*, have in common the notion of travel, but this component of meaning is not normally present in the word *hearer*, which is in any case infrequently used. The last of the set, *horror*, is clearer and sharper in meaning than *hearer*, but most learners will recognise that the word is not used here in any of the ways familiar to us in normal English usage.

Furthermore *fearer*, *farer* and even *hearer* all sound peculiar, even to advanced foreign learners of English. All three are easy enough to understand in a vague way, yet seem unfamiliar in form as well as in their mode of use here. Of the six terms, *reader*, *rider* and *horror* are in themselves the most familiar in form but equally peculiar in use. For example, the reader seems to be a specific individual, but what is he reading, and why is this important enough to be mentioned? Why does he interrupt his reading to question the rider about his destination? Indeed, what is a rider doing in the reader's house at all? – for that is where the rider's words in line 13 unquestionably locate them both.

My own readers may have noticed in my last three sentences the sudden introduction of articles before the words *reader* and *rider*. Here we have the crux of the whole matter. Both are common count nouns of the grammatical sub-class known as agential nouns: they are 'doer' nouns referring to classes or types of person. Consequently, if they are used in the singular they must be premodified by an article or a demonstrative adjective, and this is not the case in Auden's poem. Now, it is true that in English certain kinds of common count noun permit omission of the article or demonstrative in various abstract and specialised uses such as *go by car*, *go to church*, *from top to bottom*, and so on. But these seldom feature agential nouns, the majority of which are derived from a verb stem to which an agential suffix is attached, thus giving the meaning 'one who habitually or occupationally engages in' the activity denoted by the verb. They define the person referred to in terms of his role in some immediate situation or of his most charac- teristic activity or mode of behaviour, and we refer to him as *a thinker*, or *an actor*, or *a farmer*, and so on. Hence the feeling of oddity about the unmodified agential nouns in Auden's ballad. But in English it is also possible for proper nouns – personal names, that is – to be premodified by the definite or the indefinite article, as in the following:

He wants to be *a* Mozart (= a musical genius like Mozart)
I'd rather see *the* Chekhov (= the play by Chekhov, not some other play
                                            currently being performed)
They own *two* Fords (= two cars made by the firm of that name)[7]

What Auden does in the poem is invent a complementary 'rule- exception' whereby agential nouns can be used without premodifiers and so become partially converted into proper nouns, that is, the names of specific people. The latter, however, always require initial capitals, whereas Auden's have none. This has two main results. First, the six nouns in the poem become semantic hybrids uniquely blending the normally incompatible functions of identifying unique persons by name and denoting generic types, members of classes, persons identified in terms of their most characteristic activity. Secondly, the agential forms, without articles or capital letters, cleverly mask the poet's allegorical intention, for the personified abstractions of allegory are very seldom given agential nouns as names and are always assigned capital letters, e.g. Hope, Melancholy, Despair, etc. If we can bring students to arrive at these insights by the appropriate discovery-procedures, we shall have helped them to take the first steps in discovering both the theme of the poem and the genre within which it is operating.

The seeming failure of the agential nouns to form two internally homogeneous sets may now be seen in a different light if we consider all six in their interrelationships. There is a clearly foregrounded[8] scheme of parallelism, both in syntactic form and communicative function, running through the reporting clauses in the first three stanzas and repeated in reversed form in those of the final stanza, so that at equivalent places in structure of each stanza we have the six agential nouns, for example:

Speech by	Addresser	to	Addressee
1	reader		rider
2	fearer		farer
3	horror		hearer

This automatically makes the three items in each set equivalent in terms of speech-role. But, in addition, this kind of parallelism in poetry always invites us to make unusual semantic connections between items in equivalent positions. We have already observed the linguistic oddity of *fearer*, *farer* and *hearer*, and should now ask the class for their suggestions as to why Auden did not select any of the obvious choices here. If someone's most characteristic activity is the display of fear, then the word *coward* is readily available. If travel is the person's characteristic activity, then *traveller* is the obvious agential noun to describe that person. And if we need a noun which classifies a person on the ground that his most characteristic activity is using his ears to good effect, then the obvious choice is *listener*, for the verb *listen* implies a deliberate act of auditory attention rather than the involuntary process of merely *hearing* sounds, speech, music, etc. Again, if we consult the entries in a dictionary under the head *fear* we shall find no agential noun *fearer*. Likewise with the *fare* entries. Its signification as a verb in modern English is the much more general one 'to progress, to get on', whereas the meaning 'go, journey' is listed as obsolete or archaic usage. Still more important, we shall find that, as a separate item of vocabulary, the agential form *farer* does not exist, though under compounds we shall find it used as a suffix in such old-fashioned nouns as *wayfarer* and *seafarer*. On consulting the verb *hear* we shall find that there is in fact an agential noun *hearer* but that its uses are rare and restricted. Finally, we shall of course find no English verb-base *horr* to which an agential suffix can be added to give the meaning 'one who typically or occupationally *horrs*'. Auden has neatly exploited the accident that this abstract noun sounds like an agential noun if placed near the end of a string of these. We might at this point use the blackboard to tabulate these six items in derivational terms, showing the normal forms quite unmarked, the rare one queried, the invented ones starred, and the false one double-starred, thus:

Verb Base		Suffix	Verb Base		Suffix
READ	+	er	RIDE	+	(e) r
* FEAR	+	er	* FARE	+	er
** HORR	+	or	? HEAR	+	er

We should now try to see how *reader* and *hearer* might be accommodated in their appropriate sets. The pair *fearer* and *horror* share a feature of meaning we may loosely define in a negative way as 'lack or loss of courage'. By mere positional equivalence *reader* does not automatically take on this feature. In semantic contrast with its opposite number *rider*, however, it certainly suggests an intellectual, stay-at-home addiction to thought rather than to action, reading being the typical activity of this speaker. In the context provided for it here the word *rider* evokes distinctly romantic notions of the lone horseman, about to ride off through dangerous territory, and so we begin to conceive contrastively of *reader* (or Reader) as someone whose experience and knowledge, especially of danger, are second-hand, derived from books and certainly not from horseback journeys through the kind of 'badlands' he describes for Rider's benefit. This contextually unique investment of *reader* with a negative semantic feature /-heroic/ is further corroborated by the parallel contrast between the deviant forms *fearer* and *farer*. This pairing reinforces our sense of the increasing timorousness in the set of questioners. Farer may lack the more heroic characteristics of Rider but he is at least out-going, a traveller, whereas Fearer makes Reader sound almost bold. But it is the final pairing of *horror* with *hearer* which brings the pattern to its climax. Inherently the word *horror* denotes a compound of shuddering terror and loathing, and as an abstract noun it brings to its most explicit level in the poem the covert process of allegorisation. As a participant in the plot, Horror becomes the living embodiment of terrified revulsion, whereas Hearer at least sounds calm by comparison. What puzzles us is the significance of Hearer's name, for if the 'heroic' addressees in stanzas 1–3 are not to lose their common denominator at the last minute, we have to discover how the noun *hearer* can be invested with the appropriate semantic feature, just as reader was invested with suggestions of stay-at-home prudential caution.

This is where the teacher must persuade the group to think linguistically and semantically about the processes denoted by the various verbs from which these allegorical agential nouns have been derived. To read, for example, is at least an ACTIVITY, even if only of the mind and imagination, and it is a deliberate or volitional action like riding. On the other hand, to be afraid, that is, to fear things, is not an action we ourselves choose to carry out. The verb *fear*, though grammatically 'transitive', denotes a STATE or CONDITION, not an action. But in the poem Auden's invention of an agential noun derived from this verb gives it the illusory status of an ACTION verb as opposed to a 'state-of-being' or STATIVE verb.[9] This is the key to the proper understanding of the significance of this patterning of unusual agential nouns. We already know there is no English verb *horr and no agential noun meaning 'one whose typical activity is experiencing horror'. There is no equivalent verb to denote the PROCESS involved because there is no process here except that of intensely painful emotional experience. The noun *horror* denotes a pure state of dread and revulsion so intense as to paralyse all will to action. If Hearer is to belong with Rider and Farer, then, he must ACT in some way, however unspectacularly, and this means discarding the sense in which the verb *hear* denotes the merely passive perception of sounds, and selecting one which entails giving conscious and deliberate attention to sounds or speech. Hearer must become one who 'gives ear to' others.

We might now point out that we have arrived at this conclusion because we can now see Auden's motive for avoiding the 'ready-made' conventional nouns for persons characterised by cowardice, travel and attentive listening. He has invented two unique agential nouns and exploited a relatively rare one in ways which draw attention first to their own oddity and then to the double pattern of significance which together they create within the context of the poem. First, there is the pattern of unusual contrast or antonymy between each pair of interlocutors, then there is the counter-pattern of unusual similarity or synonymy which binds together all the speakers in one associative set and all the addressees in another. All the questioners share a common characteristic which at best is a recluse-like caution and at worst the paralysis of total dread and revulsion. All the addressees and ultimate respondents to the questions are united by a more adventurous or at least more extraverted temperament, and it is essentially the character of their replies which gives the final stanza the conclusive force it has. The situation within the world inside the poem is thus a series of debates or quarrels between the two sets of participants. But there is a third significant pattern within this parallelistic scheme of equivalences which is still more interesting and significant: the symmetrical and simultaneous intensification and mitigation of the semantic feature which gives unity to each of the two sets of participants. As the poem progresses we sense a marked deterioration in the morale of the questioners and an equally marked abatement of the 'heroic' overtones in the names of the more courageous set of participants, and this all turns on Auden's unusual exploitation of the contrasts between verbs which are normally active in implication and those which are normally stative. We might illustrate this pattern as in Table 8.1. This accounts in grammatical and semantic terms for our impression of a rapid diminution in the courage and capacity-to-act of the questioners. It also accounts for the counter-balancing de-romanticisation of the questioners whereby the notion of the lone horseman passes into the more general concept of a traveller of any sort and finally into the less isolated and less self-oriented figure of one who 'gives a hearing' to others. These effects must of course be read in context, and they are certainly modified by the content, manner and communicative purposes of the replies made by the 'heroes' to their respective questioners and by what these things tell us about the three characters themselves.

Table 8.1 Verb Categories and Semantic Features

Verb Category	+/− Semantic Feature 'Heroic'	Questioner	Respondent	+/− Semantic Feature 'Heroic'	Verb Category
Action 'Pseudo-active' state	−	READer	RIDEr	+ + +	Action
(None: stative noun only)	− −	FEARer	FAREr	+ +	Action
	− − −	HORROR	HEARer	+	'Pseudo-stative' action

Forms of Speech and their Communicative Functions

Before considering the postponed responses of Rider, Farer and Hearer, the class should be invited to reconsider what the three questioners say and why they say it. Just what do they hope to achieve in making these utterances? How do they expect them to affect the actual behaviour of Rider, Farer and Hearer? All three certainly ask questions, but some ask more questions than others. For example, Reader instantly adds three statements to his opening question and so allows Rider no opportunity (within the stanza at least) to reply. Fearer in his turn comes out with one long sentence which breaks down into two distinct but associated questions framed in a manner which almost inhibits any reply. Horror asks no fewer than four questions – or seems to do so, because the last two really take the form of rather insidious statements – and does so in such haste and with such rapid and unpredictable switches of topic that any addressee would be hard put to offer a full set of answers. Auden's violation of the conventions of dialogue-ballads therefore seems designed to suggest a set of questioners who either do not want any answer, or do not expect any, or do not in fact care whether they receive any reply or not. Now, the basic communicative role of a questioner is obviously that of someone who requires information. He casts his addressee in the role of an informant, someone who may be presumed to know something that he (the questioner) does not know, and places himself in the role of one who needs to acquire that knowledge. And, at first sight, Reader at least sounds as if his question is a real request for information he does not possess. The form and nature of the question presuppose not only Rider's immediate presence in the situation but also Reader's automatic presumption of his own right to ask such a question. This is important, since unless we are very intimate with the person addressed, or we are recognisable officials or householders accosting would-be intruders, we simply do not ask this question of complete or relative strangers without considerable social and communicative preamble. Indeed, much the same goes for neighbours and friends, with whom we normally exchange the customary social pleasantries before inquiring where they are heading for. The situational brusqueness of Reader's question (which is perhaps partly signalled by his exclamatory 'O') suggests great familiarity with Rider, perhaps even family kinship, as Rider's reply might indicate. We have already seen, too, that the sinister landscape to which his subsequent three statements refer must be either visible or wholly familiar to both of them. Reader's question, then, hardly seems like a straightforward request for information he does not already possess, for his statements presume a knowledge of Rider's probable route if not of his ultimate destination. They are also superfluous as information needed by Rider, since the intimacy with which Reader assumes the right to ask his abrupt question presupposes the sort of addressee who is likely to know these things about the surrounding countryside already. In informational terms, then, Reader's statements thus sound more like reminders of knowledge already shared than things Rider does not know. In terms of their tone, they sound like warnings of a thoroughly frightening kind. So, despite its interrogative mood, Reader's initial query does not really function as a request for information but takes on the force of an authoritative challenge and an implicit objection to or prohibition of Rider's intended departure (cf. 'And where do you think YOU'RE off to?'). At its very weakest, Reader's question signals an anxiety or disapproval intense enough to destroy normal good manners between intimates. At its strongest, it sounds like a stern parental warning from anxious father to errant son.

Here we might briefly tidy up a few loose ends left over from earlier stages of the discussion. We know the scene described by Reader to be a weirdly sinister blend of the industrial (or worse) and the rustic. In its topographical sense, a *gap* denotes a break or opening in a line of hills or mountains, but here its more general meaning of 'an unfilled space' transfers itself with horrid aptness to its alliterative complement *the grave*, thus fusing the two meanings of Reader's final clause:

> That defile is the location of the burial-place. . . .
> That hole is the (open) grave. . . .

The defining adverbial clause of place, *where the tall return*, tends to baffle many students but need not do so long if they are encouraged to search within the stanza for some word semantically related to *return*. The only directly related word is of course *going*, which relates directly to Rider. This in turn makes sense of the spurious referential irrelevance and anonymity of the generic noun phrase *the tall*, in which class Rider is now included because he is the only person in this scene who is going anywhere and thus the only one to whom the verb *return* has any application. The generic reference itself (on the same model of definite article plus 'plural' adjective as *the poor, the blind, the dead*) now begins to make sense as one more reinforcement of the semantic feature '+ heroic' because of its associations with *rider*. Horsemen are tall by position, are taught to 'sit tall in the saddle', and romantic heroes are tall by convention. Additionally the adjective may carry connotations of adulthood as opposed to childhood. As for *return* itself, which is alliteratively linked with *tall*,[10] we should point out that in this context it, too, ironically conflates two meanings in relation to *gap* and *grave*, implying both 'route of return to this place' and 'place of return to the earth'. Reader's warnings seem to be intended for one of a class of rash and unwary addressees who have little sense of their own inherent vulnerability to evil or of their inescapable mortality.

We have now seen that if we ask what Reader needs or wants to know the answer is really 'Nothing'. His only query takes the form of a *wh*-type question,[11] so he is ostensibly asking for just enough relevant information to satisfy his immediate curiosity about Rider's intended destination. In fact the functions of his question prove to be very different. In a similar way, Fearer's two queries seem at first to be of the kind requiring a simple 'Yes' or 'No' answer. On closer inspection, however, they prove to be much subtler: they beg the questions they appear to ask. Fearer neither needs nor expects either of the relevant answers from Farer because his questions are all rhetorical ones, that is, questions to which the questioner already knows the answers or presumes to do so. Here the teacher will probably have to explain that rhetorical questions have the same communicative functions as very assertive statements. The result is that a negative rhetorical question has the same communicative force as a very emphatic positive statement. Thus Wordsworth's well-known negative question, *Will no one tell me what she sings?*, however wistful in tone, in fact presupposes the answer 'Yes' and so is equivalent to the positive assertion 'SOMEONE must be able and willing to tell me what she is singing!', just as Shylock's 'If you prick us, do we not bleed?' is equivalent to 'OF COURSE we bleed if you prick us!'[12]

Conversely, positive rhetorical questions such as 'Can the leopard change his spots?' obviously have the force of strong negative assertions ('No leopard can change its spots!'). As a result they expect negative replies – if, indeed, they expect any at all – mainly because their implied propositions tend to be inherently absurd. In face-to-face debate, therefore, questions of this sort are deliberately designed to put the addressee at an acute disadvantage by leaving him only unpalatable options by way of response. He may deny what his questioner implies to be self-evident by replying 'Yes, some leopards can and do change their spots', but then has to prove this or be seen to hold absurd beliefs. Alternatively, he may concede defeat explicitly by replying 'No, leopards cannot change their spots'. In the last resort he may choose to be non-committal, signalling a position of stalemate by refusing to reply at all. And of course silence often is the option chosen. The purely dramatic effect of this arises, as Leech (1969: 184) points out, from our feeling that despite its built-in assumptions, the question still demands an answer but does not get one. This effect is of course only a temporary one in Auden's poem, but it is none the less present until stanza 4, where Farer uses the only other available option, a witty retort which is relevant but not strictly an answer to the question. The main point to be emphasised here is that in dialogue or debate any negative proposition of dubious probability carries much more weight if the addressee is openly challenged to refute it. The process of challenge itself, however, remains inexplicit and therefore undramatic unless the negative assertion is recast in the form of a positive question. If the addressee tries to rise to the challenge, he is soon overwhelmed by the realisation that, if he is to avoid committing himself to the defence of logical absurdities, he must either answer 'No' or hold his tongue. This is of course precisely why the addresser has chosen the positive rhetorical-question form. His own powerful convictions are thereby made to appear logically irrefutable in open debate, especially if his addressee seems unable to reply at all.

Now, both of Fearer's questions are rhetorical ones and both are positive in form, so both presuppose the answer 'No!' Moreover, the first of them challenges Fearer to defend an absurd proposition. Fearer thus adopts the deflatory debating ploy we have just examined, but the additional insidiousness with which he exploits it may not be immediately obvious to inexperienced readers. It should be pointed out to them that, because of its 'branching' or elliptical structure, Fearer's whole sentence consists of a single interrogative main clause, *do you imagine* followed by two subordinate clauses operating as complements to the main verb, *imagine*. Furthermore, although they now know why Fearer does not make negative assertions such as 'Dusk will NOT delay on your path to the pass', they still have to consider why he does not simply ask DIRECT questions of the positive rhetorical kind, such as 'Will dusk delay . . . '?' and 'Will your diligent looking discover the lacking . . . ?' This should lead them to recognise that he uses *imagine* as a 'reporting' verb, putting the content of the propositions he is challenging into two 'reported' clauses,[13] and assigning these to Farer as his (Farer's) propositions.

Main Clause (Reporting)	Subordinate Clause: Complement (Reported)
Do you imagine	that dusk will delay on your path to the pass?
Do you imagine	(that) your diligent looking (will) discover the lacking (that) your footsteps (will) feel from granite to grass?

The class should now be urged to consider why Fearer claims to be reporting not Farer's utterances but his 'imaginings' and to specify the contextual implications of Fearer's use of *imagine*. Here the teacher can point out that this verb (1) belongs to a fairly large set of reporting verbs denoting mental processes which are inherently unvoiced or 'silent' and (2) is a member of a special sub-set of such verbs that we frequently use when we report our own mental activities to others without making any claim to absolute certainty about the truth or factuality of the propositions we entertain. This sub-set includes, for example, *assume, believe, conclude, deduce, expect, fancy, feel, guess, hope, infer, presume, suppose* and *think*. It should not take students long to perceive that what all these have in common is the way in which they contrast with such verbs as *know, be certain, realise, understand, be aware that*, all of which entail the speaker's presupposition that the content of his reported complement clause is true in the sense of being a *fact*. Indeed, *know* is the key contrastive verb here, and once this has been grasped the learners should again arrive fairly quickly at the recognition of the differing degrees of factual certainty implied by these verbs. It may be wise to confine the investigations to four verbs only – *know, believe, think* and, of course, *imagine* – but the presuppositions and implications of our everyday uses of all four should be thoroughly explored, preferably with the aid of a good dictionary which cites sentences exemplifying their typical uses. It should emerge from this that, as listed here, these four verbs are arranged in diminishing order of commitment in relation to the user's certainty about the truth or factual status of the mental propositions that he entertains himself or that others report themselves as entertaining. In this way it should become clear that a proper understanding of Fearer's whole utterance turns on our recognition of the differences between (1) knowing some proposition to be a fact, (2) believing with conviction, but without the absolute factual certainty of knowledge, that some proposition is reasonably probable, (3) thinking some proposition is a reasonable possibility, (4) imagining that some proposition may just be logically feasible as a matter of mere conjecture, and (5) 'imagining things', that is, indulging in mental propositions of a highly improbable or even impossible kind.

The inherent ambiguity of *imagine* as a mental-process-reporting verb should by now be more evident to the class. Used positively and non-pejoratively in colloquial conversation it is virtually synonymous with *think* or *believe* in the sense 'consider something to be probable or possible'. But as soon as it is used positively to report a question expressing an inherently improbable or impossible proposition it assumes pejorative value and rhetorical function. The point can be reinforced by showing that this is why face-to-face questions beginning 'Can you imagine . . . ?' are likely to occur much more frequently than those which begin 'Do you imagine . . . ?' In the former, the auxiliary verb *can* only questions whether the addressee is at all ABLE to envisage some unusual state of affairs: it does not ascribe to him any serious entertainment of it as a proposition. Moreover, it presupposes any person's imaginative ability to be in direct ratio to the degree of feasibility inherent in the proposition to be imagined. Consequently 'Can you imagine being rich?' has in theory a relatively high probability of being asked and of receiving a modestly positive reply, whereas 'Can you imagine a horse with seven legs?' has relatively low probability on both counts. 'Can you imagine a horse with four legs?' is therefore unlikely to occur at all since the proposition itself makes no real demand on the addressee's powers of imagination. On the other hand, rhetorical questions beginning 'Do you imagine . . .' in no way question the addressee's ability to imagine some particular state of affairs. The auxiliary *do* automatically presupposes that ability: what it asks is whether or not the addressee's mode of mental operation in this instance is in fact the process of imagining. All questions of this type may therefore be reformulated as follows: 'Is it a FACT that you IMAGINE such-and-such to be the case?' By using this formula the questioner immediately signals his scepticism about the reliability of imagination as a mental process and so simultaneously discredits both the mental calibre of the addressee and the truth-value of the proposition, regardless of the fact that it is the very form of the question itself which imputes the challenged proposition to the addressee. This is why questions beginning 'Do you imagine . . . ?' tend to sound impolite at least, even when the discredited proposition is merely one of commonplace improbability (e.g. 'Do you imagine that car is actually going to start?'). It is when the imputed proposition violates all the canons of logic and common sense that the deflatory effect of the question becomes most powerfully insulting.

It follows that, unless their complement clauses express simple logical conjectures based on knowledge shared by questioner and addressee alike, questions beginning 'Do you imagine . . . ?' are rhetorical and offensive. Fearer's first question is an unusually blatant example, since it imputes to him the proposition 'Dusk will delay on my path to the pass'. The absurdity of this arises inevitably from Fearer's own combination of the Subject noun *dusk* with the verb *delay*. Used in this intransitive way, *delay* necessarily presupposes a human agent as its subject, since only human beings are capable of choosing to be slow or late in doing something. The noun *dusk*, on the other hand, denotes a natural cosmic event. As a result, Farer is instantly classified as the sort of person capable of believing that the larger processes of natural law will voluntarily suspend themselves to suit his personal purposes, in that the sun will deliberately stop orbiting the earth to let him (Farer) reach the pass before nightfall. Fearer's second question, however, does not impute to Farer any proposition which is inherently absurd in the same way. Stripped of the obscurities created by Fearer's elliptical syntax and unorthodox usage, that proposition is simply 'I shall find what I want by seeking it with care and persistence', which expresses nothing more unacceptable than Farer's confident belief in a reasonable probability. Like the first, this second proposition, too, is automatically discredited by Fearer's question-begging main clause ('*Do you imagine*') but this time the move is a logically invalid one. As if this were not enough, Fearer's expression of the proposition – the words he puts into Farer's mouth or mind – in fact negates the reasonableness of the proposition at every syntactic step. Fearer's second complement clause is in fact a series of self-cancelling propositions.

To validate this point the teacher will need to direct the group's attention to the abnormality of Fearer's uses of the verbs *discover* and *feel*, and the participles *looking* and *lacking*. Here again, appeal to dictionary citations of the normal uses of these words should lead to a deeper interpretation of this clause, and so to a fuller realisation of what Fearer is up to in the whole of his long sentence. Because the verb of the complement-clause here is *(will) discover*, it is clear that *your looking* is to be interpreted not as 'looking AT' but 'looking FOR' something. We can therefore analyse Fearer's utterance grammatically as follows:

S(ubject)	V(erb)	O(bject)
Your diligent looking	will discover	the lacking, etc.

But the subject of this clause is itself the nominalisation of yet another, an implied or underlying independent clause

S   V   O A(dverb)
You will be looking for X diligently.

We are bound to insert the unknown item 'X' because *look for* is a phrasal transitive verb and so must take a direct object (O_d). This in turn is because *look for* denotes an ACTION process necessarily involving two entities, the 'looker' and the 'looked-for'. The former, being the agentive participant or ACTOR, is necessarily an animate being, whereas the other, the thing or person affected by the action and so definable as the GOAL, may be either an animate being or something inanimate. Now, in nominalising this underlying clause in order to use it as the subject of his actual utterance, Fearer breaks the basic rule by omitting *for X*, with the result that the goal of Farer's search, being linguistically unrealised, becomes in a way 'unreal' for Fearer and Farer and certainly unknown to Auden's readers who are, so to speak, eavesdropping on this conversation. We shall have to examine the full implications and consequences of this at a later stage. What requires immediate attention is what results from Fearer's transformation of this underlying clause into a nominal group or noun phrase (NP) functioning as the subject of *discover*: a curiously unnecessary complication in the meaning of his utterance. Fearer seems to say the same thing twice over in different words while at the same time missing out something vitally important. For *discover* is itself a transitive verb expressing an actor–action–goal process, so it, too, requires an animate actor, and in this instance that actor must be Farer himself. So, by sticking to the normal conventions of communication and the rules of prescribed grammatical usage, Fearer could simply have asked the straightforward question

S   V   O_d
(Do you imagine that) you will discover the lacking, etc.?

Instead he replaces *you* with the genitive pronoun group *your diligent looking*. Here the teacher should explain that, despite their 'possessive' appearance, genitive groups of this type refer neither to the relevant person's physical or other attributes nor to his material belongings. What they do is provide a convenient linguistic device for naming people's states and conditions (e.g. *Jack's being in quarantine*) or their actions (e.g. *Jill's guitar-playing and your singing*). They are often called 'verbal nouns' or gerunds because they commonly function as subject or object groups in independent clauses. So they are more accurately described as subjective genitives because they nominalise underlying independent clauses in which the corresponding non-genitive group functions as the subject: *Jack was in quarantine, Jill will be playing the guitar and you will be singing.*[14] As a result, the topic or subject of Fearer's second question is not Farer himself but his future action of looking for X, and one important consequence is that as readers of the poem we are much less aware of Farer's situational role as the actor in a goal-directed action than we should have been if Fearer had used the conventional SVOd structure *You will discover X.* Fearer's odd way of expressing himself thus has the effect of linguistically demoting the actor so that he becomes assimilated to his action. Situationally, therefore, we might say that Fearer seems here to become totally identified with his own activity: looking for X.

Even if this were not the case, we should still think Fearer's utterance a very odd one indeed, for the following reasons. Fearer describes what Farer will discover as *the lacking/Your footsteps feel.* But, as a rule, when the verb *discover* is immediately followed by a nominal group (as opposed to a relative clause beginning *that, what, how,* etc.) that group itself denotes either (1) some concrete entity or matter of fact (e.g. *the American continent, old Roman ruins, a hole in your shoe*) or (2) some abstract but demonstrable principle (e.g. *the law of gravity, the solution to the problem, the molecular structure of the atom*). Also, the primary sense in which *discover* tends to be used is 'be the first person to find out or make known the existence of something hitherto unknown'. More colloquially it may be used to mean 'realise, become aware of something for the first time', and of course in this sense one may personally experience or realise for the first time something that has long been known to others though not necessarily to many. Obviously both kinds of discovery can be made by accident but in the poem the words *Your diligent looking* leave us in no doubt that Farer is going to be engaged in a deliberate and intensive search. Here the class should be asked to formulate clearly the grounds on which anyone undertakes a real search of this kind. It should be obvious to them that the seeker must feel some compelling wish or need to find the object of his search, but it may not be so immediately apparent to them that he is unlikely to contemplate a search at all unless he has good reason for believing

(1) that the object or goal of his search actually exists;
(2) that he can define and therefore recognise it if he finds it;
(3) that it is by nature something that can be found by diligent searching;
(4) that he has some idea of how to search for it and where it may be.

Fearer's phrase therefore suggests that Farer will not be hoping just to stumble across something whose existence has been hitherto unsuspected. He must be looking for something already known or believed to exist but difficult to find and certainly 'known' to Farer himself only as a concept and not as something of which he has first-hand experience. Alternatively, if it is something he has already once possessed or experienced, then he must have lost it or experienced it far away and perhaps some time ago, since he is by definition a traveller in search of something. But Fearer does not use the verb *find*, which might suggest the recovery of something lost, nor does he use *rediscover*, which would indicate the reliving of a former experience. As a traveller by vocation, Farer might of course be simply hoping to come across something new and strange, at least to himself and to others like himself, but the notion of persistent effort conveyed by *diligent looking* suggests that Fearer is not using *discover* in its basic sense of 'be the first to come across or find out the existence of something entirely unknown'. He seems more likely to mean 'experience or realise for the first time in your life something you have only heard about at second hand'. Farer's search seems to be motivated by the need to turn his theoretical knowledge ABOUT something into experiential knowledge OF that thing.

This is where the class should be reminded that Fearer's use of *do you imagine* to negate Farer's second proposition is a dishonest rhetorical trick. The joint propositions 'I will look diligently for X' and 'I will discover X' are not at all inherently illogical or absurd, provided always that Farer is satisfied about the four conditions listed earlier. Fearer only makes them seem so by embodying them both in his second clause-complement to the verb *imagine*. This makes them the grammatical equivalent of the first proposition and so falsely suggests that their truth-value is no more acceptable than that of 'Dusk will delay on my path to the pass'. But there is a second and more sinister reason for Fearer's curiously tautological grammar here. As already noted, it identifies Farer with his action of searching and allows Fearer to introduce the notion of a deliberate search, which is realised linguistically by the NP *your looking*, without giving linguistic realisation to the goal, which would normally be expressed as *for X*. This not only makes X seem rather unreal or absent, but also creates a distinct suspicion in the mind of the reader that Fearer does not wish to name X or refer to it in any explicit way. This suspicion is further confirmed by what follows next. The combination of *discover* with the object NP *the lacking* is odd enough in itself, for reasons we shall have to investigate, but the oddest thing of all is that *lack*, whether as a noun or as a verb, itself demands either a completive phrase of the form *of X* or *in X*, or a non-genitive direct object *X*, and does not get it here. This, too, will require closer scrutiny, but for the moment it should be noted that Fearer seems determined to avoid giving this mysterious goal-element 'X' any linguistic realisation whatever. The class will not easily discover his motivation for this crucial and persistent omission, so it will be best to start from what seems on the face of it to be obvious: his prediction of Farer's failure.

Most students will readily grasp intuitively that the occurrence of *lacking* in Fearer's utterance indicates his conviction that Farer's quest will be a failure and are likely to produce the somewhat simplistic paraphrase 'He says Farer won't find what he's looking for'. That is undeniably part of Fearer's meaning, but it is a small part only. As consultation of the dictionary will prove, lack is semantically a very tricky word indeed. Its main characteristic, however (apart from its need to be complemented by another noun or genitive NP), is its expression either of partial deficiency or of total absence. Indeed, it is 'gradable' according to context, for in negative uses it can express absolute completeness (*lacking nothing*), while in positive uses it can express any degree of 'minus' from near-completeness (*lacking nothing but, lacking only*) to total deprivation or complete absence (*utterly lacking*). It is therefore not really a 'denotative' noun, for, although it is necessarily abstract in meaning, its very inability to occur without nominal complementation indicates that it does not itself denote any class of entity which has independent existence even of the kind accorded to common abstract concepts. It is simply a negative quantifier of measure expressing the gradable semantic feature / -sufficiency / and consequently can only very rarely occur as anything other than that. Lack is always and unavoidably lack OF something. Despite *lacking*'s general air of 'negativity' the class ought to find its occurrence as the O$_d$ of *discover* puzzling, because discovery is itself a positive concept. Just as the successful outcome of a deliberate search is instinctively expressed in positive terms (e.g. *Farer discovered X*), so the failure of a search is normally expressed by negation (e.g. *Farer did not discover X*), and the same obviously applies to predictive statements in the future tense. So it is both a paradox and bathos to say *Farer will discover the lack of X* and only marginally less so to say *Farer will discover that X is lacking*. To say *Farer will discover the lacking*, however, is to reinforce paradox and bathos with mystification by breaking yet another rule of normal grammar and so 'reify', i.e. make a real 'thing' out of, a free-floating minus quantity which remains unrelated to any identifiable independent entity, whether a concrete object or an abstract idea.

It therefore seems that Fearer wishes to go much farther than merely saying *You, Farer, will not discover X* in the most sarcastic way possible. To do that would be to deny only that Farer is the sort of person capable of discovering X, or that X itself is at all easy to discover, or to deny both propositions simultaneously. The built-in negativity of *Do you imagine that . . . ?* has already done more than that by falsely suggesting that both propositions are as impossible as dusk's willing suspension of its own occurrence. The point to be noted, however, is that prefacing *dusk will delay on your path to the pass* with *do you imagine* denies only the possibility of dusk's behaving like a human being: it does not deny the EXISTENCE of dusk, of Farer, of his chosen path or of the pass itself. This is where Fearer's avoidance of a direct object after *your looking (for)* becomes a clue to his motive in choosing *lacking* as the direct object of *discover*. He cannot use that verb at all, even negatively, without inserting a nominal group denoting Farer's goal, and since his implication is *you will not discover*, we should expect perhaps to find the universal pronoun *anything*. But once again this would do no more than deny Farer's capabilities as a searcher. It would also suggest that Fearer does not know what it is that Farer hopes to discover. And if Fearer does not know that, then his entire negation is meaningless. No one can confidently predict the failure of somebody else's search unless he knows, among other things, exactly what the other person is looking for. Nor can Fearer now insert the negative universal pronoun *nothing*, for that would imply a double negative (*Do you imagine that you will discover NOTHING?*) which would predict Farer's success in discovering either X itself or some equally satisfactory alternative. Already committed to the sarcastic incredulity of *Do you imagine that . . . ?* with its built-in negation, and consequently committed to the positive *(you will) discover*, Fearer can no longer avoid making a positive reference to X itself. And with diabolical ingenuity he produces a nominal group which can only be paraphrased as 'the Absolutely Non-Existent'. He not only knows what Farer is looking for, but also feels able to predict his failure with complete confidence because he claims to know for certain that X does not exist.

To elucidate this point the teacher will have to explain the difference between DENOTATIVE meaning (i.e. 'dictionary definition') and REFERENTIAL meaning, which involves the use of individual vocabulary items to make statements about actual things in actual situations. Like the whole concept of 'lack', this is another difficult topic – indeed, one of much greater intrinsic complexity. Luckily, Fearer's use of the definite article simplifies the task to some extent, as we shall see. The teacher might further simplify the problem by explaining a dictionary itself as a collection of linguistic symbols. Each alphabetically listed noun, verb, adjective, etc., is a symbol which can either be spoken or written, and each definition is a description of the physical entity or abstract concept that word symbolises or 'stands for'. Because each word has to be listed in complete isolation, the definition of what it symbolises or DENOTES has to be a classification, that is, a description of the basic characteristics of the whole class of things denoted by the word, not the individual characteristics of some unique instance. Dictionary definitions are therefore GENERIC in that they relate word-symbols to whole types or classes of real things (including abstract concepts), and a dictionary can therefore be said to be a collection of merely potential meanings or 'designations' awaiting realisation in use, when they will take on REFERENTIAL meaning by symbolising particular instances of the things denoted. In total isolation, therefore, a noun such as *book* has only generic or denotative meaning, whereas the definite singular NP *the book* REFERS TO some unique instance known to and immediately identifiable by the speaker and his addressee in some particular situation.

The very fact that a noun is listed in a dictionary therefore indicates a generally agreed public belief in the existence of the class of entities described in the word's definition, whether that class is one consisting of physical things and processes, of abstract concepts and mental processes, or even of the imaginary creatures denoted by such words as *dragon*, *unicorn* and *fairy*, for the latter do exist as imaginative concepts. In fact they all exist as generic concepts which are either concrete like *book*, or abstract like *courage*, *horror* and *faith*, or mythical like *minotaur*, *centaur*, etc. Only when we REFER TO 'a centaur I was talking to yesterday' or 'the dragon we saw at the Zoo' or 'that other unicorn, the one eating Father's azaleas' do we claim, or pretend to claim, ACTUAL existence for mythical or fictitious entities. Such references automatically confer on the referents existence as specific real facts in a specific and real situation. Now, the appalling cunning of Fearer is to do precisely that in relation to the concept 'lack'. He uses a REFERRING EXPRESSION which is, on the face of it, non-generic and therefore specific, definite and therefore certainly known to himself and Farer, and singular (i.e. non-generic once more) therefore existent.[15] This is the meaning expressed by his use of the definite article, and it indicates that he is communicatively 'pointing to' something which he himself claims he knows to exist as a fact in the world outside the language-system itself and which he predicts Farer will also learn to recognise as a fact. But the 'noun' he then uses is *lacking*, and we have already seen that because *lack* itself only denotes a variable minus quantity it normally has to be complemented by some positively denotative noun indicating the KIND of thing that is 'lacking'. Unlike even the mythic nouns (*unicorn*, *centaur*), however, 'lack' has no independent conceptual existence of its own. It does not in itself imply non-existence, only deficit or absence, and even when used to mean 'completely absent in the given instance or situation' its completive noun asserts the real existence of instances of the referent elsewhere in the world. So as Fearer uses it, namely without a completive generic common noun denoting Farer's unknown goal 'X', the 'stem' *lack* is forced by its determining definite article to assume the denotative burden itself. Like its more positive equivalents *a lot of*, *a number of*, *a quantity of*, *an amount of*, the quantifier-noun *lack* is in a relation of appositional identity of reference with its genitive case noun or 'headword', but signals 'minus quantity'. Here in Fearer's utterance, however, there is nothing for it to quantify even in its own negative way. It is no trivially facetious pun to say that what is lacking from the incomplete NP *the lacking* directly symbolises or imitates by its absence what Fearer predicts Farer will discover: the total absence of what ought to be there, at least in Farer's view. It might be a useful ploy with senior pupils or adult students to explain that when linguists and grammarians wish to indicate that the user of a sentence has chosen to omit some grammatical element or 'part of speech' which is in any case OPTIONAL they indicate the absence of that element by means of the absolute zero-symbol ∅. We can therefore use this in an unorthodox way to symbolise Fearer's deliberate omission of an OBLIGATORY element of meaning by placing it immediately after the quantifier: *you will discover the lacking ∅*, thereby indicating that we are aware that Fearer is determined to deny the existence of 'X' by steadfastly refusing to name it: for to name it would be to assert that it exists, even if only as an abstract concept or, more extremely still, a mythical one.

All this may account for our surprise at the strange combination of *discover* and *lack*, but it does not account for Fearer's unusual combination of the definite article with the participial form *lacking*. The incomplete definite singular NP *the lack* would certainly have been highly compatible with Fearer's aim of 'reifying' nullity, of making 'absolute zero' into an existing thing. His invention of a pseudo-gerund *the lacking*, however, brings it closer to the verb, e.g. the intransitive uses of *be lacking* (= be missing) and the transitive uses of *be lacking in* (= be deficient in something). The unfortunate Farer is thus left to wonder whether the absolute deficiency he is to discover will be in the world about him, in himself, or in both. Important as this may be for the tone of the whole poem, it is less important than the fact that the defective NP *the lacking* is strongly reminiscent of the earlier *your looking*. We may perhaps locate Auden's motivation for putting these linguistic oddities in Fearer's mouth in the close syntactic and phonological parallelism between the two. Both are appropriately 'lacking', that is, grammatically defective, in that *looking* should be followed by *for X* and *lacking* is followed neither by *of X* or *in X*. Each therefore draws attention to itself by its grammatical deviance, each consists solely of a determiner plus an *-ing* participle, and the two verb-stems (*look-/lack-*) differ only slightly in terms of the medial vowel-sounds which alone distinguish them in meaning here. Moreover, in recognising that we expected the noun *lack* in the second instance we may now realise that we might well have expected the noun *search* in the first. The resultant sentence would still have been rather odd, but two very important components of Fearer's meaning would have disappeared. The first is his sly suggestion that both the process of looking and the state or condition of lacking are likely to continue indefinitely. For, as the teacher should explain, although *-ing* participial forms are often called 'present participles', this is often a misnomer. The time-reference of *-ing* participles is entirely dependent upon that of the finite verb to which they are most directly related, which in this instance is the elliptical *(will) discover*. Both participles thus have future time-reference but non-completive or continuative ASPECT,[16] and so the two suggest an action-process and a state of affairs continuing indefinitely in the future. This should be no surprise to us now that we see how Fearer describes what Farer will 'discover'. This device in turn supports the even more sly suggestion that, since there will be no real discovery to be made, the already slight difference between *your looking* and *the lacking* is cancelled out and the two take on the same meaning. Just as Farer is identified with his own dogged action of looking for X, so that endless activity itself becomes identified with the 'lacking' which will itself be the only thing he might possibly discover.

As if all this were not sufficiently negative and destructive, the restrictive or defining relative clause which closes Fearer's speech neither really justifies his use of the definite article before *lacking* nor defines, in any normal sense the word, the nature of the lack itself. Again it would be surprising if it did, now that we are aware of what he means by *discover the lacking*. The non-elliptical form of the relative clause is *(that) your footsteps (will) feel from granite to grass* but this itself implies yet another underlying clause of the form

S	V	O$_d$

Your footsteps will feel the lacking (etc.).

Obviously the normal way of expressing such a prediction is simply to say *You will feel the lack of X* or *You will feel that X is lacking*. But Fearer's actual words make his already equivocal utterance still more paradoxical. His substitution of the possessive pronominal group *Your footsteps* for the normal subject pronoun *you* has very complex results. First, it demotes Farer for the third time from his full human status as the actor in a human action, assimilating him in this instance to the tread of his own feet on the ground. Secondly, in doing that it completely nominalises and so partly suppresses the fact that his manner and means of looking for 'X' is the action of walking in search of it. Thirdly, it makes that action itself the very channel of information through which he will 'make his discovery'. Fourthly, it thereby predisposes both Farer and readers of the poem to interpret *feel* not as a verb denoting a vague emotional-cum-intuitive process of being or becoming aware of something in a non-physical way, but as one of physical perception through direct contact. Finally, by making *the lacking* the direct object of both verbs (*discover* and *feel*), Fearer releases his ultimate paradox. Because it expresses only a minus quantity or measure, *lack* used as a quantifying noun can only be an abstract one indirectly expressing a non-physical, non-independent 'thing', namely someone's mental awareness of a deficit or total absence. So, even when it is used to quantify nouns denoting countable concrete objects, in itself it implies some person's mental awareness (or recognition or realisation) of some degree of insufficiency or the total absence of those things. In Fearer's weird utterance it becomes abstract to the nth degree. We have just seen that his omission of the obligatory headword is itself linguistically symbolic, miming the fact of utter absence by being absent when its presence is linguistically and semantically essential. We saw that this could in fact be symbolised by an unorthodox use of the symbol $\emptyset$ to indicate not the absence of an optional grammatical element but the absence of an obligatory one. Now, in semantics and symbolic logic, the same zero-symbol is employed for a very special purpose. It is used to signify the 'empty' or null class of entities, a class which has no members at all, not even mythical or fictional concepts like *unicorn* or *centaur*. There is only one way in which such a class of entities can be given linguistic realisation and that is on the model of GENERIC definite singular noun phrases which denote vast and vague entities or classes of entities by using an attributive adjective as the headword instead of a noun. Examples are *the best*, *the worst*, *the good*, *the beautiful*, *the sublime*, *the ridiculous* and of course the vast anonymous class *the dead* (cf. Reader's *the tall*). In the extreme case of Fearer's deviant NP *the lacking*, we seem to be invited to treat *lacking* as just such an abstract adjectival headword, so that the whole becomes a generic adjectival NP paraphrasable perhaps as 'the Non-Existent', which must by definition also be 'the Unknowable'. Yet, having thus equated *the lacking* with 'that which is unknowable because non-existent', Fearer proceeds to insist that Farer will in fact get to 'know' or realise or recognise the Unknowable, form some mental awareness or dim conception of it, and that mental recognition or realisation will arise out of a concrete physical perception, as the verb *feel* here indicates. It will come to Farer through the soles of his feet as he walks in perpetual search of the perpetually Unknowable. The Non-Existence of the Unknowable will be 'known' as a palpable absence through Farer's 'having his feet on the ground' – one at a time, at least! – in the literal sense, and perhaps in the metaphorical sense as well. This paradox is further reinforced by the pair of prepositional phrases of direction *from granite to grass*. These are co-ordinated in logical and temporal sequence in the implied context, and so clearly predict Farer's passage on foot from rock-hard terrain to some softer and more fertile ground, the complete absence of determiners giving both nouns a massive generality of reference. But, as with *looking* and *lacking*, the parallelism of structure (directional preposition + generic noun) combines with the reverse rhyme which links the two

(*GRanite/GRAss*) to minimise their differences in meaning. Not even an improvement in 'the going underfoot' will itself be acceptable to Farer as the goal of his quest. It will not even be a consolation for his failure to attain that goal. Granite and grass will become virtually the same thing and therefore a matter of indifference to him, except as a constant reminder that his goal will continue to elude him no matter where he goes. And when we recall that the positive rhetorical question *do you imagine (that)* makes its reported complement clauses equivalent to *dusk will NOT delay on your path to the pass* and *you will NOT discover the lacking your footsteps (will) feel from granite to grass*, Fearer's verbal vicious circle is complete. If it is predicted that Farer will NOT discover 'the lacking' as it has been defined by Fearer's sophistries and equivocations, it can only mean that the message will never get through from his feet to his head. He will be too identified with his obsessional pursuit (*your looking*) of a chimera (*the lacking*) to do more than feel a vague physical sensation of absence-of-something-or-other as his feet touch the ground.

The perverse logic of this remarkable sentence may be very difficult to put across in the classroom, but the full significance of Fearer's use of *imagine* as his reporting verb and the logical (or ontological) difficulties of the prediction *discover the lacking* may be clarified a little if the teacher can get the class to explore and define the difference in meaning between *discover* and *invent*. If we suppose Fearer to be stating the truth of the matter, and Farer's goal 'X' is really '*Ø*', the Non-Existent, he could not possibly discover it in any sense whatever of the verb *discover*, for only things which already exist as physical facts or as abstract but unexplored logical possibilities can be discovered, the fact of their existence having remained either universally unknown or personally unrealised until the moment of discovery. So, if Fearer is right, it follows that the only way in which Farer could 'discover' his personal goal would be to create it, that is, cause it to exist. Now, the only way in which a human being can bring into existence something of a kind or class that never existed before is by inventing it. But material inventions (for example, the steam engine, radio) are the results of human acts of creative design, not discoveries made by travellers, who can only discover already existing things. Farer is by definition a traveller in search of something and, if that something does not already exist, the only way in which he can bring it into existence is by the other sort of invention, namely mental invention, an act of pure imagination. This would have to be the invention of a purely hypothetical concept, some totally new 'thought'. It could not be anything for which an existing dictionary description exists, as it does for such purely mythical concepts as centaurs, dragons, fairies, etc., for Fearer has slammed the door against even that sort of concept by defining the goal or object of Fearer's search as 'the Absolutely Non-Existent'. So it seems to follow inevitably that Farer's search may very well be the merely self-defeating pursuit of a delusion. That inevitability, however, arises only from Hearer's ingenious but demonic 'playing with words'. It may be no accident that the only way in which Hearer could create such a goal is by the artistic invention of a whole new world of imaginary beings such as that found in J. R. R. Tolkien's *The Lord of the Rings*.

Those of my own readers who have not long ago lost patience with the complexities raised by Fearer's second question will recognise its almost diabolical nature. While it appears to be only a simple if brutal sarcasm ('Who do you think YOU are to attempt such impossible tasks?') it is really a linguistic and metaphysical maze without a centre. The twenty words which constitute the non-elliptical version themselves linguistically ENACT the age-old problem of Appearance v. Reality, while compressed into those same twenty words is a labyrinthine sequence of underlying propositions raising all the problems about the nature of truth, knowledge, belief, existence and non-existence which bedevil those areas of inquiry where religion, philosophy, logic, semantics and linguistics all converge (and often conflict) in their attempts to explicate life's most profound mysteries. Fearer's second question is a Sphinxian riddle posed by one whose utter scepticism arises from his own pessimistic fear of failure or his hatred of the belief of others. At every verbal step he presupposes that Farer is looking for a category of experience which does not and cannot exist. Precisely because he is one who dares not undertake such a journey himself, he cannot possibly know from personal experience that what he asserts with such devious assurance is the truth of the matter. Farer's caustic retort *Yours* (that is, Fearer's footsteps) *never will* makes it clear that he sees through all these nihilistic quibblings. His is the retort of faith, that is, of confident belief without the demand for prior proof. If Fearer is right, Farer will never get to know the Unknowable only because no one can. If he is wrong, however, Fearer himself has missed the whole point of living. In Farer's view, it is better to travel hopefully than never to leave the point of departure for fear that no destination exists.

I have had to go into great depth of detail about Fearer's questions because they are the thematic heart of the poem and throw light on what has gone before as well as what is still to come. In particular, we only understand the Horror–Hearer exchange if we have grasped both the implications of Fearer's use of *imagine* and at least some of the linguistic and rhetorical trickery whereby he dismisses the goal of Farer's search as chimerical. But it is Horror, the incarnation of terrified loathing, who exemplifies both the weakness and the power of unbridled imagination, which is something very different from Farer's confident faith in a feasible concept. It might at first seem that we can simply dismiss all of Horror's questions as mere symptoms of his own extreme nervousness, but this would be to underestimate their real purposes or functions. For example, his first utterance is a *wh*-question, but of the kind that asks for additional information about something already partly known by the person asking it. *What was that bird?* therefore presupposes that Hearer, too, is also aware of the bird. What, then, is Horror asking for? Ostensibly his is a request for a fuller identification of the bird, for his question is a reversible one and can be rephrased as *That bird was what?* Yet precisely because Horror is who he is, we cannot really believe that he really wants to be told what species or variety the bird belongs to. Why, then, does he ask the question at all? The simplest answer is that, in being startled or horrified by this particular bird, he does not know whether Hearer has in fact seen it or, indeed, seen anything, and wants to know the answer to that question. Much the same is true for his second question, only this time it is a straight *yes/no* answer that is expected. *Did you see that shape in the twisted trees?* treats the trees as a 'given' element in the scene, but what is in question is named with greater particularity as *that shape*, not *the shape* or *a shape*, thereby implying that Hearer must surely have seen it. The question therefore tends to presuppose the answer *yes* because of the conviction implied by Horror's use of the selective demonstrative *that*, which also distances the shape in the trees from both participants.[17] What the class should be encouraged to notice, however, is that this distancing is not just in space but also in time. Horror might well have asked 'What *is* that bird?' and 'Do you see that shape?' But his questions are both in the past tense and so refer to the very immediate past. The interesting implication of this is that Horror is asking questions about things which he claims were perceptible a moment or so ago but are no longer perceptible, either because Horror and Hearer have themselves moved on a few steps or because the bird and the shape themselves are no longer there. This puts Hearer in a difficult position. If he was in fact aware of these things which have upset Horror but has said nothing about them, then if he is to be honest he must answer *yes*, thereby confirming and worsening Horror's obvious panic. On the other hand, if he was not aware either of the bird or of the shape, he may honestly answer *no*, but all that establishes for certain is his own failure to perceive them. He can neither verify for himself that they were in fact there, nor effectively or in good faith contradict Horror by denying that they were there, because it is now too late to do either. Horror is therefore able to remain convinced of the reality of the bird and the shape, and will remain horror-stricken, while Hearer cannot disprove their reality even if he feels strongly inclined to do so.

With this in mind the class should quickly see that Horror's third and fourth questions are markedly different. In the first place, their time-reference is to the immediate present, not the immediate past. Hearer should therefore be able to answer them without hesitation, for this time they involve things that he ought to be able to perceive without difficulty. Moreover, they should be easy to answer honestly since they are essentially questions directly involving himself and not involving Horror, except in his role of terrified observer. For Horror does not say 'Behind US swiftly the figure comes softly?' or 'The spots on OUR skins are a shocking disease?' His questions focus on Hearer alone (*Behind you . . . The spot on your skin . . .*). There is also a third change in Horror's method of asking questions, for these ones are posed as positive declarative questions. This means that they are really state-ments given the appearance of being questions by means of a rising intonation towards the end – a fact explicitly signalled by Auden's use of a final interrogatory punctuation mark. Declarative questions are *yes/no* questions of a very special kind. They presuppose the answer *yes* and, unlike any other kind of question, they permit, for that very reason, the addition of a declarative clause of the kind represented by *I presume*, *I expect*, *I suppose*, *I assume*, thereby indicating explicitly that the questioner himself has little doubt that the answer must indeed be *yes*. Much the same communicative effect can be produced by making a downright positive assertion followed by a question tag such as *doesn't it?* or *isn't it?* Horror's third and fourth questions can therefore be paraphrased as follows without alteration of their meaning:

Behind you swiftly the figure comes softly, I presume/doesn't it?
The spot on your skin is a shocking disease, I suppose/isn't it?

and it is significant that in this particular case *I imagine* could do duty as the mental-process clause without seriously weakening the assertive value of either line in any way.[18] This shift from authentic interroga-tives to assertive rhetorical questions is in fact a crucial clue to Horror's motivation in asking all four questions. As we saw, his first two ques-tions are utterly ambiguous in this respect. When they were asked Hearer was in no position to know whether the bird and the shape were (1) real things actually perceived by Horror, (2) mere 'appearances', that is, actual things Horror had mistaken for a bird and a 'shape', or (3) sheer baseless fantasies. Now, however, those first two questions are bound to take on the character of malicious inventions, because Horror's third and fourth questions are clearly attempts to demoralise Hearer by means of suavely horrible insinuation. Here it should be emphasised that the main characteristic of declarative questions is their casual tone, whereby the speaker shows that he takes the answer as a foregone conclusion: so that when the questions themselves are positive, as Horror's are, he implies that the answer is bound to be *yes*. Now, these two questions are also disturbing in their content, the one about the figure being eerie and the one about the spot being repulsive. Nevertheless, Horror's tone is now clearly that of someone rather casually seeking final confirmation of something he already presumes to be a fact. What, then, are we to make of his own emotions at this point? They can scarcely be those of sincere horror. A genuine horror-struck person would either make positive statements like 'I'm sure there's someone following us!' and 'My God! that spot could be the first signs of leprosy!' or use negative questions with positive question tags which clearly signal that the questioner hopes the answer is *no*: 'That's not someone following us, is it?' and 'That spot can't possibly mean cancer, can it?' The evidence seems to point to the fact that in these two questions Horror's own alarm (if any) is a mere pretence he no longer needs to maintain, and this of course destroys the credibility of his earlier panics.

Fearer's first two questions now retrospectively take on the character of deliberate attempts to deceive Hearer into assenting, however tacitly, to the reality of the uncanny presences Horror claims to have perceived. We know that, because of Horror's clever timing of these questions, Hearer cannot disprove their built-in postulates: that the bird and the shape must exist because Horror knows that they were actually there. Nor can Horror prove that they were there, because his testimony rests on alleged subjective experiences for which the objective evidence (if any) is no longer available. Nevertheless, the two questions together combine a question-begging effect similar to that of the notorious *yes/no* question 'Have you stopped beating your wife yet?' with the unnerving effect of the self-questionings and doubts bred in an addressee by the belated asking of questions like 'Did you turn the gas off before we left?' This mixture of imposed presuppositions and self-doubt now forms the pseudo-objective basis on which Horror moves in for the kill. He next tries to convince Hearer of the real presence of a sinister figure which is shadowing him (Hearer) and to sow the doubt in his mind that a spot on his skin, possibly unnoticed till now, is symptomatic of some dreadful and hitherto unsuspected infection. The technique resembles the rebriefing phase of a brainwashing process or the suggestions of a hypnotist, in that both are attempts by an outsider to create and manipulate the content of someone's mind. The difference is that Horror only uses the simple device of positive rhetorical questions which presume the answer *yes* as a foregone conclusion. Now, these particular questions are not only 'presumptive' (that is, based on assumptions he believes or pretends to be self-evident): they are also PRESUMPTUOUS. The spot-on-your-skin question is socially arrogant to the point of impossibility, in that not even one's closest intimates are likely to ask such a question and, in the unlikely event of being forced to ask it, will certainly not use this question-begging form with its casual tone and its odiously offensive innuendo that the disease cannot be decently named and so can only be described as 'a shocking' one. In this respect Horror's final question ought to remind students of Reader's high-handed assumption of his right to question Rider about where he is going. It should also remind them of the insolent scepticism of Fearer's use of *do you imagine* as his cover-question.

Above all, Horror's final questions are psychologically not only presumptuous but also pernicious. They allow Horror to pretend to a knowledge of what is going on in Hearer's mind, and this he can do with all the more assurance because he himself is supplying the content for Hearer's mind to work on. In a sense it no longer matters whether or not there really is a figure pursuing Hearer in a sinister manner or whether there is any real possibility of Hearer's having a shocking disease. What matters is whether or not Horror can convince Hearer that these things are facts, which in turn depends on how successful he has already been in making Hearer wonder whether or not there really was a frightening bird nearby and a menacing shape among the trees. If there really is a spot on Hearer's skin, he may well begin to wonder whether it does betoken some horrifying infection. If there is no spot, his evil exploitation of the suggestive power of declarative questions allows Horror to invent it by simply asserting that it is there, so Hearer is quite likely to start anxiously searching for it. That would seem to be the theory underlying Horror's behavioural and rhetorical tactics here, and on the face of it they might work, given a suitably nervous Hearer. We know that they fail, however, because Hearer's clever retort (*They're looking for you*) shows that he is in no way deceived. The cleverness lies in Hearer's avoidance of any outright denial that Horror's inventions exist. He simply turns the tables on Horror by presupposing that they do exist but denying that they have anything to do with himself. This point can be reinforced if the teacher points out that line 16 demands a strong metrical stress on Hearer's last word, *you*. Hearer's sentence therefore implies '. . . and not for ME'. This neatly bundles together under the plural pronoun *they* all the menacing presences Horror has conjured up verbally, assumes them to be there in fact, but neatly shifts the role of their goal or quarry back on to Horror himself, thus indicating that he knows what Horror has been up to, particularly in his final pair of declarative questions.

This is where the class can be confronted with the final challenge to discover links for themselves. For example, what about the route of the journey? Reader refers to *that valley* and *that gap*, both of which are topographical terms implying hills or mountains, and one meaning of *gap* is a defile or pass through mountainous country. Fearer talks of Farer's *path to the pass* and foresees a transition from mountainous *granite* to the softer *grass* of a valley on the far side. But his scepticism about Farer's alleged belief that *dusk will delay* implies negotiation of the pass at nightfall, while Horror and Hearer seem to be benighted in more fertile surroundings where even birds and trees assume a sinister and alarming character. A clear if somewhat starkly symbolic route therefore seems to run through the three stanzas, at least as far as *the twisted trees*. So perhaps we have one journey but three different travellers, each suffering from deep psychological division within himself.

Here the teacher might profitably remind the group how *looking* and *lacking*, *granite* and *grass* were made contextually synonymous through parallelism in syntactic function and similarity in sound, since the pairs of agential nouns or covert allegorical names are also syntactic parallels and share the same basic sound pattern in each case ($r*d*r$, $f*r*r$). Here, surely, we have Auden's main motivation for using the deviant agential nouns *fearer*, *farer*, *horr-or* and *hearer*. In each pair the two names are identical, differing just enough in sound to make significant distinction in meaning which is then neutralised by the context, so that the two become merely slightly different ways of referring to the same person in a slightly different guise or role:

> rEAder – rIder
> fEArer – fArer
> hOrror – hEArer

The class is already aware that the common feature / − heroic/ unites the three questioners and that the similar feature / + heroic/ unites the respondents, and is likewise aware of the intensification of that feature in the questioner-set, which is counter-balanced by the moderation of 'heroism' in the respondent-set. They may even observe that the least romantically assertive hero, Hearer, now shares the same distinguishing vowel sound as the two less panicky members of the unheroic group. The inference is fairly obvious: we do not even have three separate but psychologically split personalities. All the names refer to the same person at three different stages on a single journey. This can be confirmed from further investigation of the way in which many pairs of words throughout the text are brought into unusual equivalence in this way by the same sort of device of 'pararhyme' (e.g. *midden/ madden*)[19] or by alliteration plus similarity of syllabic structure (e.g. *gap/grave*). The cancelling out of antitheses or the reinforcement of associations by these means is a pattern which is fundamental to the whole poem and which sustains its underlying theme, and the teacher should encourage the class to seek these out and assess their contribution to the meaning of the poem as a whole. The same is true of the ways in which the masculine-ending rhyme-words reinforce connections in meaning (*twisted trees/shocking disease*), thereby contrasting with the non-rhyming feminine endings with which they alternate.

The class should also try to assess why these very assertive patterns in sound and syllable-structure do not figure in the replies of the respondents themselves, for in the final stanza the pattern is maintained only in the reversed sequence of the pairs of names, which signals the reversal in speech-roles and the rhetorical turning of the tables on the questioners. Most important of all, however, will be the need to establish the true identity of *he* and *them* and the location indicated by *there* in line 16. Still to be accounted for, too, is the strangely non-energetic closure this line gives to an otherwise energetic poem, for its repetition of the same half-line gives a slight dying fall to the end of the poem, as if all contentious passion were truly spent. Since the near-identical names simply denote in each case two aspects of the same person, and all the names in fact refer to the same protagonist, there is no great difficulty here. Superficially, there is a clash between the singularity of the pronoun *he*, which would normally only refer to Hearer, and the plurality of *they*, which is at odds with the fact that only Horror appears to represent the anti-heroic group in stanza 3. But we now know that at each stage of the journey each questioner 'contains' or subsumes the earlier ones, so, for a start, Horror includes both Fearer and Reader. On the other hand, Hearer seems to shed his earlier and more assertively romantic selves, that is, Farer and Rider. Now, Hearer's name probably signifies among other things that Horror's sinister presences are no more substantial than the words his addressee hears when Horror refers to them. Also, he has just referred to these presences collectively as *they*. So the narrator's use of *them* in line 16 probably indicates that Hearer left Horror-Fearer-Reader there among the 'horrors' they have conjured up verbally in the landscape of stanza 3. This leaves Hearer as the sole survivor because he has already, in becoming the wiser Hearer, dropped Farer and Rider from his own psychological constitution. But the repetitive content of line 16 suggests a still more satisfying answer to this problem, for *them* may well refer to all six characters as well as to the nightmare entities of the third stage of the journey. In this case, the *he* who emerges from the whole series of debates may be none of those represented by the allegorical agential nouns, but an anonymous true Self, an altogether new man born out of this three-stage struggle between thesis and antithesis. This nameless but more modest hero has now (as Hearer) given a hearing to the arguments of all his anti-Selves and so can drop even his final role as the man who listens to the other fellow's whole case before making any judgement or giving any reply. And, as the evenly balanced and quiet repetition of the final line indicates, he is a fully integrated personality in whom there are no more oppositions. The see-saw of conflicting inner forces has come to rest, and the *he* who gets off it and walks away is his own man, no longer identified with any of them. It may even be that *there* actually represents *this house* and the whole journey has in fact been one undertaken in anticipatory imagination, and the now anonymous hero is ready to leave having heard all sides of the case.

Though the model is the ballad, the mode or genre is allegory, and Auden's would appear to be an allegorical parable on the theme of secular self-salvation. Teachers who know Bunyan's *The Pilgrim's Progress* well enough will detect a strong resemblance between the protagonist of this poem and Bunyan's Valiant-for-Truth and might wish to compare the poem not merely with Valiant's hymn ('Who would true valour see . . .') but also with its whole immediate context, in which Valiant tells how his parents and others '. . . used all means imaginable to persuade me to stay at home', painting for him horrific verbal pictures of the Valley of the Shadow of Death and a country of mountains and dark woods that are full of danger and haunted by a foul fiend.[20] Auden's dramatic parable of life as a dangerous pilgrimage which must none the less be undertaken has an anonymous Everyman as its hero and the Quest for the Good as its narrative core. Its underlying theme is the triumph of self-integration over internal psychological divisions, of disciplined, informed and rational courage over both mere rashness and mere cowardice. Since the allegory is partially concealed by the avoidance of initial capital letters for the unusual names of the characters, few learners will perceive the underlying theme unless they are led to discover it by paying attention to the 'how' of the 'poem', from which the 'what' is never separable, and even those few who may intuitively sense its presence in the poem will remain unable to validate their opinion unless they are taught how and where to look for the evidence that will confirm the real existence of the goal of their search – the significance of the poem itself. They can only know where they are going if they know how to get there.

I sincerely hope no teacher will have been daunted by the mere length of this paper. Auden's is both a deeply serious poem and an ingenious one, but the complexities of its rhetorical implications are in fact much easier to handle in classroom dialogue than in the formal expository mode of an article such as this. Experienced teachers will immediately recognise, however, that several sessions would be necessary to arrive at any group interpretation which is adequate to the demands the poem makes on any reader who truly wants to understand it. The immense pedagogic value of such an approach is that a communicative focus on the problems of comprehension raised by any poem at all inevitably demands discussion of what is communicatively abnormal and grammatically unorthodox, which in turn necessitates constant appeal to what is normal in these respects, especially in some analogous context-of-communication. This means that work in the practical criticism of poetry can be directly linked to the teaching of basic communication skills. Nor need anyone be afraid of the linguistic aspects of this sort of approach to teaching competence in the reading of poetry. There is very little in this interpretation of Auden's poem which cannot be acquired through familiarity with a good modern grammar of English which links form to meaning, a good citation dictionary of contemporary English, and a little disciplined thinking about how people really do talk to each other and what they are trying to do by means of the things they say and the ways in which they say them. The rest comes from the delight and challenge of the poetry itself. As for this particular interpretation of ' "O Where Are You Going?" ' I claim only that it is as consistent as I am personally able to make it with the facts known about how the English language works to communicative effect.

Notes: Chapter 8

1 See especially Leech (1969) and Widdowson (1975). Other introductory surveys are Cluysenaar (1976) and Traugott and Pratt (1980).

2 Readers already familiar with linguistics will find a much more condensed treatment of W. H. Auden's ' "O Where Are You Going?" ' in Carter (1979), where very similar interpretative conclusions are proposed.

3 Compare Leech (1969: 189–98) on the 'world within the poem'.

4 For the text of Sandburg's 'Grass', with a brief commentary, see Leech (1969: 162–3).

5 For the contextual importance of deictic words in poetry, see Leech (1969: 191 ff.); also Leech and Svartvik (1975: sections 69–79, 87–90).

6 See Beach (1957: 95–6); Everett (1964: 27–35); Fuller (1970: 74); Hoggart (1951: 56); Hynes (1976: 94); Spears (1963: 57–8, 73).

7 On names with articles and on agential nouns, see Quirk and Greenbaum (1973: section 4.23, app. I.29, app. I.13).

8 On foregrounding and Parallelism, see Leech (1965: 68–75; 1969: 56–8, 62–9, 79–86). Widdowson (1975: 39 ff., 60–2, 118) also deals with these under the heading of 'equivalence'.

9 For dynamic or actional v. stative uses of verbs, see Quirk and Greenbaum (1973: sections 2.8, 2.16, 3.35); also Leech and Svartvik (1975: sections 123–7).

10 Students should be reminded that it is the main stressed syllables of words which normally carry alliterative sound-patterns in verse, not necessarily their initial syllables; cf. Leech (1969: 91–3).

11 For the implications of questions of the *wh*- and *yes/no* types, consult the sections listed under these headings in Quirk and Greenbaum (1973) or Leech and Svartvik (1975).

12 For an informative account of rhetorical questions, see Leech (1969: 184–6).

13 See 'Reported statements and questions' in Leech and Svartvik (1975: sections 264–8).

14 On subjective genitives, see Quirk and Greenbaum (1973: section 4.70).

15 Some help with the difficult topic of reference and referring expressions may be found in Searle (1969: 77 ff.).

16 For progressive or continuative aspect in verb phrases, see Quirk and Greenbaum (1973: sections 2.8, 2.16, 3.2, 3.27, 3.33–5) and Leech and Svartvik (1975: sections 109, 122, 131, 134).

17 Carter (1979: 39) rightly implies that 'Did you see *a* shape in the twisted trees?' would create less tension since it would presuppose neither Hearer's awareness of

any shape nor the actual existence of one among the trees. The same applies, of course, to Horror's first question: the question 'O was that a bird?', while still asserting the presence of something disturbing which may or may not be a bird, makes far fewer presuppositions than what Horror actually says here.

18 On declarative or 'tag' questions, see Quirk and Greenbaum (1973: section 7.50) and Leech and Svartvik (1975: section 250).

19 Pararhyme and other sound patterns within equivalent syllables are discussed in Leech (1969: 89–102). See especially section 6.4 on 'The interpretation of sound patterns' (95 ff.).

20 See the Everyman's Library edition of *The Pilgrim's Progress* (1907, repr. 1948), pp. 349–57, especially pp. 354–5.

References: Chapter 8

Beach, J. W. (1957), *The Making of the Auden Canon* (Minneapolis, Minn.: University of Minnesota Press).

Carter, R. A. (1979), 'Poetry and conversation: an essay in discourse analysis', *Nottingham Linguistic Circular*, vol. 8, no. 1 (mimeo.), pp. 28–41.

Cluysenaar, A. (1976), *An Introduction to Literary Stylistics* (London: Batsford).

Everett, B. (1964), *Auden* (Edinburgh: Oliver & Boyd).

Fuller, J. (1970), *A Reader's Guide to W. H. Auden* (London: Thames & Hudson).

Hoggart, R. (1951), *Auden: An Introductory Essay* (London: Chatto & Windus).

Hynes, S. (1976), *The Auden Generation* (London: Bodley Head).

Leech, G. N. (1965), ' "This bread I break": language and interpretation', *A Review of English Literature*, ed. A. N. Jeffares, vol. VI, no. 2, pp. 66–75.

Leech, G. N. and Svartvik, J. (1975), *A Communicative Grammar of English* (London: Longman).

Quirk, R. and Greenbaum, S. (1973), *A University Grammar of English* (London: Longman).

Searle, J. R. (1969), *Speech Acts* (Cambridge: CUP).

Spears, M. K. (1963), *The Poetry of W. H. Auden* (New York: OUP).

Traugott, E. C. and Pratt, M. L. (1980), *Linguistics for Students of Literature* (New York: Harcourt Brace Jovanovich).

Widdowson, H. G. (1975), *Stylistics and the Teaching of Literature* (London: Longman).

Introduction to Chapter 9

John Sinclair's chapter focuses on Wordsworth's 'Tintern Abbey', and makes acute observations and a convincing analysis of that poem in terms of concepts like 'arrest' (the ways in which our expectations are held up rather than utilised) and 'extension' (the way structures are unexpectedly expanded). These two concepts can be seen to operate at various linguistic levels in the poem. However, the main thrust of the chapter is towards a coherent methodology and theory for stylistics in general. He argues for (1) a sensible understanding of the nature of stylistic analysis – particularly in the light of hitherto extremist arguments between the so-called subjective literary criticism and the so-called objective linguistic analysis (see Introduction to this book, Section II); (2) an awareness of a probable total inventory of linguistic and textual conventions, shared in some measure by all uses of language, literary or otherwise; (3) the need for an adequate theory of literary communication, against which to measure and undertake individual practical stylistic analyses; (4) a particular marking out of points of interest in a text, where linguistic detail and literary interpretation clearly come together. He terms such points 'focusing categories', or 'focats' for short.

Sinclair's contribution is more theoretical than other chapters in the volume so far. There is a clear resolution to build the theory from definable linguistic observations and categories, and to produce a model of analysis which can go beyond elucidation of a single extract of Wordsworth's poetry. The orientation may be termed *linguistic* stylistic rather than practical or literary stylistic, but there is much that is revealed to be of real relevance to a literary analysis of 'Tintern Abbey'.

9 Lines about 'Lines'

JOHN SINCLAIR

In this chapter I want to argue, or at least assert:

(a) that in stylistics the fashionable contrast between subjective (literary) and objective (linguistic) standpoints is unrealistic. It is equally unhelpful to view a text as a communication between individuals subject to no rules, or to see it as a rigid pattern with a known communicative value. Extreme positions of subjectivity and objectivity both fail to account for the meaningful patterning of a literary text, or indeed any text at all.

(b) that stylistics need not have an unfortunate air of *ad hoc*-ness, sleight of hand. This arises from a failure to devise an adequate theory of literature. The present corpus of stylistic comment consists of applications in search of a theory.

(c) that in the explication of the relationship between linguistic details and literary interpretation there are intersection points of particular interest, which we shall call focusing categories or *focats*.

The example I have chosen is Wordsworth's 'Lines Composed a Few Miles above Tintern Abbey'. From a fairly full analysis, I shall select some important features.

(1) The metrical units and the meaningful units are offset against each other. Most sentences end mid-line; only half the lines are end-stopped: the comma is the popular end-line mark, semicolon mid-line. Contrast this with heroic-couplet poetry, where most lines are end-stopped, most sentence boundaries are also line boundaries; commas are the regular mid-line mark, with semicolons ending lines.

An effect of offsetting grammar and metre is that there are very few places in the poem where all the reader's current expectations are met. Whenever the grammar allows a break, the metre presses on, and vice versa. A text in this grammetric form may be better suited to mood-creation than to argument.

(2) If one were to range English structures on a single scale from 'tight' to 'loose', this text would show a prominence of 'loose' structures – structures like simple co-ordination, apposition, addition. Here are some typical examples; to list exhaustively would be to reprint the text. (Quotations are from the Oxford Standard Authors edition, text 5, 2nd edn, 1936.)

A   *Co-ordination*

   (i) sentences: And now (58)
                     And so (64)
                     Nor perchance . . . (111)
                     Nor wilt thou then (155)

   (ii) clauses: and in thy voice I catch . . . (116)
                     and read/My former pleasures . . .
                                        (118–19)

   (iii) groups: A lover of the meadows and the woods,
                                        (103)
                     In darkness and amid the many shapes
                     Of joyless daylight; (51–2)

   (iv) words: Faint I, nor mourn nor murmur: (86)
                     many recognitions dim and faint (59)
                     these steep and lofty cliffs (5)

B   *Apposition*

        These plots of cottage-ground, these orchard-tufts, (11)
        I bounded o'er the mountains, by the sides
        Of the deep rivers and the lonely streams,
        Wherever nature led! (68–70)
        When these wild ecstasies . . .
        when thy mind/Shall be . . .
        oh! then,/If solitude. . . . (138–43)

C   *Addition* – non-defining relative clauses, e.g. lines 6, 12, 81
        these orchard-tufts,/Which, at this season
        with their unripe fruits,/Are clad in one
        green hue (11–13)

(3) From even these few examples it can be seen that many of the 'loose' structures in the poem are further organised by a type of superficial parallelism which I shall call simply *copying*. Through the partial repetition of words and structures, pairs, triples and larger units are formed. The repeated items form a frame within which some new items are introduced. This feature pervades the poem.

        Felt in the blood, and felt along the heart; (28)
        An appetite; a feeling and a love, (80)
        And all its aching joys are now no more, (84)
        And all its dizzy raptures. (85)

(4) An examination of these copied strings shows that the second or subsequent item tends to be longer and/or more complex than its predecessor. Again, one is spoilt for choice of examples.

        With warmer love – oh! with far deeper zeal
        Of holier love. (154–5)

> The sounding cataract
> Haunted me like a passion: the tall rock,
> The mountain, and the deep and gloomy wood,
> Their colours and their forms, were then to me
> An appetite. . . . (76–80)

> neither evil tongues,
> Rash judgements, nor the sneers of selfish men,
> Nor greetings where no kindness is, nor all
> The dreary intercourse of daily life. . . . (128–31)

Note that *copying* can assert itself without dependence on syntax: for example, in the opening phrases of the poem.

> Five years have past; five summers, with the length
> Of five long winters! (1–2)

Here copying takes over from syntax to give a repetition of *five* to which is added *long*, cognate with *length* in the head-phrase. It is not clear whether *with* means 'plus' (that is, one summer plus one (long) winter equals one year), or describes an attribute of the previous five summers (each of the previous five summers has dragged on like a winter). It doesn't matter which, since the repetitive effect of the *five* and the elongation afforded by *long* suggests clearly enough that it has been a long time.

Let us establish, roughly at first, a distinction in the stylistic patterning.

> these steep and lofty cliffs,
> That *on a wild secluded scene* impress
> Thoughts. . . . (5–7)

The italicised prepositional phrase is front-placed in its clause. The conjunction *that* leads us to expect a clause, and *wild* may be subject or adjunct in such a clause. Prepositional phrases are optional in most clauses, but in a relative clause introduced by *that* a verb is obligatory. The reader must somehow store the memory of the structure so far while he is interpreting *on a wild secluded scene*, and then when he comes to *impress* he can confidently allocate *that* to the role of subject, since the subject must precede the verb in a relative clause, and no other item has presented itself.

One effect, then, of the sequence of elements in this clause is what I shall call *arrest*. The category of arrest – a focusing category or focat – is in general terms the introduction of an optional element at a place in structure where the structure is syntactically incomplete. If, in the structure AXB, A predicts B, but not X, then X is an arresting element.

There are many complications. For one thing, we cannot hold to an absolute requirement that A predicts B without any possibility of an alternative continuation of the structure. At the end of line 6 *impress* is a verb which is nearly always transitive. The preposition *on* gives confirmation of this; if the preposition was *with*, there is the possibility of the structure terminating at the end of line 6 – a remote possibility. It is, then, a subjective choice of the critic whether the example below puts the prepositional phrase into a position of arrest:

> He impressed with weighty rhetoric his point that. . . .

A second major difficulty is shown in the phrase *a wild secluded scene*. *A* predicts the noun; *wild* is rarely a noun and, if so, is uncountable and so cannot have *a* as its deictic, so *wild* is an adjective; *secluded* cannot be a noun, so must be another adjective. It would seem that the simple definition above forces us to see this fairly regular structure as heavy with arrest, and a focat that arose so frequently and naturally would be of little value in stylistic description. So we add the following to the definition of arrest:

> If (in the same structure AXB) X is a regular selection in the structure (that is, in its normal position), and is of a different grammatical class from A, then it is not an arresting element.

One or two questions are still begged; 'regular' is not exactly clear, and grammatical classes may be set up at different depths of delicacy, or detail. But the effect of this rider is that *secluded* is an arresting element, since it is a member of the same grammatical class as *wild* (that is, it is understood here as a quality adjective), but *wild* is not considered to be arresting. This adjustment is, I hope, satisfactory to one's intuitions.

What of the structure ABX, where neither A nor B predicts X? Again we must except the cases of structures developing in their normal way, and pick out those where additional elements extend the structure beyond expectation. Take the case ABX_1X_2, where X_1 and X_2 are members of the same grammatical class. X_2 is an *extension* of the structure.

Now we need a gloss on 'normal'. Adjuncts and prepositional phrases following the S-P-O part of a clause are normal; adjectives in front of nouns, and so on; distinctive elements of a particular structure. But there are a number of recursive devices in English grammar which operate fairly generally; co-ordination, juxtaposition, apposition are examples. Such structures will be classified as *extensions* whenever they occur.

There are marginal cases. The relative clause is one. A recursive structure, it cannot, however, be selected at any point but is normally dependent on a closely preceding noun. The conventions followed here are: (*a*) 'non-defining' relative clauses, being totally unpredicted, are always extension; (*b*) a single 'defining' relative clause is normal, but subsequent ones in the same structure are extensions. Convention (*b*) applies to prepositional phrases ('Tell me the price of the toy on the shelf in the window of that shop across the street'), strings of possessives ('It used to be the gentleman's wife's mother's dog's), phased predicators ('I found him helping her watch them spy on me'), and other recursive structures which require a particular syntactic environment.

Language structure is layered: there are structures within structures; clauses within sentences, words within groups, and so on. Since arrest and extension can feature at any layer, it will be possible to have arrest within arrest, extension within arrest, etc. Each combination will produce a distinctive effect.

There follows in Figures 9.1 and 9.2 an analysis of two sentences of 'Tintern Abbey', in terms of the two focats of arrest and extension. The grammatical layer, or *rank*, is noted, and the nature of the environment of a focat. Embedding of one focat within another is shown. First-order arrest is in square brackets, second-order in diamond brackets. Extension is underlined with the boundaries marked by small vertical lines. Items framed by the copying structures noted above are asterisked.

The first sentence (Figure 9.1) starts with two brief arrests and then embarks on a series of extensions by apposition. The second appositional nominal group, *that blessed mood*, introduces a non-defining relative clause. At this point (line 38) the structure is fairly extended; the relative clause continues the appositional group which is all an extended explanatory gloss on *another gift*. Then the structure changes. The relative clause is arrested between subject and predicator by a second clause (line 39) which begins in the same way as the first, and in fact turns out to be virtually a rephrasing of the first clause subject. But it is substantially longer and contains within it another arrest – *and the weary*. (The descriptive system adopted here does not formally recognise the use of long words like *unintelligible*, which obviously increases the effect of arrest at the end of line 40.)

There is a break in the patterning at *is lightened*; all the syntactic predictions are fulfilled; but the sentence develops a further extending appositional group, so off we go again. This one carefully follows the words of its predecessor, with *serene* framed in the structure, reminding one of the similar adjective arrest two lines above: however, the remainder of the structure does not involve arrest; line 42 is a simple relative clause with only initial resemblances to lines 38 and 39.

The sentence changes into its second phase at the beginning of line 43. *Until*, makes it clear that a new main clause is on the way, and its

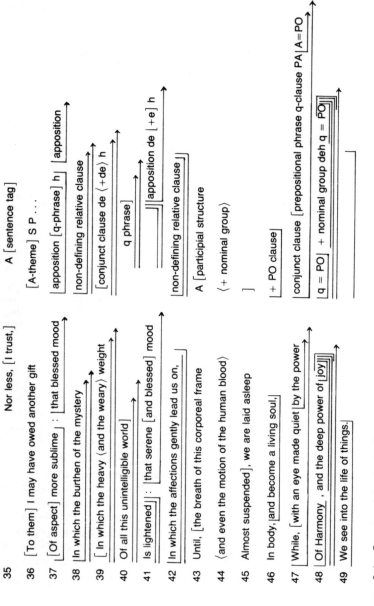

35   Nor less, [I trust,]   A [sentence tag]

36   [To them] I may have owed another gift   [A-theme] S P ...

37   [Of aspect] more sublime : |that blessed mood   apposition [q-phrase] h | apposition

38   In which the burthen of the mystery   non-defining relative clause

39   [In which the heavy ⟨and the weary⟩ weight   [conjunct clause de ⟨+de⟩ h

40   Of all this unintelligible world]   q phrase]

41   Is lightened‖ : |that serene [and blessed] mood   ‖apposition de ⌊+e⌋ h

42   In which the affections gently lead us on,   non-defining relative clause

43   Until, [the breath of this corporeal frame   A [participial structure

44   ⟨and even the motion of the human blood⟩   ⟨+ nominal group⟩

45   Almost suspended], we are laid asleep   ]

46   In body, |and become a living soul,   + PO clause

47   While, [with an eye made quiet |by the power   conjunct clause [prepositional phrase q-clause PA |A=PO

48   Of Harmony , and the deep power of |joy‖   q = PO | + nominal group deh q = PO‖

49   We see into the life of things.   q = PO + nominal group deh q = PO

Figure 9.1 Structural Analysis, lines 35–49.

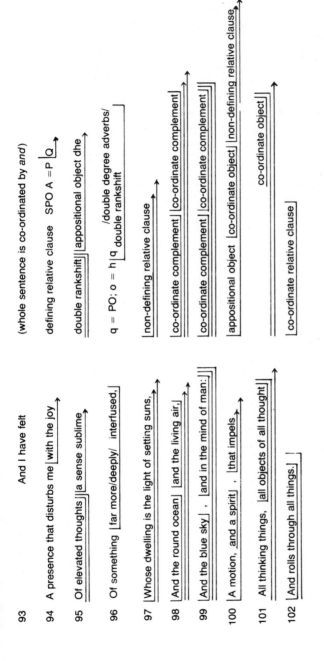

Figure 9.2 *Structural Analysis, lines 93–102.*

comma notes that the following nominal group is not the subject, but a digression as regards the predicted elements of the clause. It turns out to be a participial structure, but by the end of line 43 all we know is that it is an arresting nominal group. There is then in the following line a further arrest as the co-ordinate nominal group develops, copied from the first; and one need not wonder at the occurrence of *suspended*, just before the subject *we* that was predicted by *Until*. As before, the major arrest is followed by a period of modest extension in line 46, but the pressure builds up again with *While*, (47), which has the same predictive power as *Until*. In this case the arresting structure is a front-placed prepositional phrase within which there are surprises; *made quiet . . . joy* is a rankshifted qualifier of *an eye* which itself is governed by *with*. *Of harmony* is a further stage in rankshift and therefore constitutes further extension; there is then even more extension in the co-ordinate nominal group, a copying structure framing *deep*. At the end of line 48 the syntax is pushed very hard; an extension of an extension within an arrest which stretches the arrest out; that whole pattern being an extension which is the third time that a highly arresting structure has been developed in the sentence. All this accumulated energy spills over into the last clause, *we see into the life of things*.

A rather weak clause, the last one. None of the fine rolling phrases of the rest of the sentence. And yet the whole sentence has been building up to it. The sentence, having arrived at its main point, might have continued expansively for several lines as many of the sentences in 'Tintern Abbey' do – but no. One short clause, mainly composed of frequent grammatical words and the almost empty noun *things*. The effect, as I see it, is to invite the reader to attach greater profundity to that little clause; to see it as a visionary distillation of the message. Wordsworth has had several false starts in trying to describe the vision; first by developing the noun mood, then switching to a description of a state of being, and having two stabs at that.

Assume that Wordsworth had finished at the end of line 46. Then the last few words of line 46 would suddenly assume great importance: they are powerful words, too, but somehow their individuality is not fully felt when one reads them as contributory to the effect of the sentence as a whole.

Such an interpretation of the sentence assumes a link between the detailed linguistic facts of the text and the impression the text creates. We are entertaining the suggestion that Wordsworth's syntax accurately models his meaning; suspends itself when the meaning is suspense; builds up a tension by repeating the same arresting devices several times, and then in the quiet last clause suggests an ultimate depth of meaning. Lines 39 and 40 are presumably only present to assist the syntax – they scarcely add anything to the meaning; 44 adds very little, and so on. These are cases of copying, where in addition to the syntactic patterning there is close similarity to a previous structure, so that the two are almost compared to each other.

The poet, in effect, harnesses the process of decoding, interpreting, understanding the language, and makes it work to his purpose. The meaning of the text is supplemented by the reader feeling himself acquiring the meaning.

Not all the sentences in the poem are of this particular type; more commonly they have some arrest at the beginning, and then develop into multiple extensions. Some are exceptionally extended, and I have chosen the sentence at line 93 (Figure 9.2) as a contrasting example. It is a description of the all-pervading Spirit of Nature.

The sentence begins with extension by rankshift; extends at *a sense sublime* by apposition and repeats the rankshift extension, tacks on a non-defining relative clause and within that begins to extend the complement. There are four extensions to the complement, three of them sharing *and the (adjective noun)*. The last is slightly different. Next the sentence returns to its original appositional extension with *A motion*, parallel to *a sense* and *A presence*, and extends it to *a spirit*. A third relative extension follows, and its object is extended through apposition. Finally a co-ordinate clause to the relative clause rounds off the sentence. Twice, at the end of lines 99 and 102, three extensions are simultaneously operating.

Again it is a short, simple clause, *And rolls through all things* – an attempt to express the ultimate generalised perception of a personification of the energy in the universe. Again it is the build-up, the movement of the sentence, that charges the words and phrases with most of their meaning. The sentence is almost intolerably extended – there are more than a dozen places where one could sensibly put a full stop, but on and on it goes.

The list of nominal groups in lines 97–9, if isolated, runs close to bathos with the hoary old cliché *the blue sky*; but, since its value here is mainly to pull out the triple extension, we do not experience any let-down.

Poetry, it is sometimes argued, tries to say the unsayable – and succeeds, paradoxically. We see Wordsworth wrestling with ideas for which words are too limiting; concepts perhaps not precisely grasped by the poet. We can avoid this paradox by a hypothesis that poetry, in common with many varieties of a language, uses two routes of communication: one conventional, where words are built into phrases along accepted lines, decoded in a manner that in principle could be automated; and the other a problem-solving system, where unique combinations are suggested that have no conventional meaning. Though they are latent in the structure of the language, the language does not typically make use of them. By this route the meaning of a latent pattern is assessed in relation to the conventional, precise and basic meaning.

In fact the two routes are not separate and extreme. Continuous variations can be observed between writing that relies heavily on the conventional patterns and writing that is virtually governed by the latent patterns.

For simple presentation in the above account, I followed a linear decoding technique as if a reader read a text word by word and received the meaning at each word space. This is unlikely to be what actually happens, and in any case we assume that a sensitive interpretation of a text requires that the reader knows the whole text intimately. In which case his reading relates the linguistic details to his total knowledge of and feeling for the text.

I have tried in Figure 9.3 to flow-chart the process of analysis. First of all there is the reading and full critical understanding of the text. This is an essential step; stylistics may be heavily descriptive but its analysis must be interpreted through the impressions created by the work as a whole.

This 'total meaning' is not normally written out, since any verbalisation of it would involve selection and ordering, and thus would pre-empt areas of great concern to linguistics. Any 'critical reading' or explication set out at the beginning of a study would give guidelines, which, however accurate, could not be demonstrated to be relevant, comprehensive and sufficiently detailed.

The second stage of the process is the analysis of one area, perhaps sentence structure, rhyme or antonymy. In practice, the larger grammatical units offer the more fruitful starting-point, but there is no restriction. The procedure is independent, too, of which analytical system is followed.

The third stage is called *scan*. The analytical data are examined for patterns to see whether any aspects of the symbols in the display is worth following up. A decision is made: namely, a return to further analysis if no likely lead arises from the analysis, or a description of some aspect of the patterning. Three initial categories are suggested: *profusion* and *scarcity*, which cover the disproportionate occurrence of a symbol in the text, and *regularity*, which covers the distribution of the symbols in repeated sequences. What is profusion in one portion of a text may of course be identified as one of a regular sequence of profusions in the text as a whole.

At this point the nature of the patterning under attention should be described exactly. The next step is to consider how it relates to the unanalysed 'total meaning'. It is used in fact as a possible category for analysis of the total meaning. If the patterning is not accidental, but is meaning-bearing, then the attempt is made to establish what meaning can be assigned to it. There is another decision, then, as to whether or not such a relationship can be at least provisionally suggested. If the decision is negative, the pattern is stored for future use. If positive,

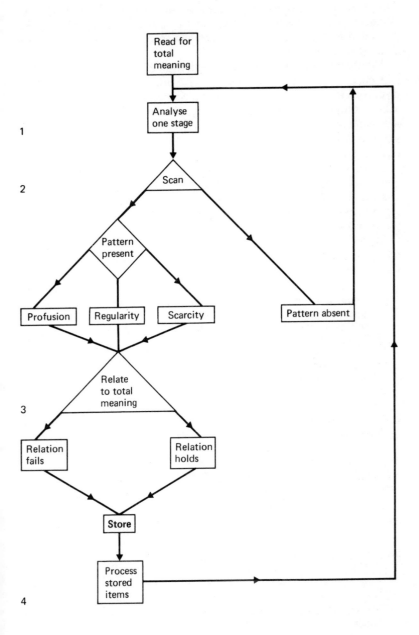

Figure 9.3 *Procedural chart for analysis and interpretation.*

then a focat comes into existence – a category which relates latent linguistic patterning to meaning. At times it has value only for the particular text, and only its frequent recurrence in other texts gives it generality. It, too, is stored.

Whether or not a focat is established, the store is now processed. The existence of a focat may suggest how other stored data might be displayed to add to the original data. Since authors do not normally follow comprehensive and rigorous stylistic rules, it is likely that a focat will attract evidence from several structural areas. Also, new data, not yet assigned to a focat, may provide missing parts of a pattern and relate other unassigned data still in the store.

When work on the store is finished, the process repeats itself, and continues until there is no data from the linguistic analysis left. If the analysis were perfect, and the judgement of the analyst infallible, then the process should end with the store empty, and the total meaning of the text analysed into focats.

Judgement is required at four points in the process: since some of them are similar to critical evaluative statements they merit a brief view. The points are marked in the figure.

(1) Which area to analyse. In any piece of work, the analyst will play hunches and follow clues, but since the whole text will be fully analysed and processed it does not matter in which order the analysis is examined. Hence the method is not suitable for long texts.

(2) Is there a latent pattern present? This is a matter for individual judgement and clearly involves the interpretation of the text. Notice, however, that the decision is recoverable; it is possible to locate disagreements about the meaning of texts by comparing decisions at this stage.

(3) Does the pattern analyse some of the total meaning? Again, this is a subjective decision; and, if the answer is positive, the meaning must be accurately defined in a focat specification. Evaluation of a literary nature is more important here, but note that the process specifies the points at which decisions are made, and this puts an effective limitation upon the critical statements that result.

(4) Processing the store. At this stage ingenuity is limited least by evidence, and decisions are at their most tentative.

With these points in mind, we return to the original assertions.

(a) Subject-object. I have here presented an argument based on the objective description of a text. There are no intended deviations in the basic grammatical description from the way I would describe any text written in English. The observations have led to groupings inspired by

 (i) a generalised, subjective analysis of syntactic forms, e.g. 'tight' and 'loose';

(ii) a subjective perception of the communicative value of the poem. There is room to manoeuvre with criteria of this nature, and the main danger is over-plausibility – discovering relationships between (i) and (ii) which arouse suspicion in other critics. (The other side of the coin is to convince linguists that they cannot describe human communications adequately without having recourse to subjective decisions. But that is not an aim of the present chapter.)

(*b*) The special language of literature. One is reminded of the old story of the rabbit running for its life through the forest because it was unable to prove to Senator McCarthy that it was not a squirrel. All the stylistic features that I have described in this and previous papers are to be found in a full range of texts; arrest is commonplace in oratory, extension is a major feature of conversation. Some literary text may deviate statistically in its density of usage, its particular exploitation of features; but such deviation is itself commonplace.

(*c*) and (*d*) The *ad hoc* nature of stylistic comment. If the text under analysis here is the only one which provides evidence for setting up the focats of arrest and extension, and each successive text requires a unique focat apparatus, then there is no defence against the charge of *ad hoc*-ness. But, if further work suggests, and it does, that a great proportion of stylistic analysis can be effected through a small and finite set of focats, then the groundwork of a theory of literary communication emerges. Most of the other levels of language have yielded to analysis based on the assumption of a set of configurations of a rather small and finite inventory of elements. There is every chance that style will be similarly describable.

Suggestions for Further Work: Chapter 9

1 Take any literary text, not one necessarily singled out as being of linguistic interest, and work through the flow-chart (Figure 9.3). How successful is this method? Do you feel the need to modify the chart in any way? Take the same approach with a non-literary text. Once again, do you feel the need to modify the chart in any way?

2 Examine other Wordsworth poems in terms of 'arrest' and 'expansion', for example, extracts from *The Prelude* or *The Excursion*.
Examine Philip Larkin's poem 'First Sight' in terms of 'arrest' and 'expansion'. The poem is discussed with particular reference to these categories in another essay by John Sinclair (1966). The following extracts from T. S. Eliot's *Four Quartets* are examples of several similar passages from the poems which make up that volume which lend themselves to interesting analysis with reference to Sinclair's categories:

> Where is the end of them, the fishermen sailing
> Into the wind's tail, where the fog cowers?
> We cannot think of a time that is oceanless
> Or of an ocean not littered with wastage
> Or of a future that is not liable
> Like the past, to have no destination.

We have to think of them as forever bailing,
Setting and hauling, while the North East lowers
Over shallow banks unchanging and erosionless
Or drawing their money, drying sails at dockage;
Not as making a trip that will be unpayable
For a haul that will not bear examination.

('The Dry Salvages', II)

the whine in the rigging,
The menace and caress of wave that breaks on water,
The distant rote in the granite teeth,
And the wailing warning from the approaching headland
Are all sea voices, and the heaving groaner
Rounded homewards. . . .

('The Dry Salvages', I)

Knowing myself yet being someone other –
And he a face still forming; yet the words sufficed
To compel the recognition they preceded.
And so, compliant to the common wind,
Too strange to each other for misunderstanding,
In concord at this intersection time
Of meeting nowhere, no before and after,
We trod the pavement in a dead patrol.

('Little Gidding', II)

Compare Sinclair's analysis of 'Tintern Abbey' with the extract from
the same poem discussed in Widdowson (1975: 42–4).

3   Are there writers you are intuitively aware of who make use of either of
these two devices? Consider and examine some work of the following:
Ernest Hemingway, Richard Brautigan, Henry James, Thomas Car-
lyle, Jane Austen. How useful are these focats? How large a part do
they play in a description of the author's style? What other factors need
to be taken into account?

4   Take a piece of writing you have identified as interesting in terms of
either 'arrest' or 'expansion' and rewrite it, obliterating this feature.
How does the overall meaning of the text change?

References: Chapter 9

Sinclair, J. McH. (1966), 'Taking a poem to pieces', in Fowler, R. (ed.), *Essays on Style
and Language* (London: Routledge & Kegan Paul), pp. 68–81.
Widdowson, H. G. (1975), *Stylistics and the Teaching of Literature* (London: Longman).

Introduction to Chapter 10

This chapter by Mick Short takes the points about free indirect speech made in a previous chapter by Carter several stages further in linguistic subtlety and refinement. Short makes an important distinction between speech presentation and the representation of thought, and shows how a continuum exists, with each point marked in precise linguistic terms, which allows the analyst a clear measure of such factors as the degree of the character's independence of the author's viewpoint, the nature of authorial intrusion and the kinds of fusion between author and character (and reader) allowed by such styles of representation. Short shows that the rather loosely applied term 'stream of consciousness' is in need of some more precise definition and that a stylistic approach of this kind can resolve certain questions of interpretation by a principled appeal to the linguistic facts. (The passage he takes – from Joyce's *A Portrait of the Artist as a Young Man* – is one over which several critics are in dispute and is regularly cited as a formative example of 'stream of consciousness' in modern fiction.) The chapter will be of particular interest to advanced students of language and literature and to those with a special interest in accounting for technical and formalistic development in prose fiction.

10 Stylistics and the Teaching of Literature: with an Example from James Joyce's *A Portrait of the Artist as a Young Man*

M. H. SHORT

. . . So far the examples I have used have been from poetry.[1] I will now demonstrate the relationship between stylistics and interpretation and effect by an extended (though by no means complete) analysis of a prose passage, namely, the evocation of the epiphany which Stephen experiences in *A Portrait of the Artist as a Young Man* when he sees the girl on the seashore (Penguin edition, pp. 171–2.)[2] An epiphany for Joyce is a moment when an abrupt spiritual awakening is experienced in which thoughts, feelings, attitudes, and so on, cohere to produce a new and sudden awareness:

> By an epiphany he meant a sudden spiritual manifestation, whether in the vulgarity of speech or of gesture or in a memorable phase of the mind itself. He believed that it was for the man of letters to record these epiphanies with extreme care, seeing that they themselves are the most delicate and evanescent of moments. (*Stephen Hero*, I)

In this particular epiphany the vision of the girl on the seashore acts as the final catalyst which makes Stephen decide to replace a religion which has become increasingly meaningless and unreal by a belief in life and art:

> 1 There was a long rivulet in the strand and, as he waded slowly up its course, he wondered at the endless drift of seaweed. (1) Emerald and black and russet and olive, it moved beneath the current, swaying and turning. (2) The water of the rivulet was dark with endless drift and mirrored the highdrifting clouds. (3) The clouds were drifting above him silently and silently the seatangle was drifting below him and the grey warm air was still and a new wild life was singing in his veins. (4)
> 2 Where was his boyhood now? (5) Where was the soul that had hung back from her destiny, to brood alone upon the shame of her wounds and

in her house of squalor and subterfuge to queen it in faded cerements and in wreaths that withered at the touch? (6) Or where was he? (7)

3   He was alone. (8) He was unheeded, happy and near to the wild heart of life. (9) He was alone and young and wilful and wildhearted, alone amid a waste of wild air and brackish waters and the seaharvest of shells and tangle and veiled grey sunlight and gayclad lightclad figures of children and girls and voices childish and girlish in the air. (10)

4   A girl stood before him in midstream, alone and still, gazing out to sea. (11) She seemed like one whom magic had changed into the likeness of a strange and beautiful seabird. (12) Her long slender bare legs were delicate as a crane's and pure save where an emerald trail of seaweed had fashioned itself as a sign upon the flesh. (13) Her thighs, fuller and softhued as ivory, were bared almost to the hips, where the white fringes of her drawers were like feathering of soft white down. (14) Her slate-blue skirts were kilted boldly about her waist and dovetailed behind her. (15) Her bosom was as a bird's, soft and slight, slight and soft as the breast of some darkplumaged dove. (16) But her long fair hair was girlish: and girlish, and touched with the wonder of mortal beauty, her face. (17)

5   She was alone and still, gazing out to sea; and when she felt his presence and the worship of his eyes her eyes turned to him in quiet sufferance of his gaze, without shame or wantonness. (18) Long, long she suffered his gaze and then quietly withdrew her eyes from his and bent them towards the stream, gently stirring the water with her foot hither and thither. (19) The first faint noise of gently moving water broke the silence, low and faint and whispering, faint as the bells of sleep; hither and thither, hither and thither; and a faint flame trembled on her cheek. (20)

6   – Heavenly God! cried Stephen's soul, in an outburst of profane joy. (21)

7   He turned away from her suddenly and set off across the strand. (22) His cheeks were aflame; his body was aglow; his limbs were trembling. (23) On and on and on and on he strode, far out over the sands, singing wildly to the sea, crying to greet the advent of the life that had cried to him. (24)

8   Her image had passed into his soul for ever and no word had broken the holy silence of his ecstasy. (25) Her eyes had called him and his soul had leaped at the call. (26) To live, to err, to fall, to triumph, to recreate life out of life. (27) A wild angel had appeared to him, the angel of mortal youth and beauty, an envoy from the fair courts of life, to throw open before him in an instant of ecstasy the gates of all the ways of error and glory. (28) On and on and on and on! (29)

(Both paragraphs and sentences are numbered for ease of reference.)

The main burden of my analysis will consist of an examination of the way in which Joyce manipulates points of view and the presentation of Stephen's thoughts in the passage. I will also try to show that the moment of epiphany suddenly occurs in sentence 21. But first I would like to try to sort out a critical disagreement over the sexuality of the description. Jane H. Jack (1964) believes Stephen's perception of the girl to be sexual as well as aesthetic:

. . . in the most profound moment of his youth he portrays himself near 'the wild heart of life'. The erotic imagery is identical in significance with 'the seaharvest of shells', the arid grasses and the earth. The word mortal is used twice of the girl he finds wading. The word grapples sex to life and therefore to his art. . . .

Richard Ellman (1959), on the other hand, describes the girl as Stephen's 'secular correlative of the Virgin Mary', and Eugene M. Waith (1964) supports the 'unsexual' view:

Profoundly moved, but not sexually aroused, he looks at her for a few moments, then turns away and strides off across the sand. . . . Stephen has 'fallen' in that he has taken a beautiful body as an object of contemplation instead of the religious mysteries with which he occupied his mind after his confession and communion, yet his excitement is what he is later to describe as 'the esthetic emotion'. . . . Instead of plunging Stephen again in the mire of sensuality, this 'fall' advances him towards the artistic goal he envisages. . . .

I would like to support Ellmann and Waith in opposition to Jane Jack. First of all, the evidence which she advances is not particularly convincing. There is no obvious reason why the seaharvest of shells, arid grasses or the earth should be erotic. Moreover, *mortal* does not have inherent sexual connotations, and in both the expressions in which the word occurs – 'the wonder of mortal beauty, her face' (17), 'the angel of mortal youth and beauty' (28) – it is collocated with *beauty*. In the first instance it premodifies *beauty* in a phrase which itself postmodifies *wonder*, the whole phrase being in apposition to *face*. In the second case it premodifies *youth* and *beauty* in a phrase postmodifying *angel*. Sexual descriptions do not usually concentrate on girls' faces or angels, and it is significant that the second instance of *mortal* occurs in a paragraph of ninety-six words in which *life* is repeated three times and the verb *live* occurs as well. This would seem to indicate a more standard interpretation of the word, as having to do with the living as opposed to the immortal. Its collocation with *angel*, which occurs twice in the same sentence, also supports this view. Mortality appears to have more to do with the right to err and sin, and hence is opposed to the Catholic proscription which Stephen rejects. In sentence 27, 'to live, to err, to fall, to triumph, to recreate life out of life', *to live* and *to recreate life out of life* are paralleled with verbs to do with the opposing notions of failing and triumphing. In sentence 28 *error* is also co-ordinated with, and hence paralleled to, *glory*, a synonym for triumph. Mortality is thus strongly associated with the set of words to do with sin, error and triumph.

Is there any other evidence which could be brought forward to support either view? Nouns like *bosom* and *thigh* do appear in the description of the girl in paragraph 4. But they are overtly associated, like many other aspects of the girl's description, with birds by the explicit use of simile. Moreover, the paragraph is structured so that we move up the girl towards her face. The subjects, and hence topics, of the main clauses, in order, are *a girl*, *she*, *her long slender bare legs*, *her thighs*, *her skirts*, *her bosom*, *her long fair hair* and *her face*. The sequencing involves a progression, with the face occurring in the final, climactic position at the end of the paragraph. The head is the only part of the girl's body which is referred to by two topic phrases. An examination of the syntax of the final clause of the paragraph, 'and girlish and touched with the wonder of mortal beauty, her face', also supports the view that the girl's face is the most important part of her. If we produced a 'normalised' version of this clause, we get 'and her face was girlish and touched with the wonder of mortal beauty'. It is thus obvious that the clause is transformationally rearranged in order to foreground *face*. It occurs in the end-weighted position in the sentence and also as the final word in the paragraph. Thus, the evidence of inter- and intra-sentential sequencing, with its emphasis on *face*, confirms the lexical evidence indicating that the description of the girl is aesthetic rather than sexual.

The discussion above provides an example of how concentrated attention to relevant linguistic evidence can help to decide critical disagreements. I now want to move on to examine Joyce's manipulation of point of view in the passage. However, in order for the reader to follow the argument he will have to be familiar with stylistic theories of speech and thought presentation. In particular, my analysis rests on the account of this area put forward in chapter 10 of *Style in Fiction* by G. N. Leech and M. H. Short (1981), to which the reader should refer if the following shorthand account is unclear. I give a brief description of the account here as it differs in significant ways from earlier work in the field (see McHale, 1978).

Besides the categories of Direct Speech (DS) and Indirect Speech (IS) which a writer has available to him, he also has the possibility of using Free Direct Speech (FDS) or Free Indirect Speech (FIS). Examples of the four types are:

(1) He said that he liked it there in Bognor. (IS)
(2) He said, 'I like it here in Bognor!' (DS)
(3) I like it here in Bognor! (FDS)
(4) He liked it there in Bognor! (FIS)

In speech presentation (in this case direct character speech in the novel) what was said in one speech situation is reported in another. In DS the distinction between the two discourses – that is (character–character) v. (narrator–addressee) – is made clear by the distinction between the repor*ted* and the repor*ting* clause, the former being marked off within inverted commas and being relatively independent syntactically. The reported clause also contains linguistic features appropriate to the embedded speech situation. Hence, if present time is referred to, the present tense is used along with near time- and place-deictics (cf. the present tense and the adverb *here* in (2) above). The other linguistic levels might also be appropriately marked; for example, colloquial lexis and indications of the phonological character of utterance might be used. In our example the exclamation mark is a graphological indication of intonation and tone of voice. If the speech is reported in the indirect mode (IS), then the reported clause becomes grammatically subordinated to the reporting clause, and the feature originally appropriate to the embedded speech situation will change to suit the higher one. The most common type of novel narration, and that which occurs in *A Portrait of the Artist*, is relatively formal, third person, and past tense. Hence in our examples the present tense in (2) becomes past in (1), the near deictic *here* becomes the remote *there* and the exclamation mark is omitted. Free Indirect Speech (FIS) is a hybrid of DS and IS. In our example (4) the subordination of the reporting clause associated with IS is missing and the exclamation mark associated with the more direct form is retained; but the tense and deixis are appropriate to the non-embedded speech situation. Free Direct Speech (FDS) has the reported clause of DS, but may omit either or both of the features which indicate the presence of a narrator, namely the reporting clause and the quotation marks. Our example (3) gives the most extreme form. The four modes of speech presentation are distributed along a cline which moves from a situation where the character's words are apparently given verbatim, without any narrative interference, to one where the formulation of the utterance is apparently completely under the control of the narrator:

In FDS and DS we are told what the character said in the words that he used. In IS we are told what the character said, but in the narrator's words. FIS is a hybrid between the two. Moreover, as DS is the norm for the presentation of speech, the use of FIS is usually perceived by readers as indicating narratorial intervention. It is thus often used for distancing, irony, or both.

But in order to understand the functions of the modes of speech presentation we need to relate it to Narrative Report (NR) via the Narrator's Report of Speech Acts (NRSA):

(5) He expressed his pleasure at being in Bognor. (NRSA)
(6) He liked Bognor. (NR)

The narrative report of events, scenes, etc., are obviously completely under the control of the narrator. The narrator's report of a speech act is the verbal equivalent of the report of an act. This can be seen by comparing sentences like 'John hit Mary' (NRA) with 'John swore at Mary' (NRSA). In NRSA the narrator's control is even greater than in IS. In DS what the character said (that is, its propositional content) and how he said it are given. In IS what the character said is reported. In NRSA only the kind of speech act that he used need be indicated. Thus:

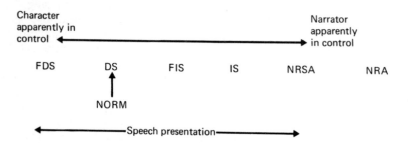

The categorisation of the presentation of character THOUGHT is essentially the same as that for speech presentation except for one important difference, namely that the norm for thought presentation is not DT but IT, because it is semantically implausible to suggest that we can directly observe the thoughts of others:

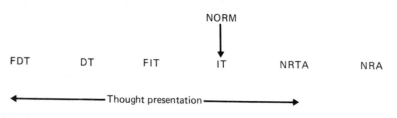

This difference is important because it explains the difference in effect obtained when the Free Indirect category is used for speech and thought. Because FIT, in opposition to FIS, is a movement from the norm towards the character end of the continuum, it is perceived by readers as representing closeness with that character, the direct observation of the articulation of his thoughts. It is for this reason that FIT is so commonly used in stream-of-consciousness writing; it apparently allows us to observe a character's unconscious thoughts as they appear.

To interpose an account of speech and thought presentation at this point may seem somewhat laborious. But a knowledge of the categorisation of thought presentation is essential to the understanding of the finer workings of Stephen's epiphany. I will now go through the passage indicating changes in the mode of presentation and how they are used, bringing in other stylistic markers to support the analysis. In particular, I will refer to some of the lexical patterning which occurs. For ease of reference, I include a table indicating the patterning of the particular morphemes which I will discuss (Table 10.1).

Table 10.1 *Morpheme Occurrence in the Passage*

Paragraph	Number of words	Morpheme occurrence*									
		wild	*alone*	*drift*	*silent*	*quiet*	*faint*	*gentle*	*soft*	*life*	*still*
1	88	1	0	5	2	0	0	0	0	0	1
2	51	0	0	0	0	0	0	0	0	0	0
3	63	3	3	0	0	0	0	0	0	1	0
4	140	0	1	0	0	0	0	0	4	0	1
5	102	0	1	0	1	1	4	2	0	0	1
6	11	0	0	0	0	0	0	0	0	0	0
7	56	1	0	0	0	0	0	0	0	1	0
8	96	1	0	0	1	0	0	0	0	4	0

* There are of course many more repetitions in the passage than this table would suggest. This is just a partial analysis of particularly interesting repetitions relative to the interpretative points which I want to make.

We might start by noting that, although the whole passage is seen from Stephen's point of view, this does not mean that his thoughts are rendered throughout. The first sentence begins with narrative report of the scene in front of Stephen and then moves into NRTA with 'he wondered at the endless drift of seaweed'. The rest of this paragraph consists of narrative report from Stephen's point of view but not a representation of the workings of his mind. We see what Stephen sees, and the scene is located with respect to him by phrases like *above him* and *below him*. The water under his feet and the sky above his head are portrayed in some detail, forming a backdrop with him in the middle. Moreover, there is an obvious internal – external contrast. The sky and water are described in terms which portray them as slow-moving and quiet. The word *drift* occurs twice in the first paragraph, and *drifting* three times. *Silently* occurs twice, we are told that the air is *still*, and Stephen himself moves *slowly*. The verbs of movement (e.g. *swaying*, *turning*) also suggest slowness. Then, in the last clause, Stephen is *described* internally ('a new *wild* life was *singing* in his veins'), where *wild* and *singing* contrast with the suggestions of slow movement and quiet with which the scene has been imbued.

The point about the first paragraph, then, is that it is largely an external description of the scene as we infer Stephen must have witnessed it. Although the workings of his mind are not represented as such, we experience what he experiences. An interesting example of this is the effect of the lack of conjunction reduction at the beginning of sentence 2: 'emerald and black and russet and olive, it moved . . .'. Note that the formation of a list structure in English would normally demand the deletion of the first two *ands*, to produce 'emerald, black, russet and olive . . .'. Joyce's refusal to reduce the conjunctions makes us feel that Stephen views the colours in the seaweed not as one agglomerated whole, but one at a time; first he notices its emerald quality, then its blackness, and so on. Lack of conjunction reduction, with similar effects, occurs elsewhere in the passage, in sentences 9 and 10 for instance. Although we see what Stephen sees, because the sentences are in the NRA and NRTA modes they are under the narrator's control; this means that the reader also takes the description to be a reliable one.

The second paragraph, on the other hand, is entirely in FIT and so moves directly into Stephen's mind. All three sentences are questions with third-person pronouns and past tense, there is no introductory thinking clause, and the deictic *now* in sentence 5 is appropriate to Stephen's immediate situation. The whole paragraph could possibly be interpreted as direct authorial address to the reader, but we must assume that the omniscient author would have no need to ask such questions, and therefore FIT is the most obvious interpretation. Hence the movement into Stephen's mind at the end of the first paragraph, where his new, wild state of mind is described metaphorically, is taken farther by the free indirect presentation of his thoughts themselves.

The third paragraph can be seen either as narrative report of Stephen's mental state and position, or alternatively as FIT. Formally, either interpretation would be consistent with the facts. There are no reporting verbs, the tense is past, and the third-person pronoun is used. There is considerable lexical repetition and the use of parallel forms both at a syntactic and phonetic level. These choices could be consistent either with a 'poetic' description on the part of the narrator or with an emotionally charged series of character thoughts. The most reasonable explanation, however, would be that sentences 8–10 are FIT, as they appear to be answers to the questions asked in 5–7. Stephen's view is that he is alone (*alone* occurs three times in this paragraph), and yet at the same time he appears to be surrounded by children, girls and their voices. This inconsistency, both in terms of this paragraph and with the description in paragraph 1, where no figures were mentioned, reinforces the suggestion that it is Stephen's thoughts that we are witnessing. This distinction also accounts for another apparent inconsistency, namely, that in this paragraph the adjective *wild* is predicated not only of Stephen (as it was in paragraph 1), but also of the air. This conflicts with the description of the scene in the first paragraph with its repetition of *silently* and the phonaesthetic morpheme *drift*. We infer here that Stephen *thinks* that his surroundings are wild because of the mood he is in, whereas we know that they are not because of what the narrator has previously told us.

It should now be becoming clear that the paragraph divisions in this passage coincide with changes in type of presentation. The end of a paragraph does not necessarily mean a change in presentation type, as paragraphs 2 and 3 show; but the type of presentation does not change (as it does in many other novels and at other places in this one) in the middle of a paragraph. This effect of the paragraphing helps the reader notice the conflicts between the narrator's and Stephen's perceptions of the scene. Paragraphs are also strongly associated with different aspects of the situation. Hence 1 describes the general scene around Stephen, then in 2 Stephen asks questions, which are answered in 3. Paragraph 4 describes what the girl looks like, whereas 5 describes what she does. This use of paragraphs is reflected in the grouping of some of the lexical items. Paragraph 1 contains all five of the occurrences of the morpheme *drift* in the passage and both of the occurrences of *silently* (the morpheme *silent* does occur once each in 5 and 8, but as a noun). *Soft* occurs four times, but only in paragraph 4, and *faint* also occurs four times, but only in paragraph 5, which also contains both of the occurrences of *gently*. *Alone and still* occurs twice, once at the beginning of each of the two paragraphs about the girl. When these points are taken together with the fact that words from common associational groupings tend to go together (cf. *still, quiet, faint, gently, soft, silence* and *whispering* in 5) it is very apparent that Joyce is using paragraph structure strategically to signal shifts from internal thought to the perception of externals and from one aspect of the description to another.

The fourth paragraph moves us back out of Stephen's mind to a description of the girl he sees in the water. Every sentence in this paragraph begins with a subject noun phrase referring to the girl or some part of her. The description is, however, from Stephen's point of view. This is indicated, for instance, by the locative phrase *before him* and the non-factive verb *seem* in sentence 12. Lexically this paragraph seems consistent with the first (also narrative report from Stephen's point of view). The girl, like the air earlier, is described as *still*; and *soft*, which has associations with *silently* and partial phonetic similarity with *drift*, occurs four times. It is also foregrounded by its occurrence in the balanced repetitive phrase 'soft and slight, slight and soft'.

Paragraph 5 continues the narrative report of 4. The girl is again described in the first sentence of the paragraph as *alone and still*, and the noise which she makes with her foot in the water is described in minimal terms by the repeated use of *faint* and *gently*, verbs like *stirring* and *whispering*, simile ('soft as the bells of sleep'), and by the density of onomatopoeically appropriate fricatives and sibilants. The return to the description of the girl's face with 'a faint flame trembled on her cheek' is also consistent with this.

After the soft, external description of the previous two paragraphs, the single sentence of paragraph 6 (which is foregrounded for this reason alone) marks a sudden and extreme shift. We move from very little noise to a lot with the exclamation, *cried* and *outburst*. Moreover, we move from one end of the presentation scale (Narrative Report) to the other with Direct or Free Direct Thought (there are no quotation marks, but it is arguable that the dash is equivalent to them for Joyce). The suddenness of the change is increased by an inversion which places the exclamation next to the narrative report with which it contrasts. Although the use of *cried* and *outburst* at first sight suggests that we are being presented with speech, the fact that *Stephen's soul* is the subject of *cried* indicates that we are witnessing his thoughts. The use of 'noisy' terminology is thus designed to bring out as strongly the soft/loud contrast between the description of the girl and Stephen's reaction. But, more importantly, this, along with all the other features which make the single sentence of paragraph 6 stand out, indicates that this is the sudden moment of change and realisation which characterises the epiphany. The fact that DT and FDT are structurally like soliloquy also gives the impression that the realisation marked by the exclamation is a conscious one.

Paragraph 7 returns to Narrative Report from Stephen's point of view. But now it describes *him*, and so is emotionally highly charged. It contains literally untrue statements which are metaphors for strong emotions ('cheeks were aflame', 'body was aglow'), loud utterance words (*crying*, *singing*), the word *wildly*, which links with paragraph 3, and the heavy repetition of 'on and on and on and on'. In the last paragraph this highly charged description gives way to the interior portrayal of emotional thoughts. Except for sentences 27 and 29 (which because of their verbless, exclamatory nature are perhaps best treated as FDT) the paragraph is in FIT. Stephen's highly individual perception of events is marked by statements made to himself which the reader must take as untrue. It is hard to interpret the fact that the girl looked at him because she felt his eyes on her as a 'call', and she was certainly not a wild angel, as Stephen appears to assume. The portrayal here is consistent with the individual view of paragraphs 3 and 7, and the linking of emotional involvement ('on and on and on and on') with sin ('to err, to fall') helps explain why Stephen's original outburst of joy was *profane*. That he has decided to throw over religion for life and beauty together can be seen in the description of the wild angel as 'the angel of mortal youth and beauty'.

We have passed briefly over many aspects of this passage (e.g. phonetic patterning and lexical repetition), and ignored others altogether (e.g. the passage's 'poetic' quality and the lexical items associated with religion). But it should now be clear why it is an 'epiphany' passage and why it marks Stephen's rejection of religion for life and beauty. I hope that the reader will also understand more clearly how Joyce strategically manipulates variation in the mode of presentation of Stephen's thoughts and perceptions in conjunction with lexical repetition and paragraph structuring to achieve the climactic outburst which characterises the end of the passage.

Notes: Chapter 10

1   This chapter is an abridged version of a much longer paper by M. H. Short entitled 'Stylistics and the teaching of literature: with an example from James Joyce's *A Portrait of the Artist as a Young Man*' and published in *ELT Documents 110: Language and Literature* (British Council, forthcoming). The extract here is reproduced by kind permission of the British Council. Readers are referred to the longer essay for a cogent account of some basic principles and strategies in teaching stylistics [Ed.].

2   The reader may well object that this piece of prose is a particularly poetic example. Though this is true, it should become apparent that the points which I want to make do not relate to the 'poeticality' of the passage.

Suggestions for Further Work: Chapter 10

Examine the passages that follow for forms of speech presentation, outlining the various types you find. How do these forms affect the passages' 'meaning'?

1(a)   (*Background notes*: Lord Decimus (starchy but influential aristocrat) is being lionised at a party at the house of Mr Merdle (rich but monosyllabic merchant), attended by social-climbing sycophants Bar, Bishop, Physician, etc. Bar carries his professional mannerisms with him into the drawing-room, and is hence described as addressing a fictitious jury, etc.)

Lord Decimus nevertheless was glad to see the Member. He was also glad to see Mr Merdle, glad to see Bishop, glad to see Bar, glad to see Physician, glad to see Tite Barnacle, glad to see Chorus, glad to see Ferdinand his private secretary. . . .

Bar, who felt that he had got all the rest of the jury and must now lay hold of the Foreman, soon came sliding up, double eye-glass in hand. Bar tendered the weather, as a subject neatly aloof from official reserve, for the Foreman's consideration. Bar said that he was told (as everybody always is told, though who tells them, and why, will for ever remain a mystery), that there was to be no wall-fruit this year. Lord Decimus had not heard anything amiss of his peaches, but rather believed, if his people were correct, he was to have no apples. No apples? Bar was lost in astonishment and concern. It would have been all one to him, in reality, if there had not been a pippin on the surface of the earth, but his show of interest in the apple question was positively painful. Now, to what, Lord Decimus – for we troublesome lawyers loved to gather information, and could never tell how useful it might prove to us – to what, Lord Decimus, was this to be attributed? Lord Decimus could not undertake to propound any theory about it. This might have stopped another man; but Bar, sticking to him fresh as ever, said, 'As to pears, now?'

(Charles Dickens, *Little Dorrit*, II, ch. 12)

(*b*)   Here arises a feature of the Circumlocution Office, not previously mentioned in the present record. When that admirable Department got into trouble, and was, by some infuriated member of Parliament, whom the smaller Barnacles almost suspected of labouring under diabolic possession, attacked, on the merits of no individual case, but as an Institution wholly abominable and Bedlamite; then the noble or right honourable Barnacle who represented it in the House, would smite that member and cleave him asunder, with a statement of the quantity of business (for the prevention of business) done by the Circumlocution Office. Then would that noble or right honourable Barnacle hold in his hand a paper containing a few figures, to which, with the permission of the House, he would entreat its attention. Then would the inferior Barnacles exclaim, (obeying orders), 'Hear, Hear, Hear!' and 'Read!' Then would the noble or right honourable Barnacle perceive, sir, from this little document, which he thought might carry conviction even to the perversest mind (Derisive laughter and cheering from the Barnacle fry), that within the short compass of the last financial half-year, this much-maligned Department (Cheers) had written and received fifteen thousand letters (Loud cheers), twenty-four thousand minutes (Louder cheers), and thirty-two thousand five hundred and seventeen memoranda (Vehement cheering). Nay, an ingenious gentleman connected with the Department, and himself a valuable public servant, had done him the favour to make a curious calculation of the amount of stationery consumed in it during the same period. It formed a part of this same short document; and he derived from it the remarkable fact, that the sheets of foolscap paper it had devoted to the public service would pave the footways on both sides of Oxford Street from end to end, and leave nearly a quarter of a mile to spare for the park (Immense cheering and laughter); while of tape – red tape – it had used enough to stretch, in graceful festoons, from Hyde Park Corner to the General Post Office. Then amidst a burst of sacred exultation, would the noble or right honourable Barnacle sit down, leaving the mutilated fragments of the Member on the field.

(Charles Dickens, *Little Dorrit*, II, ch. 8)

(*c*)   Yvonne he thought, with sudden tenderness, where are you, my darling? Darling. . . . For a moment he had thought her by his side. Then he remembered she was lost; then that no, this feeling belonged to yesterday, to the months of lonely torment behind him. She was not lost at all, she was here all the time, here now, or as good as here. The Consul wanted to raise his head and shout for joy, like the horseman: she is here! Wake up, she has come back again! Sweetheart, darling, I love you! A desire to find her immediately and take her home (where in the garden still lay the white bottle of Tequila Anejo da Jalisco, unfinished), to put a stop to this senseless trip, to be, above all, alone with her, seized him, and a desire, too, to lead immediately again a normal happy life with her, a life, for instance, in which such innocent happiness as all these good people around him were enjoying, was possible. But had they ever led a normal happy life? Had such a thing as a normal happy life ever been possible for them?

(Malcolm Lowry, *Under the Volcano*, ch. 28)

(*d*) Such was her situation, with a vacant space at hand, when Captain Wentworth was again in sight. She saw him not far off. He saw her too; yet he looked grave, and seemed irresolute, and only by very slow degrees came at last near enough to speak to her. She felt that something must be the matter. The change was indubitable. The difference between his present air and what it had been in the octagon room was strikingly great. Why was it? She thought of her father – of Lady Russell. Could there have been any unpleasant glances? He began by speaking of the concert gravely, more like the Captain Wentworth of Uppercross; owned himself disappointed, had expected better singing; and, in short, must confess that he should not be sorry when it was over. Anne replied, and spoke in defence of the performance so well, and yet in allowance for his feelings so pleasantly, that his countenance improved, and he replied again with almost a smile. They talked for a few minutes more; the improvement held; he even looked down towards the bench, as if he saw a place on it well worth occupying; when, at that moment, a touch on her shoulder obliged Anne to turn round. It came from Mr Elliot. He begged her pardon, but she must be applied to, to explain Italian again. Miss Carteret was very anxious to have a general idea of what was next to be sung. Anne could not refuse; but never had she sacrificed to politeness with a more suffering spirit.

A few minutes, though as few as possible, were inevitably consumed; and when her own mistress again, when able to turn and look as she had done before, she found herself accosted by Captain Wentworth, in a reserved yet hurried sort of farewell. 'He must wish her goodnight; he was going; he should get home as fast as he could.'

'Is not this song worth staying for?' said Anne, suddenly struck by an idea which made her yet more anxious to be encouraging.

'No!' he replied, impressively, 'there is nothing worth my staying for'; and he was gone directly.

Jealousy of Mr Elliot! It was the only intelligible motive. Captain Wentworth jealous of her affection! Could she have believed it a week ago – three hours ago! For a moment the gratification was exquisite. But, alas! there were very different thoughts to succeed. How was such jealousy to be quieted? How was the truth to reach him? How, in all the peculiar disadvantages of their respective situations, would he ever learn her real sentiments? It was misery to think of Mr Elliot's attentions. Their evil was incalculable.

(Jane Austen, *Persuasion*, ch. 20)

(*e*)   Mrs Bast (she had never known them; had lived in Glasgow at that time) wondered, putting her cup down, whatever they hung that beast's skull there for? Shot in foreign parts no doubt.

It might well be said Mrs McNab, wantoning on with her memories; they had friends in eastern countries; gentlemen staying there, ladies in evening dress; she had seen them once through the dining-room door all sitting at dinner. Twenty she dared say in all their jewellery, and she asked to stay help wash up, might be till after midnight.

Ah, said Mrs Bast, they'd find it changed. She leant out of the window. She watched her son George scything the grass. They might well ask, what had been done to it? seeing how old Kennedy was supposed to have charge of it, and then his leg got so bad after he fell from the cart; and perhaps then no one for a year, or the better part of one; and then Davie Macdonald, and seeds might be sent, but who should say if they were ever planted? They'd find it changed.

She watched her son scything. He was a great one for work – one of those quiet ones. Well they must be getting along with the cupboards, she supposed. They hauled themselves up.

At last, after days of labour within, of cutting and digging without, dusters were flicked from the windows, the windows were shut to, keys were turned all over the house; the front door was banged; it was finished.

(Virginia Woolf, *To the Lighthouse*, ch. II, 9)

2   For further reading, see Leech, G. and Short, M. H., *Style in Fiction* (London: Longman, 1981), especially ch. 10. Also Quirk and Greenbaum (1973: 341–6); Page, N., *Speech in the English Novel* (London: Longman, 1973); and Jones, C. (1968), 'Varieties of speech presentation in Conrad's *The Secret Agent*', *Lingua*, vol. 20, no. 2, pp. 162–78.

References: Chapter 10

Ellmann, R. (1959), *James Joyce* (New York: OUP).

Jack, J. H. (1964), 'Art and *A Portrait of the Artist*', in Connolly, T. (ed.), *Joyce's Portrait* (London: Peter Owen), pp. 156–66.

Jones, C. (1968), 'Varieties of speech presentation in Conrad's *The Secret Agent*', *Lingua*, vol. 20, no. 2, pp. 162–78.

Leech, G. N. and Short, M. H. (1981), *Style in Fiction* (London: Longman, 1981).

McHale, B. (1978), 'Free indirect discourse: a survey of recent accounts', *Poetics and the Theory of Literature*, vol. 1, no. 3, pp. 235–87.

Quirk, R. and Greenbaum, S. (1973), *A University Grammar of English* (London: Longman).

Waith, Eugene M. (1964), 'The calling of Stephen Dedalus', in Connolly, op. cit., 114–23.

Introduction to Chapter 11

In this challenging chapter Deirdre Burton argues for a new stylistics, aware of its theoretical presuppositions and committed to giving students equipment with which to unmask ideologies. She argues that no method of literary analysis can pretend to be neutral or objective and that stylisticians should stand up and be counted.

In an analysis of a passage from Sylvia Plath's *The Bell Jar* Deirdre Burton provides an explicit and linguistically detailed model for analysing power relations in texts, whether fictional as here or in the 'real' world. The model contains detail enough to be replicable and can be applied successfully in many different contexts; it also provides a basis for creative writing by students. As we see from a wealth of examples from work by her own students, rewriting different elements in the model can produce radically different accounts of the ways in which reality is perceived and structured. The chapter encourages fuller literary appreciation of how writers manage texts, but also leads directly to greater participation by readers in the world which they have to manage. The tightness and rigour of the suggested analytical procedures mean that hard work is needed to master them, but it also means that links and transitions between literary analysis and political commitment can be effected in a clear and principled way. Whatever your 'political' standpoint, and whatever your reaction to the kind of feminism unravelled here in Sylvia Plath's text, Deirdre Burton shows that such a link cannot be ignored.

This is a stimulating chapter and comes fittingly towards the end of this book, opening up new directions and possibilities. It is also a deliberately provocative chapter to which the author would welcome soundly argued responses. For example, readers might object that rewriting texts and recognising 'fictions' is, indeed, *doing* something with literary analysis beyond the literary text itself but that at heart the procedures developed here are no more than a sophisticated academic game-playing which cannot fundamentally alter realities. Or would such an objection only reveal a defensive, 'neutral' desire to leave things the way they are?

11 Through Glass Darkly: Through Dark Glasses

On stylistics and political commitment – via a study of a passage from Sylvia Plath's *The Bell Jar*

DEIRDRE BURTON

I Introduction

And where do you go from here? You've taken some poem or conveniently sized piece of prose. You've spent time and effort mastering a sensible descriptive grammar of English. You've meshed understanding and knowledge of both to produce a rigorous analysis of the language used to construct your text, together with a "relevant" sensitive interpretation. You have talked about "effects", "foregrounded features", "overall impressions", and so on. Very nice. Very satisfying. But what are you going to *do* with it? What now?

Don't misunderstand me. I am not, in any way, suggesting that I see no value in this sort of analytical method *as far as it goes*. Certainly, given, say, the shamefully scant attention generally paid to analytical skills in English language work in secondary education in Britain at the moment, I can see very good reasons for teaching explicit and rigorous methods for analysing the linguistic structures in texts. This can be seen as extremely useful preparatory material for worthwhile intellectual work in both literary studies and linguistics. On the one hand, it means that all students have, at the very least, a "way in" to articulating their understanding, interpretations, or confusions about *any* literary text. This seems to me to be a considerable advance on the vague and slippery, "competitive sensitivity" approach that often passes as a method of text explication in English literature classes, and which disenables many a bewildered student, who would love to do good work if only he or she could work out the rules of the game. On the other hand, an awareness of the fascinating complexity and organisation of linguistic structure available as the meaning potential[1] of the language, together with a certain degree of confidence in recognising and being articulate about structural choices and their resultant meanings, opens up the way to a substantial number of nice areas of study in linguistics *per se*; both the standard core elements in theories of language-and-mind and language-in-use, and the various inter-disciplines like psycholinguistics, sociolinguistics, language-in-education, computational linguistics, and so on.

However, while all this is very much to the good in first-order pedagogic terms, it is some of the taken-for-granted, pretheoretical notions of practising stylisticians with which I wish to take issue here. To put my main point simply (and crudely), I am unhappy with the tacit assumption behind almost all the work in this field, that presumes that it is the legitimate task of the stylistician to observe and describe phenomena in a 'neutral'[2] and 'objective' way. More particularly still, I wish to take issue with the assumption that any such work *can* be done in a politically neutral way.

Historically, it is easy to see why stylistics has gone overboard on the 'objective', 'scientific', 'simple descriptive' approach to text. As an antidote to the extreme, élitist, elusive and determinedly dogged 'sub-jectivity' of traditional literary criticism in the twentieth century, recourse to the precise technicalities available within linguistics – an exciting, promising and challenging discipline available to many a discontented (and puzzled) modern languages graduate – was a wel-come release from the vagueness and precarious lucky chance of insightful reactions to literature available in other models of debate. However, while linguistic models clearly do concern themselves with the precise organisation of phenomena, and the relationships of generalisation and abstraction to particulars, as well as the intricacies of the networks between theory and data, it is only the epistemologi-cally naive who could believe that all this bears any simple relationship to 'objectivity'. There is no space here to rehearse the relevant argu-ments in the philosophy of science (and interested readers should refer to the following at least: Popper, 1977, 1979; Kuhn, 1962, 1967; Lakatos, 1970, 1976; Feyerabend, 1975, 1978; Tarski, 1956; David-son, 1967), but I take it as axiomatic that *all* observation, let alone description, *must* take place within an already constructed theoretical framework of socially, ideologically and linguistically constructed real-ity, whether the observer/describer of observations is articulately aware of that framework or not. (For further discussion, see: Burton, 1981; Burton, in preparation *a* and *b*. Also, see Lakoff and Johnson, 1980, who offer a very neat discussion of 'rational subjectivity' as a possible mediation between the artificially constructed contradictions in the subjective/objective dichotomy.) I also take it that any work which does not explicitly acknowledge its theoretical boundaries is open to analysis for its theoretical presuppositions, and *cannot avoid* demonstrating such presuppositions in some way.

This brings me to the question of 'political neutrality'. Again, I take it as unquestionable that there is no conceivable 'a-political' work in this, or any other, society. By which I do not mean that it is always easy to perceive or discuss or explain the precise and delicate relationships that obtain between any instance of work and its political status or political inference. Again, given that the focus of this chapter must – in time, dear Reader – be the practical analysis and discussion of the language in some text, there is no space to discuss this in detail, but see, for example, Barthes, 1967, 1970, 1972, 1977; Derrida, 1976; Foucault, 1970, 1972, 1977; Lacan, 1977; Althusser, 1969, 1977.

However, I maintain that, as with observation and theory, and description and theory, any writer that supposes that he or she is politically neutral in their writing is merely naively supporting and demonstrating the (largely unseen and unnoticed) political bias of the status quo. What follows from here depends very largely on how you feel about the status quo. Let me state my own political biases as clearly as possible in a simple, bland way. It is clear that we live in a classist, racist and sexist society, and that is, at the very least, a highly unsatisfactory state of affairs. I believe that, of these three major and massive injustices, sexism is the most deep-rooted (psychologically), the most pervasive, the most difficult to perceive, the most resistant to change – yet available as a locus for important and essential radical impetus to the reorganisation of all the unequal and oppressive power-structures in our society. (See Millett, 1969; Rich, 1977; Jaquette, 1974; Daly, 1978; Berger and Kachuk, 1977; Ardener, 1975; Delamont and Duffin, 1978.) I also believe now that all academic work should be committed in some way (and there are many; see Burton, 1981) to influencing long-term improvements in issues of human rights. Each to his or her own, of course – in terms of skills, and powers of perception, analysis, and influence. What we cannot, I think, support any longer is the self-indulgence of the mythological 'knowledge for its own sake'. *All* knowledge is contained and produced within an ideological framework. It is essential to distinguish between work which supports an oppressive dominant ideology and work which challenges it, and to state clearly which it is that you are doing. As all methodological components of theories are intricately related to the goals of those theories, responsible academics must continually state and refer to both the lower-order and high-order constraints of the particular work they are doing, in order to make sense of that work.

Linguists and literary critics (and therefore also the hybrid stylisticians) have an especially obvious responsibility here. All linguistic work owes ultimate allegiance to the higher-order disciplines of cognitive sociology, political sociology, or the philosophy of mind. Whichever intellectual direction linguists choose, the recurrent questions and problems ultimately to be faced are to do with the specifically *cultural* human issues: thought; consciousness; action; interpretation; meaning; interaction; cultural and historical processes and influences;

and so on. To be politically irresponsible in such areas is to be seriously culpable. Similarly, literary criticism (of whatever traditionalist persuasion) is again concerned with products and processes of human society in such a way that *not* to examine and act upon the political implications of literature, Literature and literary criticism *per se* is to be seriously at fault. (See Coward and Ellis, 1977; Belsey, 1980.)

In that a great deal of highly valued post-Romantic literature is specifically that which co-operates in constructing and maintaining the dominant ideology, and in that a substantial body of literary criticism in general (stylistics in particular) colludes in that construction and maintenance by 'appreciating' and 'describing' texts which hide the problems, conflicts and oppressions in that ideology, this polemical introduction is a plea for a radical rethinking of the contribution that stylisticians could be making to society. In European Marxist-structuralist writing there is a repeatedly stated appreciation of the powers of the non-authoritarian, open literary text in the first instance, a belief in the value of critically deconstructing any text in the second instance. If deconstruction[3] is the means whereby readers may begin to burst the bubble of the dominant ideology, then close analysis of the linguistic construction of texts and their 'realities' is essential, and a linguistic method, by virtue of its generalised tools and procedures, is an excellent strategy with which to begin such work.

II Some General Background Remarks

The piece of prose fiction I am going to consider in some detail, is a short passage from Sylvia Plath's autobiographical[4] novel *The Bell Jar*. It is a passage which details her experience of electric-shock treatment as a 'remedy' for severe depression. Readers may care to look ahead at this point, to Section III below, where the text is given, in order to contextualise general points made here. Essentially, in Section IV, I will be analysing aspects of clause construction and, in a preliminary reading of the passage, readers may find it useful to pay specific attention to the simple question 'who does what to whom?'.

Here, then, I want to consider two issues as preliminaries to that analysis. First, I want to map out a model of some relevant features of clause construction in general, against which *any* text can be charted, and our Plath text will be charted. Secondly, I want to discuss why this type of analysis is particularly relevant to the issues raised in the introduction, and similarly why this specific text was chosen for analysis.

The model of processes and participants in the structure of clauses that I shall draw here is adapted from ideas in the work of Michael Halliday (1970, 1973, 1978). Among other things, he offers a model of the underlying semantic options available in English as *types* or processes which are expressed in the clause – the essential unit of construction in any text. My simplified map of those options – with demonstration examples – is reproduced in Figure 11.1. Readers wanting an expanded description should consult Berry (1975: Vol. 1, 149 ff.) for a clear and precise exposition; a gentle guide. As she says:

In English grammar we make choices between different types of process, between different types of participant, between different types of circumstance, between different roles for participants and circumstances, between different numbers of participants and circumstances, between different ways of combining processes, participants and circumstances. These choices are known collectively as the *transitivity* choices. (p. 150)

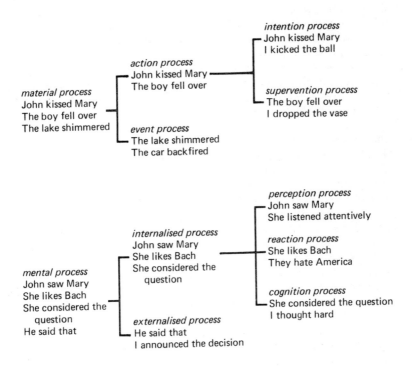

Figure 11.1 *Process options.*

Here we shall be dealing with a limited and simplified version of some of these choices, which brings us to several central points which can be made in relation to the semantic map in Figure 11.1. First, it should be understood that the question "who *does what* to whom?" only makes interesting sense when asked against a background knowledge of all possible options or 'ways of doing' that are available for use in the language. This sign-system relationship is, I take it, a commonplace in linguistic-semiotics (Saussure, 1916; Firth, 1957; Halliday, 1978), but the force of it might need restatement here. The point being that, although one might, certainly, approach the processes of the text in an insightful, intuitive way, and observe some relevant patterns of choice there, this map of meaningful options allows us clarity and precision and neatness in analysing the processes realised in this text, *compared* with (*a*) any other text, (*b*) the absences (Macharey, 1978), in this text – the relevant 'other choices' that could have been made – the 'noticeable absences' (Sacks and Schegloff, 1973). Thus, it allows us really to see 'what it means' to have chosen particular prominence for, say, one type of process.

Let me quickly also try to explain why processes and participants are a strong place to begin analysis given the arguments in Section I above. If the analyst is interested in 'making strange'[5] the power-relationships that obtain in the socially constructed world – be it the 'real' world of public and private social relationships or the spoken and written texts that we create, hear, read, and that ultimately construct *us* in that 'real' world – then, crucially, it is the realisation of *processes* and *participants* (both the actors and the acted upon) in those processes that should concern us. Ultimately, I want to suggest, with Sapir (1956), Whorf (1956) and Vološinov (1930), that the 'world' is linguistically constructed. But rather than a crude Whorfian view, which might lead us to believe that we are trapped and constrained by that linguistic construction, I want to suggest a far more optimistic line of thought. Simply, once it is clear to people that there are alternative ways of expressing 'reality', then people can make decisions about how to express 'reality'; both for others and themselves. By this means, we can both deconstruct and *reconstruct* our realities to an enabling degree.

And this brings me to an explanation of why the Plath text seemed peculiarly appropriate to a feminist-linguistic polemic.

Where the topic of "women and literature" is concerned, there are three immediate areas of thought and study that are being researched:

(1) Images of women in literature written by males – particularly in relation to details of social history. This is, of course, work that draws upon, and contributes to, a 'new' feminist version of that history. (See Rowbotham, 1973*a*, 1973*b*.)
(2) Images of women in literature written by feminist women. This may well involve *finding* them in the first place. (See Showalter, 1977; Rich, 1977.)

(3) Images of women in literature by women who were not/are not feminists – either by 'free' choice, or because they were unaware that that choice was available to them.

Sylvia Plath's work and life can clearly be seen in relation to the third point here. Reading her prose, poems and letters, and reading about her, in the context of the raised consciousness and women's support groups of the 1970s and 1980s, is a moving, and disturbing, experience. It is so easy for *us* to locate her contradictions, dilemmas and pressures as they are expressed by her texts. It is so easy to see her writing herself *into* a concept of helpless victim, and eventually, perhaps, into suicide itself.[6] Her texts abound in disenabling metaphors, disenabling lexis, and – I wish to demonstrate here – disenabling syntactic structures.

To return to the mood of Section I, I want to assert the importance of perceiving those sorts of forces, pervasive in the language around us, and would maintain that both individuals and social institutions require analytical access to knowledge about the intricacies of the relationship between linguistic structures and reality, such that, with that knowledge, reality might be reconstructed in less damaging ways – and again, I would emphasise, with regard to both individuals and social institutions.

I do not, by any means, wish to suggest that only women 'are' victims, or construct themselves as such. If this were a text written by a man (and there are, of course, similar texts), then it would be open to similar sympathetic analysis and discussion. However, that seems to me to be a job for somebody else to do, given that life is short and we must follow our immediate priorities. My general message is: stylistic analysis is *not* just a question of discussing 'effects' in language and text, but a powerful method for understanding the ways in which all sorts of 'realities' are constructed through language. For feminists who believe that 'the personal is political' there is a burning issue which has to be investigated immediately, and in various triangulated ways. We want to understand the relationships between severe and crippling depression that many women experience and the contradictory and disenabling images of self available for women in models of literature, the media, education, folk-notions of the family, motherhood, daughterhood, work, and so on. It is just these contradictions, it has been argued, that are influential in breakdowns of various sorts. As with so much in this chapter, this is a truncated version of a complex and problematic area of discussion, whose complexities are unfortunately minimised here. Suffice it to say that the contradictions that abound in the language of Sylvia Plath's texts make her an important woman to study from a feminist perspective. Any reader with any other radical political commitment should see what follows as a model to appropriate and to be made relevant to his or her own convictions.

III The Text

The wall-eyed nurse came back. She unclasped my watch and dropped it in her pocket. Then she started tweaking the hairpins from my hair.

Doctor Gordon was unlocking the closet. He dragged out a table on wheels with a machine on it and rolled it behind the head of the bed. The nurse started swabbing my temples with a smelly grease.

As she leaned over to reach the side of my head nearest the wall, her fat breast muffled my face like a cloud or a pillow. A vague, medicinal stench emanated from her flesh.

'Don't worry,' the nurse grinned down at me. 'Their first time everybody's scared to death.'

I tried to smile, but my skin had gone stiff, like parchment.

Doctor Gordon was fitting two metal plates on either side of my head. He buckled them into place with a strap that dented my forehead, and gave me a wire to bite.

I shut my eyes.

There was a brief silence, like an indrawn breath.

Then something bent down and took hold of me and shook me like the end of the world. Whee-ee-ee-ee-ee, it shrilled, through an air crackling with blue light, and with each flash a great jolt drubbed me till I thought my bones would break and the sap fly out of me like a split plant.

I wondered what terrible thing it was that I had done.

IV Analysis

On reading the passage, readers[7] repeatedly formulate the following sorts of responses:

(1) the persona seems quite helpless;
(2) the persona seems "at a distance", "outside herself", "watching herself", "detached to being with – and then just a victim";
(3) the medical staff seem more interested in getting the job done than caring.

In order to understand something of what is happening in the language of this passage, that gives rise to such responses, the following instructions enable us to get a firmer grasp of the persona's 'reality' as constructed in the clause-by-clause make-up of the text as a whole:

(1) isolate the processes *per se*, and find which participant (who or what) is "doing" each process;
(2) find what *sorts* of process they are, and which participant is engaged in which type of process;
(3) find who or what is *affected* by each of these processes.

First, then, here is the text repeated with sentences numbered for ease of reference, and processes isolated and underlined.

(1) The wall-eyed nurse *came* back. (2) She *unclasped* my watch and *dropped* it in her pocket. (3) Then she *started tweaking* the hairpins from my hair.

(4) Doctor Gordon *was unlocking* the closet. (5) He *dragged out* a table on wheels with a machine on it and *rolled* it behind the head of the bed. (6) The nurse *started swabbing* my temples with a smelly grease.

(7) As she *leaned over to reach* the side of my head nearest the wall, her fat breast *muffled* my face like a cloud or a pillow. (8) A vague, medicinal stench *emanated* from her flesh.

(9) 'Don't worry,' the nurse *grinned* down at me. (10) 'Their first time everybody's scared to death.'

(11) I *tried to smile*, but my skin *had gone stiff*, like parchment.

(12) Doctor Gordon *was fitting* two metal plates on either side of my head.

(13) He *buckled* them into place with a strap that *dented* my forehead, and *gave me a wire to bite*.

(14) I *shut* my eyes.

(15) There *was* a brief silence, like an indrawn breath.

(16) Then something *bent down* and *took hold* of me and *shook* me like the end of the world. (17) Whee-ee-ee-ee-ee, it *shrilled*, through an air crackling with blue light, and with each flash a great jolt *drubbed* me till I *thought* my bones *would break* and the sap *fly out* of me like a split plant.

(18) I *wondered* what terrible thing it *was* that I *had done*.

Given this simple skeleton analysis, we can abstract out the actors in each process,[8] and spell out the lexical realisation of each of the processes associated with them:

Sentence No.	Actor	Process
1	nurse	came back
2a	nurse	unclasped
b	nurse	dropped
3	nurse	started tweaking
4	doctor	was unlocking
5a	doctor	dragged out
b	doctor	rolled
6	nurse	started swabbing
7a	nurse	leaned over to reach
b	nurse's body part	muffled
8	nurse's body contingency	emanated
9a	n.a.	n.a.
b	nurse	grinned
10	n.a.	n.a.
11a	persona	tried to smile
b	persona's body part	had gone stiff
12	doctor	was fitting
13a	doctor	buckled
b	doctor's equipment	dented
c	doctor	gave . . . to bite
14	persona	shut

Sentence No.	Actor	Process
15		was
16a	something (electricity)	bent down and took hold
b	something (electricity)	shook
17a	something (electricity)	shrilled
b	electricity part	drubbed
c	persona	thought
d	persona body part	would break
e	persona body part	fly out
18a	persona	wondered
b	–	was
c	persona	had done

The analysis is simple, but the resultant table above gives access to a clear, general picture of who is doing what and when in the persona's description of the 'world' around her. The first half of the text gives the Nurse and Doctor performing all actions (1–10). We have a brief mention of the persona as actor (11), and then the Doctor and his equipment dominate the action (12, 13). We have another brief mention of a negative persona as actor (14), the electricity as actor in a very positive sense (16–17) and finally the persona as actor – in a hypothetical sense at least. We shall be able to say more about the types of process below. A simple counting of actors and their actions shows us very little:

nurse (including body parts) as actor: 8
doctor (including his equipment) as actor: 7
electricity as actor: 4
persona (including body parts) as actor: 7

This is interesting in view of the often expressed pre-analytic response, "the persona doesn't *do* anything". Clearly, we can see what readers 'mean' when they say that, but we have to pursue the analysis further, and rephrase the response to capture the 'reality' of the text. What this analysis does lay bare is the *succession* of actors in the scene. The Nurse, for example, drops out after sentence 9, although she has certainly played the major part in the action till then (eight clauses out of eleven), and has been the focus of the persona's (and therefore our) attention. The Doctor, his equipment and the persona interact together, then he drops out and is superseded by a succession of clauses where the 'something' takes over very forcefully. Finally the persona is left acting alone.

Charting through the *types* of processes involved allows us much more room for discussion:

1   nurse came back = material-action-intention
2a nurse unclasped = material-action-intention

b nurse dropped = material-action-intention
3   nurse started tweaking = material-action-intention
4   doctor was unlocking = material-action-intention
5*a* doctor dragged out = material-action-intention
b doctor rolled = material-action-intention
6   nurse started swabbing = material-action-intention
7*a* nurse leaned over to reach = material-action-intention
b nurse's body part muffled = material-action-supervention
8   nurse's body contingency emanated = material-event
9*a* n.a.
b nurse grinned = material-action-intention
10 n.a.
11*a* persona tried to smile = material-action-intention
b persona's body part had gone stiff = material-event
12 doctor was fitting = material-action-intention
13*a* doctor buckled = material-action-intention
b doctor's equipment dented = material-action-supervention
c doctor gave . . . to bite = material-action-intention
14 persona shut = material-action-intention
15 – was = relational
16*a* something took hold = material-action-intention
b something shook = material-action-intention
17*a* something shrilled = material-action-intention
b something drubbed = material-action-intention
c persona thought = mental-internalised-cognition
d persona's body part would break = material-action-supervention
e persona's body part fly out = material-action-supervention
18*a* persona wondered = mental-internalised-cognition
b – was = relational
c persona had done = material-action-intention

Here, the overwhelming fact revealed by the analysis is the definite preponderance of the selection of the option material-action-intention; twenty clauses out of thirty make this choice. A closer consideration brings out the following interesting features of the text. First, all the Nurse's actions are material-action-intention processes; though where the Nurse's body is the actor we have supervention or event processes, so that the effect is of her deliberately carrying out determinate actions, in the persona's environment, while her body produces contingent, 'accidental', yet none the less substantial effects on her thought-world also. Similarly all of the Doctor's actions are material-action-intention processes, but, like the Nurse's body, his equipment produces effects on the environment tangentially, as it were. The electricity is also only represented in terms of material-action-intention processes. Thus, all three of these major actor-participants are seen as overwhelmingly 'in control' of whatever events take place. They are presented and given as being in charge of the construction of the reality that the persona perceives and expresses.

But what of the patient herself? Her attempt at what is (technically) a material-action-intention process (11*a*) fails. Her related body-part action is similarly only an 'accidental' event, that is, beyond her control (11*b*). At sentence 14, she succeeds in a material-action-intention process but, whereas all the other actors are doing constructive, concrete tasks by that option, her contribution is to shut her eyes – to remove herself from the scene. At 17*c* and 18, she has the only mental-internalised-cognition processes in the passage – a fact which makes it absolutely clear that the piece is very much – and only – from her point of view. At 17*d* and *e* we are given two possible (but hypothetical) supervention processes for her body parts – so, again, material actions that are *not* part of the actual reality, but only subordinated possible outcomes of others' actions. And, finally (18*c*), her 'successful' material-action-intention process is located away in the past, in mysterious circumstances.

This further analysis, then, gives us a little more scope in the way of accounting for our understanding of the persona's conception of her world. The next analysis, which isolates who or what is *affected* by each process takes us a little further:

1   nurse affects ϕ by intention process
2a   nurse affects persona's possession by intention process
 b   nurse affects persona's possession by intention process
3   nurse affects persona's possession by intention process
4   doctor affects equipment by intention process
5a   doctor affects equipment by intention process
 b   doctor affects equipment by intention process
6   nurse affects persona's body part by intention process
7a   nurse affects persona's body part by intention process
 b   nurse's body part affects persona's body part by intention process
8   nurse's body contingency affects ϕ by event process
9a   n.a.
 b   nurse affects persona by intention process
10   n.a.
11a persona affects ϕ by intention process
 b   persona's body part affects ϕ by event process
12   doctor affects equipment by intention process
13a doctor affects equipment by intention process
 b   doctor affects persona and equipment by intention process
14   persona affects persona's body part by intention process
15   ϕ affects the environment by relational process
16a something affects persona by intention process
 b   something affects persona by intention process
17a something affects ϕ by intention process
 b   something affects persona by intention process
 c   persona affects persona's body part by cognition process
 d   persona's body part affects ϕ by supervention process
 e   persona's body part affects ϕ by supervention process

18a persona affects φ by cognition process
  b φ affects φ by relation process
  c persona affects φ by intention process (hypothetical)

Reading this skeleton gives us a firmer grasp of the abstract reality of the persona's world. Massively, it is the Nurse who affects both the persona's possessions and body parts (2a, 2b, 3, 6, 7, 8) and, in one instance, the whole of her (9b). The Doctor, on the other hand, uses his intention processes to affect equipment (4, 5a, 5b, 12, 13a, 13c) and, in one localised area, via the persona's body part (13a) and the equipment (13b), the persona herself (13c). At this point he disappears from her world view. The electricity, not surprisingly, continually affects the whole persona (16a, b, 17a, b).

And the patient herself? At 11a she affects nothing – despite her intentions. At 11b her body part affects nothing. At 14 she successfully affects her own body – but remember that this is her escapism clause. At 17c she again 'successfully' carries out a cognition process on her own body – but remember that the resultant effect is only hypothetical. At 17d and e, 18a and c, the remaining clauses which have the persona as actor, the persona and her body parts still affect nothing at all.

This third analysis, then, gives us a much neater and more delicate way of addressing ourselves to readers' responses. Obviously we could discuss much more in this text, and I do not mean to suggest that this is a 'full analysis'.[9] Nevertheless, by pursuing these important sets of related features in this way, we have begun to refine our understanding of the 'reality' presented by this text. Section V suggests how constructive use might be made of this understanding.

V Follow-up Activities

I want, here, to suggest a few follow-up activities that are closely related to the types of analysis in Section IV, and which have worked well with students recently. I should perhaps stress that I do not see them as optional extras, but as a constructive part of a move towards students' knowledge and power over the relationships that obtain between linguistic structures and socially constructed meanings. I shall include a few pieces of work by them,[10] though, sadly, limitation of space prevents extensive reproductions, and one of the most interesting aspects of this sort of enterprise is the comparison and further analysis of substantial numbers of students' materials.

The first activity is to rewrite the paragraph from the point of view of either the Nurse or the Doctor, while – and this is crucial – *staying as close to the words of the original text as possible*. "Do you just mean paraphrasing it?" asked one student, puzzled by that restriction, until, in doing the work, he realised that by considering each word so closely, and in trying to decide whose point of view it represented, he was coming to (1) know the text very thoroughly and (2) see how the semiotic of the text depends heavily on the interplay between networks of syntactic choice and networks of lexical choice. This sort of exercise is the quickest (and most reliable) way I know of demonstrating that the apparent simplicity of the type of analysis given in Section IV is – while substantial as an orientation and clarification heuristic – by no means the whole story.

Here, then, are two rewritten versions; (1) the paragraph from the Nurse's point of view and (2) the paragraph from the Doctor's point of view.

(1)   I returned to the patient's bed. I unclasped her watch and put it safely in my pocket. Then I gently took the hairpins from her hair.
   Dr Gordon unlocked the closet. He pulled out the trolly with the EST machine on it, and rolled it behind the head of the bed. I started to swab her temples with protective ointment.
   'Don't worry,' I said to her reassuringly. 'The first time everybody's a little nervous.'
   She returned a brief smile.
   Dr Gordon fitted two metal plates to either side of her head, and buckled them firmly into place with the safety strap. He gave her a wire to bite on.
   She closed her eyes.
   There was a short silence.
   Then, as she lay there, her eyes closed patiently biting the wire, her body suddenly arched upwards into the most perfect 'D' shape, held for a few seconds, then relaxed.
   We had commenced treatment!

(2)   Nurse Smith re-entered the room. She began to remove all metal objects from the patient. I unlocked the storage cabinet and, rolling out the equipment, began to prepare it for the treatment.
   The patient seemed a little afraid, so Nurse Smith said a few words of encouragement, accompanied by her usual reassuring smile, as she applied the lubricating grease to the girl's forehead. As I fastened the two metal plates in position on her temples, I could see the patient was nervous, but I wasn't unduly worried as this kind of treatment was completely foreign to her. I put the wire between her teeth for her to bite. The girl shut her eyes, and I switched on the equipment to begin the therapy.

A second activity, again closely related to the analysis in Section IV, and the overall perspective of Sections I and II, is to move on to the following passage as given in the novel:[11]

I was sitting in a wicker chair, holding a small cocktail glass of tomato juice. The watch had been replaced on my wrist, but it looked odd. Then I realized it had been fastened upside down. I sensed the unfamiliar positioning of the hairpins in my hair.

'How do you feel?'

An old metal floor lamp surfaced in my mind. One of the few relics of my father's study, it was surmounted by a copper bell which held the light bulb, and from which a frayed, tiger-coloured cord ran down the length of the metal stand to a socket in the wall.

One day I'd decided to move this lamp from the side of my mother's bed to my desk at the other end of the room. The cord would be long enough, so I didn't unplug it. I closed both hands round the lamp and the fuzzy cord and gripped them tight.

Then something leapt out of the lamp in a blue flash and shook me till my teeth rattled, and I tried to pull my hands off, but they were stuck, and I screamed, or a scream was torn from my throat, for I didn't recognize it, but heard it soar and quaver in the air like a violently disembodied spirit.

Then my hands jerked free, and I fell back on to my mother's bed. A small hole, blackened as if with pencil lead, pitted the centre of my right palm.

'How do you feel?'

'All right.'

But I didn't. I felt terrible.

'Which college did you say you went to?'

I said what college it was.

'Ah!' Doctor Gordon's face lightened up with a low, almost tropical smile. 'They had a WAC station up there, didn't they, during the war?'

The most obvious connected job is to pursue a very similar analysis, to see where the two passages are similar, and where they differ. In particular one might want to move on here to question the functions of time/place/manner circumstances, and a comparison between the types of processes the persona acts out in the present and in the past, in terms of degrees of control and precision.

Alternatively, it is very interesting to focus on the sentence 'An old metal floor lamp surfaced in my mind', and discuss how one might represent a persona who was in the process of deciding to take positive control over as many aspects of her life as possible.

Here is another student's response to that suggestion:

With a conscious effort I jerked myself out of the whole mad circus, blanked out the doctor's blandly professional, smoothly patronising face, the nurse, flapping like a billowing sheet on the periphery of my vision. I remembered before.

That summer, when we walked down to the beach on a blue-blazing afternoon, when the light tumbled from the soft waves in shards of magnesium flare and drops of honey, sand stretching, expansive, generous in a vast loving gesture from horizon to planed horizon. And then the evening, when the sun slowly sank to the very edge of the sea, tracing waves in silhouette, blazing blood and orange black water beneath. Above, blue-grey misty twilight deepening to studded shroud of deepest blue. Shape to shape we turned, black figures against carmine. And talked then. And discovered ourselves.

A third activity is one that I have only used with students who have not already discussed and analysed the Plath text in class. They were given the final analysis table of Section IV – the table which gives actions, affected entities and shorthand labels for processes. I merely said, 'Make something of that,' and refused to answer any questions. What I hoped to get back were texts with different surface structures (obviously), but which would state the 'same' "state of affairs". Here is one student's interpretation of the job:[12]

I am no longer me
I must be no longer me
It is not expedient
I am no longer me
In their world I am part of their world
They manipulate me
They use me
I am silent
I am no longer me
They are aliens
Coming at me with instruments
To do what?
To do what?
They wield power, absolute power
There is no escape
I am humiliated, used,
subjugated, enslaved, manipulated
I belong to them.
I become their equipment: experimental equipment,
A flesh machine, only a flesh machine
To be probed
Investigated
Inspected under arc lights
Nurse is a programmed flesh machine
Doctor is a programmed flesh machine.
I too: we understand our roles.
Their programme operates here
Mine operates outside in another world.
We are not men and women in this world: but we have parts to play
I am no longer me.
I am no longer me.
But I will be.

Throughout, I hope it is clear, the emphasis has been away from studying style *qua* style, towards understanding some of the relationships between language, represented thought and the sociolinguistic construction of reality.

VI Concluding Remarks

It is important to realise that, if I have given the impression that there is any simple set of relationships between language, thought and socially constructed reality, it was an unintentional and artificial contingency of the inevitable gap between the complexities of the world and the simplification process involved in any attempt at a coherent academic statement about the world. Clearly, work in semantics, pragmatics and semiotics has a long way to go before we can hope to chart the networks of meaning and significance which mediate between structure and representations of reality. However, I hope, at least, to have opened up one possible approach to the analysis and understanding of the construction of images of power-relationships in general, and to have urged the motivation for so doing.

To sum up let me offer the following programme of eight points, which I see the teacher of stylistics as pursuing. It assumes students with an interest in literature in general, but little or no linguistic knowledge. Parts 1–4 are, I take it, uncontentious; parts 5–8 are offered as a programme for radical stylistics.

(1) Stylistics can be part of a programme to enable students to handle competently a coherent and comprehensive descriptive grammar, which can then be used in either literature-oriented studies, or linguistics-oriented studies.
(2) It is always at least a 'way in' to a text.
(3) It can shift discussion to awareness of effects that are intuitively felt to be in a text in the process of reading it, and a contingent 'making strange' of those effects and feelings simultaneously. It is towards 'knowing how' as well as 'knowing that' (Ryle, 1949).
(4) It can spell out a shared vocabulary for describing the language of any text – whether those effects are straightforward or ambiguous.
(5) Crucially, stylistics can point the way to understanding the ways in which the language of a given text constructs its own (fictional) reality.
(6) It should then point the way towards understanding the ways in which language constructs the 'reality' of everyday life – and an awareness that is always *must* do so. So that, in a sense, everyday 'reality' can usefully be seen as a series of 'fictional' constructs – as texts open to analysis and interpretation in just the same way as texts marked out for literary study are.
(7) This would lead to an awareness of the importance of perceiving the constituent parts of the fictions we live *in* and *by*, if only to map them against alternative constructions of reality.
(8) Finally, this would lead to an understanding that the fictions (both large and small) that we live in and by can be rewritten. Both individually and collectively. As reform or revolution, whichever is more appropriate.

As for my title? See it as notes for a poem, on Sylvia Plath, Women,

Feminism, Radical Stylistics, academic work in general. Optimistic notes.

Notes: Chapter 11

1   I am here following Halliday. See, in particular, Halliday (1978).
2   Throughout I am using single quote marks as 'scare' quotes. They are meant to imply a certain scepticism about the terms encapsulated in them.
3   Readers unfamiliar with the term should see Belsey (1980) for an excellent discussion of this aspect of critical practice. Basically, it is a series of methods for perceiving the *cultural* and *ideological* presuppositions inherent in any text.
4   See Burton (in preparation *b*) for a discussion of the complexities of this shorthand convenience-label.
5   See Brecht (1950), Garfinkel (1967), Chomsky (1968).
6   Perhaps I should make it clear that I am here acknowledging the pervasive power of the culturation processes, and foregrounding the concept of 'self as an ideological construct' (Lacan, 1977).
7   I have taught several undergraduate classes using this text. The responses I quote here are typical, but just happen to be the most recent ones.
8   I am ignoring clauses which represent quoted speech from participants other than the persona, since I am attempting to deconstruct that part of the 'reality' which is specifically 'reality' plus her interpretation. However, compare Anita Thorpe's rewritten version, Section 5(1).
9   Compare John Sinclair's argument in this volume.
10 My thanks here to Anita Thorpe, Valerie Tiplady, Simon Davies and Pam Burt for permission to quote their work.
11 The lay-out of the page includes a small gap between the passage given in Section IV and the passage given here, indicating, I assume, a time/space shift.
12 There is no simple relationship between the surface structure of this piece of writing and the table, since even the sequence of processes has been altered. None the less, the texts are remarkably similar in underlying semantic and cultural propositions.

References: Chapter 11

Althusser, L. (1969), *For Marx*, trans. B. Brewster (Harmondsworth: Penguin).
Althusser, L. (1977), *Lenin and Philosophy and Other Essays*, trans. B. Brewster (London: New Left Books).
Ardener, S. (ed.) (1975), *Perceiving Women* (London: Malaby).
Barthes, R. (1967), *Writing Degree Zero*, trans. A. Lavers and C. Smith (London: Cape).
Barthes, R. (1970), *S/Z*, trans. R. Miller (London: Cape).
Barthes, R. (1972), *Mythologies*, trans. A. Lavers (London: Cape).
Barthes, R. (1977), *Image, Music, Text*, trans. S. Heath (London: Fontana).
Belsey, C. (1980), *Critical Practice*, New Accents series (London: Methuen).
Berger, G. and Kachuk, B. (1977), 'Sexism, language and social change', *Michigan Papers in Women's Studies*, no. 2 (Summer).
Berry, M. (1975), *Introduction to Systemic Linguistics*, Vol. I (London: Batsford).
Brecht, B. (1950), 'The street scene', in *Brecht on Theatre*, trans. and ed. J. Willett (London: Methuen, 1964), pp. 121–9.
Burton, D. (1981), 'Pass the Alka-Seltzer: she's swallowed the dictionary' (mimeo.), English Language Research, University of Birmingham.

Burton, D. (in preparation *a*), *Eccentric propositions: the sociolinguistic construction of reality*.

Burton, D. (in preparation *b*), *Seeing through language: essays on the language used by, and about, women*.

Coward, R. and Ellis, J. (1977), *Language and Materialism* (London: Routledge & Kegan Paul).

Chomsky, N. (1968), *Language and Mind* (New York: Harcourt Brace & World).

Daly, M. (1978), *Gyn/Ecology: the Metaethics of Radical Feminism* (Boston, Mass.: Beacon Press).

Davidson, D. (1967), 'Truth and meaning', *Synthèse*, no. 17, pp. 304–23.

Delamont, S. and Duffin, L. (eds) (1978), *The Nineteenth Century Woman: Her Cultural and Physical World* (London: Croom Helm).

Derrida, J. (1976), *Of Grammatology*, trans. Gayatri Chakravorty Spivak (Baltimore, Md: Johns Hopkins University Press).

Feyerabend, P. (1975), *Against Method* (London: New Left Books).

Feyerabend, P. (1978), *Science in a Free Society* (London: New Left Books).

Firth, J. R. (1957), *Papers in Linguistics, 1934–1951* (London: OUP).

Foucault, M. (1970), *The Order of Things* (London: Tavistock).

Foucault, M. (1972), *The Archaeology of Knowledge*, trans. A. N. Sheridan Smith (London: Tavistock).

Foucault, M. (1977), *Language, Counter-Memory, Practice: Selected Essays and Interviews*, ed. D. F. Bouchard and trans. D. F. Bouchard and S. Simon (Oxford: Blackwell).

Garfinkel, H. (1967), *Studies in Ethnomethodology* (Englewood Cliffs, NJ: Prentice-Hall).

Halliday, M. A. K. (1970), 'Language structure and language function' in *New Horizons in Linguistics*, ed. J. Lyons (Harmondsworth: Penguin), pp. 140–65.

Halliday, M. A. K. (1973), *Explorations in the Functions of Language* (London: Edward Arnold).

Halliday, M. A. K. (1978), *Language as Social Semiotic* (London: Edward Arnold).

Jaquette, J. (ed.) (1974), *Women in Politics* (New York: Wiley).

Kuhn, T. (1962), *The Structure of Scientific Revolutions* (Chicago: Chicago University Press: rev. edn 1970).

Kuhn, T. (1967), *The Copernican Revolution* (Cambridge: CUP).

Lacan, J. (1977), *Ecrits*, trans. A. Sheridan (London: Tavistock).

Lakatos, I. (1970), 'Falsification and the methodology of scientific research programmes', in *Criticism and the Growth of Knowledge*, ed. I. Lakatos and A. Musgrave (Cambridge: CUP), pp. 91–6.

Lakatos, I. (1976), *Proofs and Refutations: The Logic of Mathematical Discovery* (Cambridge: CUP).

Lakoff, G. and Johnson, P. (1980), *Metaphors We Live By* (Chicago: Chicago University Press).

Macharey, P. (1978), *A Theory of Literary Production*, trans. G. Wall (London: Routledge & Kegan Paul).

Millett, K. (1969), *Sexual Politics* (London: Virago).

Popper, K. (1977), *The Logic of Scientific Discovery* (London: Hutchinson).

Popper, K. (1979), *Objective Knowledge* (London: OUP, rev. edn).

Rich, A. (1972) 'When we dead awaken: writing as re-revision', *College English*, vol. 34, no. 1, pp. 18–30.

Rich, A. (1977), *Of Woman Born: Motherhood as Experience and Institution* (London: Virago).

Rowbotham, S. (1973*a*), *Woman's Consciousness: Man's World* (Harmondsworth: Penguin).

Rowbotham, S. (1973*b*), *Hidden from History* (London: Pluto Press).

Ryle, G. (1949), *The Concept of Mind* (London: Hutchinson).

Sacks, H. and Schegloff, E. A. (1973), 'Opening up closings', *Semiotica*, vol. 8, no. 4, pp. 289–327.

Sapir, E. (1956), *Culture, Language and Personality* (Berkeley, Calif.: University of California Press).

Saussure, F. de (1916), *Course in General Linguistics*, trans. W. Boskin (London: Fontana; repr. 1974).

Showalter, E. (1977), *A Literature of Their Own: British Women Novelists from Brontë to Lessing* (Princeton, NJ: Princeton University Press).

Tarski, A. (1956), *Logic, Semantics, Metamathematics* (Oxford: Clarendon Press).

Vološinov, V. M. (1930), *Marxism and the Philosophy of Language*, trans. L. Matejka and I. R. Titunik (New York: Seminar Press; repr. 1973).

Whorf, B. L. (1956), *Language, Thought and Reality*, ed. J. B. Carroll (Cambridge, Mass.: MIT Press).

Introduction to Chapter 12

As argued in the previous chapter by Deirdre Burton, there are ways in which stylistic analysis can provide tools for relating the organisation of texts to organisation of social reality. This chapter is broader still in scope. Gill Alexander is not principally concerned with an interpretation of her texts *per se*, but in demonstrating a close relationship between discourse styles and an opposition between rival or ideologically conflicting social groups. Her texts are taken from seventeenth-century prose writers, and by offering a clear model for examining pronoun usage in specific texts she is able to distinguish a series of key historical disfunctions in the way the conservative Anglicans and the more radical Puritans saw themselves in relation to God, their fellow men and the society in which they lived. It is important to assess the contribution of this chapter to the discipline of stylistics in the light of other chapters in the book, and evaluate and examine for yourself what kind of priorities stylistic analysis can or should set itself. What are the strengths and limitations of respective approaches? These are questions which link both theoretical issues and the detail of practical analysis. And in spite of differences in emphasis, what are the common principles which inform the various practices?

12 Politics of the Pronoun in the Literature of the English Revolution

GILLIAN ALEXANDER

1   Introduction

Conventional historiography agrees that the middle decades of the seventeenth century (between about 1640 and 1660) were a period of change, challenge and revolution. The period is generally labelled the English Revolution, and this chapter is concerned with the empirical study of a collection of texts which grew out of and were part of that historical process. The specific aim of the chapter is to examine the relationship between linguistic change and social conflict in an analysis of the prominent patterns of pronoun usage in the texts under consideration.[1] For the purposes of contrastive analysis the texts chosen for study are representative of both the radical and conservative elements[2] of the English Revolution. The chapter is a summary of a much larger study, and so the analysis presented can only be selective. However, the texts looked at most closely here are: Donne's *Devotions Upon Emergent Occasions*; Bunyan's *Grace Abounding*; a selection of Digger writings, principally *A Declaration from the Poor and Oppressed People of England, The True Levellers' Standard Advanced, An Appeal to the House of Commons, A Watch-Word to the City of London and the Army*;[3] and a collection of Radical courtroom testimonies. The theoretical questions implicit in this study are both semantic and sociolinguistic. First, what is the relationship between the language of a text and the belief systems, conflicts and struggles of the society it is produced in? Secondly, what is the place of linguistic analysis in the study of the function of writing in an actual historical process?

   The basic perspective which motivates this study is based on a set of taken-for-granteds concerning the relationship between language, thought, action, interaction and the social structure generally, and the operation of those dynamics at a time of revolution in particular. A brief summary of those taken-for-granteds will answer any questions concerning the reasons for undertaking this analysis.

(a)   I maintain that reality is linguistically constructed. In other words, the means we have for understanding ourselves as individuals in a physical and social environment is intricately related to the language we use. Language, in effect, constructs a perspective on reality. In this I am following the basic arguments of Halliday (1978), Sapir (1956), Whorf (1956) and Vološinov (1930).

(b)   Language is not just a collection of sentences by which we build a view of reality; it serves another important function. People *talk* to each other, and language forms a basis for *interaction*. Thus, since language serves the function of organising how groups of people communicate it is intricately related to social structure. It establishes the roles of participants relative to a social system and encodes the shared systems of value, knowledge and belief of the given society.

(c)   At any given time a specific set of concepts constitute the dominant perceptual framework of a society. All knowledge of the group is contained and produced within this dominant ideological framework. Since language is related to the perceptual structures of a society, the linguistic system plays a significant role in this process. To this extent there exists a 'dominant discourse framework'. Further, any discourse or action which opposes this dominant framework is labelled as deviant and fringe – at best eccentric, at worst insane. There is no space to discuss this in detail, but see, for example, Althusser (1969, 1977), Foucault (1970, 1972), Kuhn (1970), and Lakoff and Johnson (1980).

(d)   Historical processes labelled 'revolutionary' involve social conflict and social change. These are periods in time when the fact that it is possible to construct new perspectives on reality becomes obvious. Thus, the contradictions the dominant ideology presents for groups are challenged and systematic attempts are made to redefine and reconstruct concepts basic to how the relevant social group functions. This has crucial implications for changes in form and function at a linguistic level.

In the light of this basic perspective texts produced during the English Revolution are of great interest. The mid-decades of the seventeenth century were, more than any other period of English history, a time of conflict, challenge and change. It was a time of flux – concepts of self, society, the world, God and human potential were being challenged and reconstructed. And it was a time of noise – a linguistic self-consciousness and the complete liberty of the press between 1641 and 1660 saw a flood of printed material. Christopher Hill sums up the spirit of the age in the following terms (1972: 12):

From say, 1645 to 1653, there was a great overturning, questioning, revaluing of everything in England. Old institutions, old beliefs, old values came in question . . . there was a period of glorious flux and intellectual excitement, when, as Gerrard Winstanley put it 'the old world is running up like parchment in the fire'. Literally anything seemed possible; not only were the values of the old hierarchical society called in question, but also the new values, the protestant ethic itself.

The basic premiss of this chapter, therefore, is as follows. During the mid-seventeenth century there arose an 'oppositional discourse', a discourse which evolved to serve the purpose of the new democratic ideas which were emerging during the English Revolution. This discourse challenged and criticised the dominant, traditional, aristocratic discourse of the period. And if, as in Winstanley's phrase, 'Freedom is the man that will turn the world upside down, therefore no wonder he hath enemies' (Hill, 1973: 128), then, given the relationship between language and social structure, freedom, in a sense, demanded turning language upside down, too – both stylistically and in relation to the rule-governed events of interaction. And it was no wonder that the speaker had enemies. For in attempting to challenge the dominant discourse patterns an oppositional discourse is also demanding a social structure which would label the oppositional discourse not as deviant, but as acceptable.

Thus, the analytical section of this chapter attempts to deal with the linguistic differences between the form of a radical text and the form of a conservative text. At this level the pattern of pronoun usage in the texts is particularly significant and constitutes the object of analysis for this study. The reason for this emphasis on pronouns rests on their function in identifying the participants of the text. The pronoun 'I', for example, identifies 'self', whilst the pronoun 'you' identifies 'other'. As such a pronoun patterning in texts represents relationships between members of social groups – in effect, it reflects how relationships between the 'I', 'you', 'thou', 'we', 'him', 'her' or 'them' of a text are constructed and perceived. This is particularly significant in texts which grew out of the English Revolution since it was just these relationships which were being redefined and reconstructed. Variations in pronoun usage in these texts, therefore, reflect variation at this conceptual level. Given this, the analysis concentrates on (1) pronoun patterning in the texts at the level of clause relations and (2) patterning in dialogue, specific attention being paid to the function of pronouns in defining role relations in the rule-governed system of address.

2 Some Background Comments

The texts I am going to look at in detail were all produced during the events and debates of the mid-seventeenth century. Any readers wanting a detailed account of these events, and of the relationship of the various radical sects to each other, are referred to Hill (1972, 1973, 1977). However, a brief outline of the set of ideas which motivated the thoughts, actions and utterances of a radical and a conservative is a necessary preliminary to the analysis.

In the seventeenth century all arguments about the nature of humanity, whether radical or conservative, were expressed through the medium of theology – the relationship of humankind to God was the arena in which struggles were defined. In terms of this frame of reference, two issues were basic in the developing conflict between tradition and revolution: the doctrine of the Fall; and the related topic of the relationship of God to man. Concepts based on the nature of self, society and human potential for change were all defined in these terms.

For the conservative thinker the orthodox interpretation of the Fall explained the miserable condition of humanity. Adam's first disobedience meant that Paradise was lost and man was in a fallen state. If Adam had not fallen, there would be no inequality, no oppression, and property would be held in common. Fallen humanity, however, is greedy and proud, and a coercive state is necessary to protect society from the consequences of this post-lapsarian state. The radical view stood traditional orthodoxy on its head. From a radical perspective, far from private property, inequality and the state being the necessary and inevitable consequences of the fall, a radical argued that the introduction of private property *was* the fall – that from it followed covetousness, social inequality and the state which protects the rich. Sin here *comes from* the social system; it does not make it necessary. For a radical thinker each person is born into a state of innocence, and each person falls in his/her own lifetime owing to the sinfulness inherent in the social system.

Related to this was the whole issue of the possibility of change – of improving the state of affairs on earth. This argument was defined in terms of the relationship of God to man. For a conservative, progress on earth was impossible. Humanity inherited a state of sin from Adam's first transgression. Thus, God and with Him Paradise existed *outside* our frame of reference. Thus, compensation for the sadness of life was in heaven; it could never be on earth. The radicals, however, maintained that humanity has the potential to progress – to create the New Jerusalem on earth and in time, by in effect changing the constraining social system. The notion which made this possible was the doctrine of the 'inner light'. Essentially radicals argued that Righteousness, Truth, Justice, Christ and, ultimately, God were *within* everyone. God therefore exists *inside* our frame of reference and is the means for explaining how perfectionability is possible – the millennium on earth. Two major consequences follow on from this perspective. First, the argument that mankind is the clothing for God is the greatest argument, not only for human potential, but also for human *equality*, and this formed the basis for arguing for the levelling of the society. Secondly, it meant that the Second Coming would have explicit socio-economic consequences. From the orthodox perspective, Christ would descend from the Clouds; for the radicals, he would appear among sons and daughters if the constraining social system were changed. There would be no more buying and selling, no more private property, the earth would be a 'common treasury' belonging to the Lord, who is everyone. Winstanley presents this perspective in *A Watch-Word to the City of London and the Army*:

> If thou wouldst know what true freedom is, read over this and other my writings, and thou shalt see it lies in the community in spirit, and community in the earthly treasury; and this is Christ the true man-child spread abroad in the creation, restoring all things into himself. (Hill, 1973: 129)

Given this basic framework of debate two quite distinct perceptual paradigms developed during the English Revolution which had a fundamental effect on how a conservative and a radical made sense of their experience of the world. Ultimately these paradigmatic differences laid foundations for the existence of two conflicting discourses, which became the 'voices' in which the struggles of the revolutionary period were expressed and enacted. The essential features of these discourses were exhibited in what is conventionally labelled as the Anglican and Puritan literature of the period, and as such have established the basic premiss of several literary critical accounts of mid-seventeenth-century texts, see particularly Webber (1968) and Knights (1971).

At one extreme, then, is the Anglican understanding of experience. Three concepts are basic to Anglican prose (see, for example, Browne's *Religio Medici* and Donne's *Devotions*), and are automatically developed within the conservative perceptual paradigm. First, in holding that humanity is united in the sin inherited from Adam's first Fall a conservative Anglican sees himself[4] as representative of mankind, since all share the same sin. Secondly, from the perspective that no progress is possible on earth, the Anglican sees time as being part of the eternal present – there is nothing new under the sun. Thirdly, being in a fallen state the Anglican also sees himself in a state of conflict. Thus, Anglican writing is frequently glossed as a meditative and self-analytical style. Further, since all humanity shares the same sin, self-analysis and meditation mean the analysis of the human condition. The typically Anglican metaphor (so often occurring in Donne) is of man as a little world, for the Anglican frequently becomes the world both in metaphor and importance.

At the other extreme was radical Puritan discourse. Developing the basic ideas of a radical perspective, a Puritan understood his/her purpose as assisting in the fulfilment of God's purpose for England in establishing an earthly Utopia in time (see Watkins, 1972, for further elaboration). Here the concept of self is that of an active, time-bound being, desirous of being taken seriously as a person in a hostile and constraining world. Thus, instead of concentrating on her/his miserable condition as a fallen human, the radical concentrated on who he/she was in the here and now, and, more importantly, what she/he could be. Thus, rather than meditation, the function of Art was to be useful for creating a better life. The formal consequences of this perspective were perhaps most succinctly analysed by the Puritan Bunyan:

> I could have stepped into a style much higher than this which I have here discoursed, and could have adorned all things more than here I have seemed to do, but I dare not. God did not play in convincing of me, the devil did not play in tempting of me, neither did I play when I sunk into the bottomless pit, when the pangs of hell caught upon me; wherefore I may not play in my relating of them, but be plain and simple, and lay down the thing as it was. (*Grace Abounding*, p. 5.)

3   Analysis

Given that at a general level the existence of two distinct discourse patterns during the English Revolution is obvious, it is the purpose of this analysis to indicate some of the ways the orthodox and radical texts were operating at the *specific* level of pronoun patterning. The concern of the analysis is twofold. The first is to highlight a selection of examples which demonstrate how the pronoun patterns of a text at clause level are related to the basic perceptual systems of a social group. I am interested here in the role of pronouns in the construction of participant relations in discourse. The second concern is with the status of pronouns in the language of face-to-face interaction during the period. The emphasis at this level is on how an oppositional discourse becomes directly involved in revolutionary struggle. Radical discourse was not just a matter of changing patterns at clause level to give expression to democratic ideas, but also of active participation in the struggle those ideas motivate. It is predicted that an analysis of the role of pronouns in dialogue will throw light on this particular function of radical discourse.

3.1   Clause-Level Relations

Given that pronouns are significant in that they signify the participants of the discourse, this section of the analysis is concerned with how changing concepts of the relationship between individual members of social groups affected the dominant pronoun patterns in the texts analysed.

3.1.1   I–YOU RELATIONS

The most obvious difference between pronoun patterns in a radical and conservative text is based on the frequency of occurrence of the pronouns 'I' and 'you'. Since these pronouns are crucial in constituting author/text/reader relations, patterns developing from the use of these pronouns are central. Quite basically, the pronoun of most significance to the operations of traditional prose is the pronoun 'I', occurring most frequently in subject and object position. This pattern is crucial for example in the following extract from Donne's *Devotions*:

> s   o
> I have no other sacrifice to offer but myself and wilt thou accept no spotted
>
>   s   p
> sacrifice? Doeth thy son dwell bodily in this flesh . . . the flesh itself is the
>
> o   s   p   o
> garment and it spotteth itself with itself. (*Devotions*, expos. 13, p. 68).

Conversely the crucial pronoun in radical texts is the second person 'you' (or 'thou').

These basic differences can be substantiated in a statistical analysis of the distribution of pronouns in the texts. Given that the opening paragraphs of a discourse are functional in defining participant relations, a count was made of the occurrence of 'I' and 'you' in the first two thousand words of Donne's *Devotions*, Bunyan's *Grace Abounding*, and the Digger Winstanley's *A Watch-Word to the City of London and the Army*. The results are represented in Figure 12.1. As the graph indicates, there is an interesting reversal in the results. In Donne's *Devotions* the most significant pronoun is 'I', while 'you' is of minor importance. In the Bunyan and Digger extract, however, 'you' is relatively more significant, and 'I' less so.

These formal differences are related to the conceptual differences between a radical and conservative at a basic level. As discussed in Section 2 above, a conservative Anglican was concerned with meditation on 'self' as a symbol of the miserable condition of humankind. The motivation here is to develop a relationship with self. Thus, I-writer assumes a central position in the discourse, whilst the you-reader is given the status of an eavesdropper. The radical on the other hand viewed the process of writing as serving the end of establishing Utopia on earth. Thus a radical has a message to impress upon an audience, whether in attacking a site of power, such as the church, or in developing a relationship with a sympathetic reader. Pronoun patterns which constructed 'you'–'I' relations were therefore crucial to radical discourse.

3.1.2 I—WE RELATIONS

Given that the conservative perspective held that all men and women are grouped together by original sin, 'the miserable condition of man-

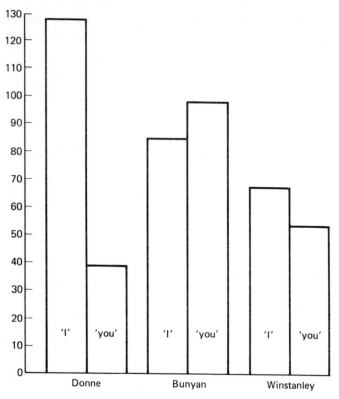

Figure 12.1 *'I' and 'you' pronoun usage.*

kind', conservative texts tend to shift interchangeably from the use of 'I' to the use of 'we'. In Donne this shift from an 'I' to an all-inclusive 'we' is hardly noticeable, reflecting Donne's belief that he is a symbol for the world. In the following extract from the beginning of *Devotions* this pattern is central:

> Variable, and therefore miserable condition of Man; this minute I was well, and am ill, this minute. I am surpriz'd with a sodaine change, and alteration to worse, and can impute it to no cause, nor call it by any name. We study health and we deliberate our meats, and drink and aire, and exercises, and we hew and we polish every stone, that goes to that building. (*Devotions*, med. 1, p. 3)

'We' in radical texts, however, serves a different function. Here 'we' usage is specifically geared towards signalling or awakening some kind of group consciousness and collective political activity. Digger writings are laced with this kind of usage. The opening of *The True Leveller's*

Standard Advanced sets out in specific terms exactly who the text represents:

> A declaration to the powers of England and to all the powers of the world, shewing the cause why the common people of England have begun and gives consent to dig up manure and sew corn upon George Hill in Surrey; by those that have subscribed and thousands more that give consent. (Hill, 1973: 77)

Thus, 'we' in this text is used to represent a specific group, not the whole of humanity. As a consequence 'we' usually takes priority over 'I' in the text:

> We are assured, and reason makes it appear to others that bondage shall be removed, tears wiped away, and all poor people by their righteous labours shall be relieved and freed from poverty and straits. (Hill, 1973: 91)

3.1.3 FIRST PERSON–THIRD PERSON RELATIONS

I am concerned here with pronoun patterning which establishes a dichotomy in the texts between one group of participants and another. Such dichotomies are inevitably marked by patterns in which the first-person pronouns occur at different positions in the clause to the third-person pronouns.

For Donne this dichotomy is inevitably used to represent the separation between a Divine God and a Fallen Humanity. God is outside humanity's frame of reference and, as a result, the pronouns 'he' and 'I'/'we' are always in syntactic opposition – they never occur in the same position at the level of clause structure. This pattern is basic in the following extract:

> s
> We are all prodigall sonnes, and not disinherited; wee have received our
>
> portion and misspent it, not bin denied it. We are God's tenants heere, and
>   s   p   o
> yet here, he, our landlord payes us our rents; not yearely, nor quarterle;
>   s   s   s
> every minute he renews his mercy, but wee will not understand, least that we
>   s   o
> should be converted, and he should heale us. (*Devotions*, expos. 1, p. 2)

As outlined in Section 2 above, however, an essential feature of the radical perspective was that such a dichotomy between God and humanity did not exist. The doctrine of the inner light held that God was *within* all of us, and hence broke down the traditional he/we division. The linguistic attempts to encode this at the level of pronoun organisation, however, were not easily acceptable. In fact when the Quaker George Fox dispelled the he/we distinction by saying 'I am the risen Christ' he was put on trial for blasphemy and imprisoned for one year.[5]

Radical texts did establish a dichotomy between first and third pronouns, but not in the religious sense. Here the all-inclusive 'we' of the orthodox voice was divided into two opposed units, 'they' and 'we'. There is, in effect, a distinct division in radical texts which might be glossed as a 'them and us' distinction. This serves to reflect the radical view that, although 'we' have the potential to create Utopia given that God is within 'us', 'they' – the 'buyers and sellers' – are preventing us. This pattern occurs frequently in Digger texts and is obvious in *Poor and Oppressed People of England*:

> We say we hope we need not doubt of their sincerity to us herin, and that they will not gainsay our determinate course; howsoever their actions will prove to the view of all others either their sincerity or hypocrisy. We know what we speak is our priviledge, and our cause is righteous and if they doubt of it, let them but send a child for us to come before them and we shall make it manifest. (Hill, 1973: 106)

3.2   Pronouns in Face-to-Face Interaction

So far this analysis has concentrated on clause-level surface operations in monologue, that is, syntactic patterns in texts where a writer communicates to a reader but does not receive a reply. The purpose of such an analysis was twofold: first, to demonstrate that two linguistic styles did exist during the English Revolution; and, secondly, to indicate ways in which the pronoun patterns of the traditional orthodox texts and the radical 'oppositional' texts are related to differences in the radical and conservative perspectives on reality. In effect, the concern so far has been to highlight obvious examples of how sentences build up a view on reality and, as a consequence, how the new levelling concepts of the English Revolution required changes in formal linguistic patterning at a basic level. The rest of this analysis, however, is concerned, not with how language encodes perspectives on reality, but with how language reflects the whole social framework in terms of which people talk to each other. I am interested here in highlighting obvious examples of how language is related to the social structure and, more specifically, to social conflict, in dialogue and the literary form based on dialogue – drama.

The general framework of this section is based on insights developed within sociolinguistics. The analysis of spoken discourse has revealed that when people talk to each other they do not just send and receive sentences, but that they take part in a highly rule-governed activity, which operates above the level of the clause (see Sinclair and Coulthard, 1975). At this level, one of the functions of language is to define 'role' relationships. That is, discourse rules embody a set of behaviours normally expected of a person occupying a specific space in the social structure. From this point of view, the rules governing the system of address are particularly interesting, and pronouns have a significant function in the dynamics of that system. This is relevant in terms of mid-seventeenth-century texts. The conflicts of the English Revolution saw an attempt to deconstruct and reconstruct the system which defines the role relationships of the participants of a discourse; the pronouns 'you' and 'thou' began to assume the status of a revolutionary tool in the developing struggle between the set of aristocratic ideas and the new set of levelling, democratic ideas.

The details of this analysis are based on a modified version of the work of Brown and Gilman (1960) who examine the relationship between the polite and familiar pronouns of address (referred to for convenience as the V and T forms, following the Latin *Tu* and *Vos*) in several European languages using the dimensions of power and solidarity. Given that during the seventeenth century in England 'thou' had the same status in the system of address as, say, *tu* in French today, the conclusions Brown and Gilman draw form a useful framework for this analysis.

As Brown and Gilman suggest, because of the system of referring to a monarch in the plural (the famous royal 'we'), that habit grew up amongst the upper classes of marking rank by calling an individual person by the second-person plural – you (V-form). This aristocratic habit led to a system of address whereby, although the upper classes called each other by the V-form and the lower classes used the T-form, the upper classes used the T-form to the lower classes and received V back. Thus, the power dimension was marked by non-reciprocity in pronoun usage. Given these terms, another variable also began to have an influence on pronoun choice – the solidarity factor. Since V-usage for the lower classes represented distance and alienation, T-usage was used when the degree of intimacy or solidarity between speakers was felt to be large. This system of address embodies the social structure in seventeenth-century English society. For the purposes of this paper a modified version of the set of rules Brown and Gilman propose can be formalised by a decision chart as in Figure 12.2. The flow-chart is entered at E and a choice is made at each box: + means 'yes', − means 'no' and = means 'neither'. If the addressee is not human (God,[6] an animal or thing), then 'thou' is selected immediately (box T). 'Child'

Prospero: Thou lying slave. . . .
Miranda: I pitied thee,
                    Took pains to make thee speak.

And 'making' Caliban speak involves teaching him non-reciprocity in pronoun address – Caliban says 'you' back to Miranda and Prospero:

Caliban: You taught me language and my profit on't
                    Is I know how to curse.

The traditional pronoun address system in seventeenth-century England, then, confirmed the hierarchical structure of the social system. However, the flood of egalitarian ideas which were voiced by the revolutionary sects during the mid-decades of the century could not be encoded in this traditional system. As a consequence, 'thou' and 'you' became explicitly involved in social conflict and protest.

The Quakers and Diggers were the innovators of this new pronoun usage, for, given that all men and women were equal in Christ, it followed from the radical perspective that no discrimination of rank should be possible in the linguistic system. Thus, George Fox describes the basis of the new system of address in these words:

. . . moreover when the Lord sent me forth into the world, he forbade me to put off my hat to any, high or low; and I was required to 'thee' and 'thou' all men and women, without any respect to rich or poor, great or small. And as I travelled up and down, I was not to bid people 'good morrow' or 'good evening', neither might I bow or scrape with my leg to anyone; and this made the sects and professions to rage. (*Journal*, p. 35)

In 1660 Fox write a fascinating grammar to formalise exactly what the terms of this pronoun battleground were; *A Battle-Doore for Teachers and Professors to Learn Singular and Plural* is a comprehensive attempt to form a grammar to protest against the traditional pronoun address system. He argues that 'thou' to one and 'you' to many was the natural and logical form of address. The grammar is therefore directed at those responsible for teaching the basic features of the linguistic system:

All you doctors, teachers, schollats and school-masters that teach people in your Hebrew, Greek, Latine and English grammars, plural and singular; that is Thou to one, and you to many, and when they learn it they must not practice it. (Fox, 1660: 5)

For the sake of comparison, the system Fox proposes can be simply formalised by a decision chart (Figure 12.3). This is an address system which completely undermines the power dimension inherent in the

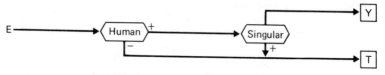

Figure 12.3 *'Radical' address system.*

sociolinguistic norms of the period. Further, given that social-norm-breaking marks the offender as eccentric and/or insane, the practice of 'thou-ing' came to define the radical sects as the lunatic fringe. Thus, Fox points out that the student who follows this singular/plural system

> is called clownish and unmannerly, if your childe practice that he hath learnt at school, which you have paid for, he is called a clown, and unmannerly and ill bred. (Fox, 1660: 5)

What effect then, does the democratic pronoun system have on the literature which evolved in terms of this oppositional discourse patterning? Again, drama is the literary form we must turn our attention to at this point, and therein a traditional definition of drama is presented with a problem. As is commonplace, the philosophy of a radical Puritan prevented him/her from creating any kind of fictional drama for us to analyse. However, if we consider why the radicals did not produce drama, then I think we are near to finding the kind of 'literary objects' in which this oppositional pronoun system was voiced. From a Puritan perspective, the highest Art a person could practise was the Art of living. They valued literature, not for its own sake, but in so far as it was functional for life. Fiction was rejected for life, drama for reality. If we are to develop this concept farther, then it is obvious that any definition of radical Puritan drama will have to be in terms of non-fiction – Puritan drama was the drama of living.

Further, when the radicals were put on trial for their beliefs, the court cases could quite easily be seen as the best 'performances' of their lives. As a 'dramatic performance'[7] these proceedings established the radical as a protagonist in his/her own drama, with the added attraction that the final appreciation of an audience would not wipe away a make-believe. An awareness of the dramatic aspect of public proceedings certainly seemed to be part of the mid-seventeenth-century consciousness. It was, for example, a commonplace in the Anglican pamphlet literature of the Civil War that the Puritans closed the theatres in order to cut off competition for their own comedies (the proceedings of Parliament) and tragedies (the trial of the King). Whilst the radicals themselves were concerned that the actual transcripts of their trials should get into print for circulation amongst a reading public. The second half of Bunyan's *Grace Abounding*, for example, is an attempt to present the proceedings of Bunyan's own trial in dramatic form. In the light of this perspective, it follows that the 'dramatic dialogue' in which a radical discourse is most coherently and directly presented in opposition to the seventeenth-century orthodox discourse is in the language of radical courtroom trials. Given this, an analysis of thou/you usage in radical dialogue contributes to our understanding of how the courtroom texts are operating.

The linguistic norms of a mid-seventeenth-century courtroom were defined in terms of the traditional, orthodox discourse rules. Thus, in terms of the pronoun system of address outlined in Figure 12.2, a courtroom is a status-marked setting. It follows from this that the pronoun usage would be reciprocal 'you'. The representatives of authority (Judge/Prosecutor) give 'you' to the defendant and receive 'you' back, as in Figure 12.4.

Figure 12.4 *Address norms.*

Any acceptable thou-usage in a courtroom was the privilege of the representatives of authority, and was usually used to express anger and contempt for the defendant. A famous example of this acceptable norm-breaking was Sir Edward Coke's attack on Ralegh at the latter's trial in 1603:

Coke: All that thou did, was at thy instigation, for I thou thee, thou traitor. (Jardine, 1832–5).

Figure 12.5 *Acceptable norm-deviation.*

Here the dynamics are as follows as shown in Figure 12.5. Within this framework of possibilities the oppositional nature of radical discourse is reflected in the fact that the radical defendant insisted on using 'thou' to the representatives of authority in the courtroom. This, in a sense, was an inversion of the dominant pronoun system of address, and as a consequence had a crucial effect on the dynamics of the courtroom proceedings. The effects of this radical norm-breaking are obvious in George Fox's trial before Judge Twysden in 1664. Fox wrote down the transcript of this trial in his *Journal* (pp. 466–70).

At the outset of the trial the conflict between the radical and the orthodox is marked by the fact that Fox's insistence on retaining his hat (a radical practice which accompanied thou-ing) had a immediate effect – the Judge is offended:

Judge: What! do you come into the Court with your hat on?
George Fox: Peace be amongst you all. The hat is not the honour that came down from God. (*Journal*, p. 466)

Further, following the traditional pronoun system of address the Judge begins by using 'you' to Fox. Fox, however, insists on inverting the reciprocal you-usage, and 'thous' the Judge consistently. Thus, orthodox phrases like 'your honour' are replaced by 'thou Judge' and 'Judge Thee'.

George Fox: As I said before, whether must I obey God or man, Judge Thee,
              Christ commands not to serve and if thee. . . . (*Journal*, p. 468)

Figure 12.6 *Radical norm-deviation.*

Again the effect of this pronoun usage is quite basic, and as such reflects a conflict between a radical and orthodox discourse. First, the Judge becomes exasperated with what is glossed as Fox's eccentric, stubborn and unacceptable behaviour, and, secondly, the courtroom proceedings break down. The business of the court is not completed. Fox is remanded in custody again until the next assizes.

The whole courtroom procedure, then, is antagonised and challenged by the radical pronoun usage. To engender such reactions the thou-ing custom was no mere eccentricity of a minority fringe, but a revolutionary weapon, embodying conflict at a basic level.

Perhaps the significance of radical pronoun usage was summed up most succinctly by Fuller in his *Church History*, Volume IV, and will serve as a useful statement to end this analysis of pronouns in seventeenth-century texts:

In a word: it is suspicious, such as now introduce thou and thee will, if they can, expel mine and thine, dissolving all propriety [property] into confusion. (*Church History*, Vol. IV, p. 132)

4 Concluding Remarks

The major conclusion to be drawn from this argument can be summarised in the slogan 'discourse as history'. More specifically, a historical process exists as a phenomenon in the interaction of individuals as members of social groups in time. Observable interaction has two forms – physical and verbal. Given this, it follows that 'discourse actions' and 'physical actions' realise the systems of belief, value and conflict of individuals within their social groups. Historical processes labelled 'revolutionary' are particularly interesting from a linguistic perspective. Since revolution involves the process of deconstructing traditional concepts and reconstructing new ones, it follows that changes will occur in the dominant linguistic patterns of the period. Further, since the changing patterns are in *opposition* to traditional patterns, the conflict between the radical and conservative elements of the 'revolution' will be enacted at a linguistic level. Pronouns are particularly significant here, for changing concepts of how individuals relate to each other in a society are reflected in the dominant pronoun patterns in texts. Perhaps the *implications* of what this chapter says for a developing stylistics are more important than what is actually said in and for itself. Clearly it follows from this argument that stylistics can have an important role to play in the study of an actual historical process – but it is more than that. *Any* given text approached from a linguistic perspective is produced within the framework of the beliefs, knowledge and values of a specific historical period. Given this, the whole programme of a developing stylistics can do no other but be placed within a historical and political context.

Notes: Chapter 12

1   This chapter is based on research carried out for two undergraduate essays submitted to the University of Birmingham in 1978. I am grateful to Tony Davies and Bob Wilcher for the historical and literary guidance they gave me at that stage, and to my linguistic supervisor, Deirdre Burton. Needless to say, I am solely responsible for any error of historical fact or linguistic judgement this version contains.

2   The term 'conservative', as represented by such figures as Donne, Laud, Browne and Filmer, is unexceptional, I think. However, the term 'radical' is problematic. As Christopher Hill (1972) argues, it is possible to refer to two revolutions during the mid-seventeenth century. The successful one established the rights of a middle/property-owning class, the other represented the struggle of a working class. The radicals I refer to were of the latter type, who challenged everything in their society, including the rising Protestant ethic itself. Thus, I refer to the various sects – most significantly, Baptists, Quakers, Seekers, Ranters, Diggers and Levellers.

3   All Digger texts referred to in this chapter are included in Hill (1973).

4   The term 'himself' is used specifically here to refer to the male section of society, since from a conservative perspective men were the representatives of mankind, and women were only part of that symbolic system when joined with a man in marriage.

5 Derby Assizes, October 1650.
6 The introduction of a non-human/human distinction in this decision chart is useful in accounting for a problem with the Brown and Gilman essay. They do not sufficiently account for the fact that the pronoun 'thou' is used for addressing God. Given that from an orthodox perspective God is the all-powerful, this is contradictory. However, for the purposes of this analysis the issue is sidestepped. It is convenient to regard God as non-human (non-mortal), and thus the system governing the choice of pronouns for humans does not apply to Him.
7 Goffman (1974) offers a frame definition of what constitutes a theatrical performance which is useful to formalise these intuitions. Court cases fulfil the necessary conditions for a theatrical performance except on two accounts. They had, for example, an audience which during the mid-seventeenth century would express its appreciation with vehemence, the transcripts were frequently published, and they had a protagonist. They did not have what Goffman calls a 'run'; in other words, the audience cannot buy tickets and see the same performance repeated night after night, and the make-believe could not be wiped away with a final applause. Both of these 'deviations' would have been an added attraction in a 'drama of living'.

Suggestions for Further Work: Chapter 12

1 One productive comparison would be with the text and discussion undertaken in the chapter by Widdowson. Plays by Shakespeare and Elizabethan and Jacobean dramatists generally are rich sources for the application of the ideas and mode of analysis explored in Gillian Alexander's chapter. The same general points are discussed in relation to *As You Like It* in an essay by McIntosh (McIntosh and Halliday, 1966), but how far can or should their points be extended to discussion within the socio-political model suggested by Alexander? There are useful articles in related areas by Lyons (1980) and Atwood (1970). Further relevant examples are contained at the end of the essay by Brown and Gilman referred to by Gillian Alexander (Brown and Gilman, 1960: 273–6)
2 The model developed here also has some considerable relevance for sociolinguistic study of language. Useful sources of academic discussion are Gumperz and Hymes (1972) and, as an example for comparative study of this topic, Bates and Benigni (1975).
3 A useful project for students of English would be an examination of how relations of power, solidarity, formality, and so on, are marked in a language such as contemporary English where there are no pronominal alternatives. How are systems of voice, tense, clause utilised to mark such relations, and where are the points of overlap with lexis, phonology, intonation, and so on? Several of D. H. Lawrence's stories make good case-studies; for example, 'Fanny and Annie' or 'Daughters of the Vicar'. A good starting-point is the dialogue between the Rigleys and Elizabeth Bates in 'Odour of Chrysanthemums', the opening to which is discussed in the chapter by Walter Nash.

References: Chapter 12

Atwood, Norman R. (1970), 'Cordelia and Kent: their fateful choice of style', *Language and Style*, vol. IX, no. 1, pp. 42–53.

Althusser, L. (1969), *For Marx*, trans. B. Brewster (Harmondsworth: Penguin).

Althusser, L. (1977), *Lenin and Philosophy and Other Essays*, trans. B. Brewster (London: New Left Books).

Bates, E. and Benigni, L. (1975), 'Rules of address in Italy: a sociological survey', *Language in Society*, vol. 4, no. 3, pp. 271–88.

Brown, R. and Gilman, A. (1960), 'Pronouns of power and solidarity', repr. in *Language and Social Context*, ed. P. Giglioli (Harmondsworth: Penguin, 1972), pp. 252–82.

Bunyan, J. (1976), *Grace Abounding* [1666] (London: Dent).

Donne, J. (1975), *Devotions Upon Emergent Occasions* [1624], ed. A. Raspa (Montreal: McGill Queen's University Press).

Foucault, M. (1970), *The Order of Things* (London: Tavistock).

Foucault, M. (1972), *The Archaeology of Knowledge*, trans. A. N. Sheridan Smith (London: Tavistock).

Fox, G. (1975), in *Journal of George Fox* [1675], ed. J. L. Nickalls (London: London Yearly Meeting of the Religious Society of Friends).

Fox, G. (1660), *A Battle-Doore for Teachers and Professors to Learn Singular and Plural* (London).

Fuller, T. (1845), *The Church History of Britain until 1648 Vol. IV* [1655], ed. Rev. J. S. Brewer (London: OUP).

Goffman, I. (1974), *Frame Analysis* (Harmondsworth: Penguin).

Gumperz, J. J. and Hymes, D. (eds) (1972) *Directions in Sociolinguistics* (New York: Holt, Rinehart & Winston).

Halliday, M. A. K. (1978), *Language as Social Semiotic* (London: Edward Arnold).

Hill, C. (1972), *The World Turned Upside Down* (Harmondsworth: Penguin).

Hill, C. (ed.) (1973), *Change and Continuity in Seventeenth Century England* (London: Weidenfeld & Nicolson).

Hill, C. (1977), *Milton and the English Revolution* (London: Faber).

Jardine, D. (1832–5), *Criminal Trials*, Vols 1–2 (London).

Knights, L. C. (1971), *Public Voices* (London: Chatto & Windus).

Kuhn, T. (1970), *The Structure of Scientific Revolutions* (Chicago: Chicago University Press).

Lakoff, G. and Johnson, P. (1980), *Metaphors We Live By* (Chicago: Chicago University Press).

Lyons, J. (1980), 'Pronouns of address in *Anna Karenina*: the stylistics of bilingualism and the impossibility of translation', in S. Greenbaum, G. Leech and J. Svartvik (eds), *Studies in English: for Randolph Quirk* (London: Longman).

McIntosh, A. (1966), 'As you like it': a grammatical clue to character', in McIntosh, A. & Halliday, M. A. K., *Patterns of Language: Papers in General, Descriptive and Applied Linguistics*, ed. A. McIntosh and M. A. K. Halliday (London: Longman), pp. 70–82.

Sapir, E. (1956), *Culture, Language and Personality* (Berkeley, Calif.: University of California Press).

Sinclair, J. McH. and Coulthard, R. M. (1975), *Towards an Analysis of Discourse: The English Used by Teachers and Pupils* (London: OUP).

Vološinov, V. M. (1930), *Marxism and the Philosophy of Language*, trans. L. Matejka and I. R. Titunik (New York: Seminar Press, 1973).

Watkins, O. C. (1972), *The Puritan Experience* (London: Routledge & Kegan Paul).

Webber, J. (1968), *The Eloquent "I"* (Madison, Wis.: University of Wisconsin Press).

Whorf, B. L. (1956), *Language, Thought and Reality*, ed. J. B. Carroll (Cambridge, Mass.: MIT Press).

Glossary

This is a glossary of the main and most frequently used grammatical and stylistic terms in the book. Definitions of this kind are dangerous. Counter-examples can often be found, and much of the discussion needs to be both amplified and qualified. The cited sources should be consulted wherever possible. It is intended that the definitions given here should be no more than a handy starting-point to enable initial stylistic analysis to be undertaken. In general, the more examples which can be generated, explored and analysed on the basis of those given here, the better will be the connections you can make between grammatical functions and literary stylistic effects.

Active

(1) Active verbs. A term sometimes used for 'dynamic verbs'. They are generally opposed to 'stative verbs' (see Quirk and Greenbaum, 1973, ch. 3).

(2) Active voice. The active voice in grammar indicates whether the subject of a verb is (*a*) the agent of the action or (*b*) exists in the state represented by the verb. For example:

    (i)   John crossed the road.
    (ii) The weather became even hotter.

Active and passive are the two main voice relations recognised in English grammar. (See also **Passive**.)

The term voice should not be confused with voice sounds, that is, sounds produced with the vocal cords vibrating: *d* and *v* are voiced consonants.

Adjunct

The adjunct is a primary category of structure in the English clause along with 'subject', 'predicate', 'object' and 'complement'. Semantically, adjuncts may represent various types of 'circumstance' attached to the process of the verb (e.g. time, place, manner, reason, etc.). The term is one used in systemic grammar and is roughly interchangeable with 'adverbial' but it also embraces 'prepositional phrases' and can be used to represent logical relations with a preceding clause:

'I *therefore* rejected his proposal.'

Adverb

An adverb can be defined with reference to both its form and its function. In form many adverbs end in the suffix -*ly* (e.g. cleverly) but some do not (e.g. often). In function an adverb can modify a verb (e.g. He ran quickly) or modify an adjective (e.g. He had a slightly pink face) or both. Adverbs can also modify other adverbs (e.g. He ran *very* quickly). When modifying adjectives or other adverbs, adverbs are sometimes referred to as sub-modifiers.

Anaphora

Anaphora or anaphoric reference occurs in the following example:

Bill started to limp. He had hurt his foot.

He relates anaphorically to *Bill* in that it presupposes a previous point of reference in the text. See **Reference**.

Antonym

A gradable opposite to a word. See **Synonym**.

Apposition

Elements of language which have equal grammatical status or which are co-referential are said to be in apposition:

I gave John, my brother, a book.

Here 'John' and 'my brother' are in apposition. To remove one or the other element does not affect the grammar or meaning of the sentence.

Article

Articles are conventionally the words *the* (definite article) or *a* (indefinite article), although some grammars extend the category to include items such as *some*, *any*. Other grammars refer to the whole group of words as determiners. Determiners and articles give definite or indefinite status to a 'noun'.

Aspect

A category of the verb which specifies whether an event, process or state of affairs is basically viewed in terms of duration ('progressive') or completion ('perfect'). But there is also 'habitual' and 'iterative' aspect.

Auxiliary

Auxiliaries are verbs which, as the name suggests, help other verbs. In sentences they cannot stand on their own. 'The man can' is meaningless except in reply to a question or in relation to some previous piece of discourse. But 'The man can help' is grammatical. See also **Modality.**

Bound clause

A term used in Sinclair (1972). Bound clauses are more widely known as 'subordinate clauses'.

Cataphora

Cataphora or cataphoric reference occurs in the following example:

He started to limp. It was strange to see Bill in pain.

He relates cataphorically to *Bill* in that it presupposes a subsequent point of reference in the text. See **Reference**.

Cohesion

An umbrella term for the ways in which different meaning relations in a text are combined intersententially. The most comprehensive introduction to cohesion is that of Halliday and Hasan (1976).

Complement

Complements are generally related to the subject of the sentence. They appear in the following examples:

That man seemed *nice*.
That girl is a *teacher of Russian*.

In both examples we understand the complements to relate to the subject *That man* and *That girl*. There can be object complements, too, as in the sentence

They considered him *very bright*

(where the complement relates to the object 'him').
Note, however, that in some versions of systemic grammar the term complement is used differently and stands for the term object in traditional grammar. For example, in the sentence

The man shot the grouse

'the grouse' would be classified as a complement. At the initial stages of analysis, systemic grammarians do not consider the distinction between 'object' and 'complement' to be sufficiently clear-cut.

Conditional

Usually a conditional clause. Conditional clauses are usually introduced by the conjunctions 'if' and 'whether'.

Conjunctives. See **Connectives**.

Connectives

(Also referred to as 'conjunctives'.)
An item used to relate successive sequences. *And*, *but because*, *so*, *then* are all connectives, but the range is wide and connectives can be categorised functionally into additive, adversative, casual and temporal. For fuller discussion of connectives see Halliday and Hasan (1976: ch. 5).

Declarative

The sentence structure standardly used to make statements. see **Interrogative**, **Imperative** moods.

Deixis
This may loosely be characterised as the 'orientational features of language'. It comprises the elements of language which locate an utterance in relation to a speaker's viewpoint, whether in space (e.g. these/those), time (e.g. now/then) or interpersonal relations (e.g. we/you). The individual words are called *deictics*.

Demonstratives
These are expressions to do with a pointing out of specific features in the environment of an utterance. For example, *this*, *that*, *these*, *those*, etc. See also **Pronoun** and **Deixis**.

Deviance
This is another complex notion which refers to a breaking of linguistic '**norms**'. See also **Foregrounding**.

Direct speech
The actual words of a speaker represented in a sentence within quotation marks. For example:

He said, 'I will never come back'.

See **Indirect Speech** and **Free Indirect Speech**.

Discourse
An umbrella term covering several different aspects of language organisation. It is used to refer to connected text beyond the level of the sentence; it can also mean a particular style or genre. 'Discourse' analysis is the linguistic examination of spoken conversation (see Coulthard, 1977). A discourse function can refer to the way in which linguistic items are used interpersonally (e.g. 'Do you want to go to bed?' – spoken by a father to a child – can function as an imperative in discourse though its grammatical *form* is that of an 'interrogative').

Endophoric
A general term used for 'reference' within a text. It contrasts with *exophoric*, which is a special term of reference to a situational context for a text.

Finite
A form of the verb in English which can be marked for 'tense', 'aspect' and 'number' (i.e. singular or plural). Finite clauses usually have a subject.

Foregrounding
In literary works this is a process of giving special attention to elements of language which are crucial to a particular effect or meaning. This is often achieved by using them in unusual contexts or unusually in relation to 'norms' of syntax, lexis, discourse, genre, etc. In certain contexts foregrounding can be brought about by achievement of a norm as well as by **Deviation**.

Free Clause
A term used in Sinclair (1972) for what is more generally designated a 'main clause'.

Free Indirect Speech
One of several techniques to represent a stream-of-consciousness narrative but still remaining within the control of the reporter of the action. Tense tends to be situated in the reporter's or narrator's viewpoint. For example:

Would she never come back?

See **Direct Speech** and **Indirect Speech**.

Grammetrics
Grammetrical relations in poetry are those affecting the congruence of grammar and metrics. For example, a grammetrical account of a poem might explore, among other things, the interrelationship between clause structure, lines in a poem and its metrical and stanzaic organisation.

Group
Group is a term used in systemic grammar. In that grammar it is the 'rank' lying between 'word' and 'clause'. There are three types of group, *nominal*, *verbal* and *adverbial*, The term corresponds roughly to that of phrase, i.e. nominal group = noun phrase.

Headword
A term used largely in systemic grammar which corresponds approximately to 'noun'. But 'noun' is a class of word. Headword is an element of group structure.

Hyponym
One of a set of specific terms in a relationship of 'hyponymy' to some more embracing or superordinate word. For example, 'oak' and 'ash' are hyponyms of *tree*. See **Synonym** and **Antonym**.

Imperative
The sentence structure standardly used to issue commands. See **Interrogative**, **Declarative** moods.

Indirect Speech
The reported words of the speaker presented in a 'that' or reported clause within the sentence. For example:

He said that he would never come back.

See **Direct Speech** and **Free Indirect Speech**.

Infinitive
A 'core' feature of the verb marked by the presence of *to* (e.g. 'to go' is the infinitive of the verb *go*).

Interrogative
The sentence structure standardly used to ask questions. See **Imperative**, **Declarative** moods.

Lexis
A general term for vocabulary. Lexical items need not be single words, however. 'It's raining *cats and dogs*' is more usually regarded as a single lexical item.

Locatives
These are expressions to do with place or position relative to an utterance. For example, *here, there, where, everywhere*. See also **Pronoun**.

Main Clause
A main clause consists of words which can be analysed into the main categories of the structure of a sentence. Main clauses can be *co-ordinated*, that is, linked by conjunctives such as *and*, and have 'subordinate clauses' related to them.

Modality
Modal verbs are a sub-class of 'auxiliary' verbs which are concerned with the speaker's attitude towards his message. Their meaning is basically to qualify the assertive power of utterances, but they can be used for prophecy, prediction, obligation, etc. 'Must', 'might', 'can', 'could', 'may', 'ought to' are all examples of modal verbs. See Halliday (1970) for further definition of modality and 'modulation'.

Modifier
Modifier is a term used to describe the elements of a nominal group in English which are positioned between the determiner and the **headword**. (Note, however, that in Sinclair (1972) a determiner/deictic is a kind of modifier.) It corresponds approximately to that of adjective. For example:

It was a very *bright* day.

'Very' here is sometimes referred to as a sub- or pre-modifier.

Mood
This is the general term used to describe different types of sentence. See **Declarative**; **Imperative**; **Interrogative**. Sentences can also be moodless. It should be noted that grammatical descriptions do not adequately account for the '**Discourse**' functions of mood.

Norm
This is a very complex notion. There are norms at different linguistic levels. In grammar this would be the most neutral and acceptable order and structure for linguistic items. 'Deviance' occurs when the 'normal' order is in some way broken, but there will inevitably be disagreement about what constitutes the norm and about variation in a norm according to context.

Object
The direct object of a sentence is usually the noun phrases or 'nominal groups' which follow the verb. Direct objects can be made into the subject of a '**passive**' sentence. An indirect object is the person or thing to which something is given, said or done (e.g. I gave him the book, *him* = indirect object; *the book* = direct object). Note, however, that stylistic variation allows objects to appear at the beginning of a sentence before the verb and subject (e.g. 'That book you gave me'). In systemic grammar the direct object of a sentence is referred to as the 'complement'.

Parallelism
Parallelism is in certain respects in contradistinction to '**deviation**', for it consists of the introduction and 'foregrounding' of regularities, not irregularities, in the language. See Leech (1969: 62–9).

Participle/Participial Clause
A subordinate clause based on the present- or past-participle form of a verb. For example, given the verb *capture* a present participle (capturing) and a past participle (captured) can be formed as a basis of the participial clauses:

Capturing the city in a week, Hannibal moved on to attack the villages.
Captured by the enemy, he still resisted bravely.

Participial clauses are 'non-**finite**'.

Passive
The passive voice is in complementary relationship to the 'active' voice. It indicates that the subject of the verb is the recipient of an action. For example:

A dog bit the man (active)
The man was bitten by a dog (passive)

But note that things are not always as simple as this. In the sentence 'He fell', 'fell' has the form of an active verb but 'he' is clearly the recipient of the action.

Person
Person in English refers to the speaker (I/we), the addressee (you) and the person referred to (he/she/it/they), but actual use is not always consistent with this general classification. Person is usually conveyed by '**pronouns**'.

Phrase
A group of words which is grammatically equivalent to a single word and which does not contain its own subject and verb. For example:

NP   VP   NP   PP
The man / pushed / his car / along the road /

contains three main kinds of phrase. These are noun phrase NP, verb phrase VP, and prepositional phrase PP. In traditional and TG grammar 'phrase' is used for 'group', which is the term widely used in systemic grammar.

Predicate
Another term for verb or element of structure in a verbal group.

Preposition
A preposition is a grammatical word and includes items such as *in*, *on*, *across*, *between*, *up*, *for*, *at*, etc. When followed by a noun phrase (or nominal group) a prepositional phrase is formed (e.g. 'in the car park').

Pronoun
A grammatical word which substitutes for a noun. There are a number of sub-types:

(*a*) personal pronouns: *I*, *we*, *he*, *she*, *they*, etc.
(*b*) interrogative pronouns: *who*, *what*, *where*, *why*, etc.
(*c*) locative pronouns: *here*, *there*, *where*, etc.
(*d*) temporal pronouns: *now*, *then*, etc.
(*e*) demonstrative pronouns: *this*, *that*, *these*, *those*, etc.

Qualifier
A qualifier is any word which qualifies, describes or identifies a 'headword' and which comes *after* a headword: see Berry (1975: 65–6). For example:

The man *next door* is a criminal.

See also defining **relative clause.**

Rankshift
Rankshift is a term used in systemic grammar to define the syntactic function of a piece of language at a level or 'rank' lower than that at which it would normally operate. For example:

The man *who came to dinner* is very old.

Here the relative clause is rankshifted to the position of qualifier in the nominal group headed by 'the man'. Traditionally, clauses in this syntactic role are termed restrictive or defining relative clauses. (See **Relative Clause**). There are many different kinds of rankshift involving shift from clause to group, from group to word and so on. The term is lucidly explained, with helpful examples, in Berry (1975: 107–16).

Reference
A type of 'cohesion' in English which depends for its interpretation on the presence of other items in a text. See, in particular, Halliday and Hasan (1976: ch. 2).

Register
A rather imprecise term which describes the kind of language use appropriate to a particular function in a situational context. For example, a legal register or a register of advertisements. Features of language are selected in accordance with content, purpose, the relation of the language user to an audience, etc.

Relative Clause

A clause which extends or adds information relative to that given in a 'Main Clause'. For example:

My brother, who lives in Scotland, is a solicitor.

This is a non-defining relative clause. In the following sentence:

My brother who lives in Scotland is a solicitor.

we have a defining relative clause. This defines some information relevant to a particular brother and, unlike the first example, carries a clear meaning that the speaker has another brother(s). The whole clause *who lives in Scotland* becomes a qualifying element identifying the '**headword**' brother.' Sometimes the terms 'restrictive' and 'non-restrictive' relative clause are employed.

Synonym

A word or phrase similar in meaning to another word or phrase. See **Antonym**.

Tense

Tense in English involves a morphological modification of the verb (e.g. I walk → I walked adds the morpheme -*ed* but it can also involve a different verb, e.g. I go → I went). It usually expresses time relative to the time of the utterance, action, event or state. The two tenses in English are *present* and *past*. See Leech (1971) for more advanced discussion. See also Quirk and Greenbaum (1973) for numerous examples in connection with tense of the terms 'progressive', 'imperfect', 'perfect'. Future Tense in English is usually indicated by an 'auxiliary' verb (e.g. I *shall* decide next week). But the present tense can also indicate futurity (e.g. I fly to Moscow on Monday) when accompanied by appropriate adverbial elements (or 'adjuncts'). Semantically, too, the simple past tense can be used to indicate deference rather than pastness (e.g. I *wondered* if I could have a word). Tense is a complicated morphological, grammatical and semantic category. Palmer (1971: 193–6) makes some useful introductory points along these lines.

Transitivity

A transitive verb is a verb which has a grammatical object affected by the 'action' of the verb. For example, in

The man *hit* the ball.

'hit' here is a transitive verb. In the sentence

An hour *elapsed*.

'elapsed' is intransitive, i.e. it can never take an object. Much work has been done on 'systems of transitivity' in systemic grammar; see Berry (1975: 149–53). For discussion of 'ditransitivity' and 'double transitivity', see Quirk and Greenbaum (1973: 370–4) and Sinclair (1972: 114–24).

References: Glossary

Berry, M. (1975), *Introduction to Systemic Linguistics: Vol. 1, Levels and Links* (London: Batsford).

Coulthard, R. M. (1977), *Introduction to Discourse Analysis* (London: Longman).

Halliday, M. A. K. (1970), 'Functional diversity in language as seen from a consideration of modality and mood in English', *Foundations of Language*, vol. VI, pp. 322–61.

Halliday, M. A. K. and Hasan, R. (1976), *Cohesion in English* (London: Longman).

Leech, G. N. (1969), *A Linguistic Guide to English Poetry* (London: Longman).

Leech, G. N. (1971), *Meaning and the English Verb* (London: Longman).

Palmer, F. (1971), *Grammar* (Harmondsworth: Penguin).

Quirk, R. and Greenbaum, S. (1973), *A University Grammar of English* (London: Longman).

Sinclair, J. McH. (1972), *A Course in Spoken English: Grammar* (London: OUP).

Further Reading: Bibliography

Part I is a select bibliography of work in language and literature which starts with introductory material and moves on to more theoretical and advanced studies in stylistics and poetics. A more extensive bibliography produced by PALA (Poetics and Linguistics Association of Great Britain) can be obtained from the Department of English and Linguistics at the Universities of Lancaster and East Anglia. Part II is a consolidated bibliography of references made in the course of this reader.

Part I

I BIBLIOGRAPHIES

Bailey, R. W. and Burton, D. M. (1968), *English Stylistics: A Bibliography* (Cambridge, Mass.: MIT Press).

Style, vol. 13, no. 2, Spring 1979: annual bibliography 1976–7; bibliography of grammatical aspects of style.

II INTRODUCTIONS AND GENERAL DISCUSSIONS

Bailey, R. W. (1974), 'Stylistics today', *Foundations of Language*, vol. II, pp. 115–39.

Chapman, R. (1973), *Linguistics and Literature: An Introduction to Literary Stylistics* (London: Edward Arnold).

Cluysenaar, A. (1976), *Introduction to Literary Stylistics* (London: Batsford).

Egan, M. (1972), 'How relevant is linguistics to criticism?', *Times Higher Educational Supplement*, 28 January, p. 13.

Enkvist, E. (1971), 'On the place of style in some linguistic theories', in Chatman, S. (ed.), *Literary Style: A Symposium* (London: OUP), pp. 47–61.

Enkvist, E., Spencer, J. and Gregory, M. (1964), *Linguistics and Style* (London: OUP).

Epstein, E. L. (1978), *Language and Style* (London: Methuen).

Hasan, R. (1971), 'Rime and reason in literature', in Chatman, S. (ed.), *Literary Style: A Symposium* (London: OUP), pp. 299–329.

Jakobson, R. (1960), 'Linguistics and poetics', in Sebeok, T. (ed.), *Style in Language* (Cambridge, Mass.: MIT Press), pp. 350–77.

Leech, G. N. (1969), *A Linguistic Guide to English Poetry* (London: Longman).

Leech, G. N. and Short, M. H. (1981), *Style in Fiction* (London: Longman).

Rodger, A. (1969), 'Linguistics and the teaching of literature', in Fraser, H. and O'Donnell, W. R. (eds), *Applied Linguistics and the Teaching of English* (London: Longman), pp. 88–98.

Sinclair, J. McH. (1982), 'The integration of language and literature in the English curriculum', in Carter, R. A. and Burton, D. (eds), *Literary Text and Language Study: An Approach to Language and Literature in the Classroom* (London: Edward Arnold), pp. 9–27.

Traugott, E. C. and Pratt, M. L. (1980), *Linguistics for Students of Literature* (New York: Harcourt Brace Jovanovich).

Turner, G. W. (1973), *Stylistics* (Harmondsworth: Penguin).

Widdowson, H. G. (1975), *Stylistics and the Teaching of Literature* (London: Longman).

III ANTHOLOGIES

Chatman, S. (ed.) (1971), *Literary Style: A Symposium* (London: OUP).

Chatman, S. (ed.) (1973), *Approaches to Poetics* (New York: Columbia University Press).

Chatman, S. and Levin, S. R. (eds) (1967), *Essays on the Language of Literature* (Boston, Mass.: Houghton Mifflin).

Ching, M. K. L., Haley, M. C. and Lunsford, R. F. (eds) (1980), *Linguistic Perspectives on Literature* (London: Routledge & Kegan Paul).

Fowler, R. G. (ed.) (1975), *Style and Structure in Literature* (London: OUP).

Freeman, D. C. (ed.) (1981), *Essays in Modern Stylistics* (London: Methuen).

Sebeok, T. A. (ed.) (1960), *Style in Language* (Cambridge, Mass.: MIT Press).

IV APPLICATIONS

Banfield, A. (1978), 'The formal coherence of represented speech and thought', *Poetics and the Theory of Literature*, vol. 3, no. 2, pp. 289–314.

Bronzwaer, W. J. M. (1970), *Tense in the Novel* (Gröningen: Wolters-Noordhoff).

Burton, D. (1980), *Dialogue and Discourse* (London: Routledge & Kegan Paul).

Edwards, P. (1968), 'Meaning and context: an exercise in practical stylistics', *English Language Teaching*, vol. XXII, no. 3, pp. 272–7.

Fowler, R. (1977), *Linguistics and the Novel* (London: Methuen).

Halliday, M. A. K. (1971), 'Linguistic function and literary style', in Chatman, S. (ed.), *Literary Style: A Symposium* (London: OUP), pp. 330–65.

Hendricks, W. O. (1976), *Grammars of Style and Styles of Grammar* (Amsterdam: North-Holland Publishing Co.).

Hirsch, D. H. (1972), 'Linguistic structures and literary meaning', *Journal of Literary Semantics*, no. 1, pp. 80–8.

Leech, G. N. (1965), ' "This bread I break": language and interpretation', *Review of English Literature*, vol. VI (April), pp. 66–75.

McHale, B. (1978), 'Free indirect discourse: a survey of recent accounts', *Poetics and the Theory of Literature*, no. 3, pp. 235–87.

Page, N. (1973), *Speech in the English Novel* (London: Longman).

Pratt, M. L. (1977), *Toward a Speech Act Theory of Literary Discourse* (Bloomington, Ind.: Indiana University Press).

Short, M. H. (1973), 'Some thoughts on foregrounding and interpretation', *Language and Style*, vol. 19, pp. 97–108.

Short, M. H. (1981), 'Discourse analysis and drama', *Applied Linguistics* vol. 2, no. 2, pp. 180–202.

Sinclair, J. McH. (1966), 'Taking a poem to pieces', in Fowler, R. (ed.), *Essays on Language and Style* (London: Routledge & Kegan Paul), pp. 68–81.

Sinclair, J. McH. (1968), 'A technique of stylistic description', *Language and Style*, vol. 1, no. 4, pp. 215–42.

Thorne, J. P. (1970), 'Generative grammar and stylistic analysis', in Lyons, J. (ed.), *New Horizons in Linguistics* (Harmondsworth: Penguin), pp. 185–97.

V FORMAL APPROACHES

Dijk, T. A. Van (1976), *Pragmatics of Language and Literature* (Amsterdam: North-Holland Publishing Co.).

Levin, S. R. (1963), 'Deviation – statistical and determinate – in poetic language', *Lingua*, no. 12, pp. 276–90.

Levin, S. R. (1965), 'Internal and external deviation in poetry', *Word*, no. 21, pp. 225–37.

Milic, L. T. (1966), *A Quantitative Approach to the Style of Jonathan Swift* (The Hague: Mouton).

Milic, L. T. (1971), 'Rhetorical choice and stylistic option: the conscious and unconscious poles', in Chatman, S. (ed.), *Literary Style: A Symposium* (London: OUP). pp. 77–88.

Widdowson, H. G. (1972), 'On the deviance of literary discourse', *Style*, vol. VI, no. 3, pp. 294–306.

VI POETICS, STYLISTICS AND LITERARY THEORY

Barthes, R. (1970), 'To write: an intransitive verb?' in Macksey, R. and Donato, E. (eds), *The Languages of Criticism and the Sciences of Man* (Baltimore, Md.: Johns Hopkins University Press), pp. 134–56.

Culler, J. (1975), *Structuralist Poetics* (London: Routledge & Kegan Paul).

Ellis, J. M. (1974), *The Theory of Literary Criticism: A Logical Analysis* (Berkeley, Calif.: University of California Press).

Fish, S. (1973), 'What is stylistics and why are they saying such terrible things about it?' in Chatman, S. (ed.), *Approaches to Poetics* (New York: Columbia University Press), pp. 109–52.

Genette, G. (1980), *Narrative Discourse* (Oxford: Blackwell).

Hawkes, T. (1977), *Structuralism and Semiotics* (London: Methuen).

Iser, W. (1978), *The Act of Reading* (Baltimore, Md: Johns Hopkins University Press).

Lodge, D. (1966), *Language of Fiction* (London: Routledge & Kegan Paul).

Lodge, D. (1977), *The Modes of Modern Writing: Metaphor, Metonymy and the Typology of Modern Literature* (London: Edward Arnold).

Matejka, L. and Pomorska, K. (eds), (1971), *Readings in Russian Poetics: Formalist and Structuralist Views* (Cambridge, Mass.: MIT Press).

Mukarovsky, J. (1964), 'Standard language and poetic language', in Garvin, P. (ed.), *A Prague School Reader on Esthetics, Literary Structure and Style* (Washington, DC: Georgetown University Press), pp. 19–35.

Riffaterre, M. (1978), *Semiotics of Poetry* (Bloomington, Ind.: Indiana University Press).

Ringbom, H. (ed.) (1975), *Style and Text: Studies Presented to Nils Erik Enkvist* (Stockholm: Åbo).

Robey, D. (ed.) (1973), *Structuralism* (London: OUP).

Smith, B. H. (1978), *On the Margins of Discourse: The Relation of Literature to Language* (Chicago, Ill.: University of Chicago Press).

Spitzer, L. (1948), *Linguistics and Literary History: Essays in Stylistics* (Princeton, NJ: Princetown University Press).
Werth, P. N. (1976), 'Roman Jakobson's verbal analysis of poetry', *Journal of Linguistics*, vol. 12, no. 1, pp. 21–73.

VII   LINGUISTIC THEORY AND BACKGROUND

Cole, P. and Morgan, J. (eds) (1975), *Syntax and Semantics: Speech Acts* (New York: Academic Press).
Coulthard, M. (1977), *An Introduction to Discourse Analysis* (London: Longman).
Giglioli, P. P. (ed.) (1972), *Language and Social Context* (Harmondsworth: Penguin).
Halliday, M. A. K. and Hasan, R. (1976), *Cohesion in English* (London: Longman).
Lyons, J. (1968), *Introduction to Theoretical Linguistics* (Cambridge: CUP).
Lyons, J. (1977), *Semantics*, Vols I and II (Cambridge: CUP).
Lyons, J. (ed.) (1970), *New Horizons in Linguistics* (Harmondsworth: Penguin).
McIntosh, A. and Halliday, M. A. K. (1966), *Patterns of Language: Papers in General, Descriptive and Applied Linguistics* (London: Longman).
Smith, N. and Wilson, D. (1979), *Modern Linguistics* (Harmondsworth: Penguin).
Trudgill, P. (1974), *Sociolinguistics* (Harmondsworth: Penguin).

Part II

Althusser, L. (1969), *For Marx*, trans. B. Brewster (Harmondsworth: Penguin).
Althusser, L. (1977), *Lenin and Philosophy and Other Essays*, trans. B. Brewster (London: New Left Books).
Ardener, S. (ed.) (1975), *Perceiving Women* (London: Malaby).
Barthes, R. (1967), *Writing Degree Zero*, trans. A. Lavers and C. Smith (London: Cape).
Barthes, R. (1970), *S/Z*, trans. R. Miller (London: Cape).
Barthes, R. (1972), *Mythologies*, trans. A. Lavers (London: Cape).
Barthes, R. (1977), *Image, Music, Text*, trans. S. Heath (London: Fontana).
Beach, J. W. (1957), *The Making of the Auden Canon* (Minneapolis, Minn.: University of Minnesota Press).
Belsey, C. (1980), *Critical Practice*, New Accents series (London: Methuen).
Berger, G. and Kachuk, B. (1977), 'Sexism, language and social change', *Michigan Papers in Women's Studies*, no. 2 (Summer), pp. 139–62.
Berry, M. (1975), *Introduction to Systemic Linguistics: Vol. I, Levels and Links* (London: Batsford).
Brecht, B. (1950), 'The street scene', in *Brecht on Theatre*, trans. and ed. J. Willett (London: Methuen, 1964), pp. 121–9.
British Council (forthcoming), *ELT Documents 110: Language and Literature*.

Brown, R. and Gilman, A. (1972), 'Pronouns of power and solidarity', in Giglioli, P. (ed.), *Language and Social Context* (Harmondsworth: Penguin), pp. 252–82.

Bunyan, J. (1976), *Grace Abounding* [1666] (London: Dent).

Burton, D. (1981), 'Pass the Alka-Seltzer: she's swallowed the dictionary', mimeo., English Language Research, University of Birmingham.

Burton, D. (in preparation *a*), *Eccentric Propositions: The Sociolinguistic Construction of Reality*.

Burton, D. (in preparation *b*), *Seeing Through Language: Essays on the Language Used by, and about Women*.

Carter, R. A. (1979), 'Poetry and conversation: an essay in discourse analysis', *Nottingham Linguistic Circular*, vol. 8, no. 1 (mimeo.), pp. 28–41.

Chomsky, N. (1968), *Language and Mind* (New York: Harcourt Brace & World).

Cluysenaar, A. (1976), *Introduction to Literary Stylistics* (London: Batsford).

Coulthard, R. M. (1977), *Introduction to Discourse Analysis* (London: Longman).

Coward, R. and Ellis, J. (1977), *Language and Materialism* (London: Routledge & Kegan Paul).

Crystal, D. (1972), 'Objective and subjective in stylistic analysis', in Kachru, B. and Stahlke, H. (eds), *Current Trends in Stylistics* (Edmonton, Alberta: Linguistic Research, Inc.), pp. 103–13.

Daly, M. (1978), *Gyn/Ecology: The Metaethics of Radical Feminism* (Boston, Mass.: Beacon Press).

Davidson, D. (1967), 'Truth and meaning', *Synthese*, no. 17, pp. 304–23.

Delamont, S. and Duffin, L. (eds) (1978), *The Nineteenth Century Woman: Her Cultural and Physical World* (London: Croom Helm).

Derrida, J. (1976), *Of Grammatology*, trans. Gayatri Chakravorty Spivak (Baltimore, Md: Johns Hopkins University Press).

Donne, J. (1975), *Devotions upon Emergent Occasions* [1625], ed. A. Raspa (Montreal: McGill/Queen's University Press).

Ellmann, R. (1959), *James Joye* (New York: OUP).

Everett, B. (1964), *Auden* (Edinburgh: Oliver & Boyd).

Feyerabend, P. (1975), *Against Method* (London: New Left Books).

Feyerabend, P. (1978), *Science in a Free Society* (London: New Left Books).

Firth, J. R. (1957), *Papers in Linguistics, 1934–1951* (London: OUP).

Foucault, M. (1977), *Language, Counter-Memory, Practice: Selected Essays and Interviews*, ed. D. F. Bouchard and trans. D. F. Bouchard and S. Simon (Oxford: Blackwell).

Foucault, M. (1972), *The Archaeology of Knowledge*, trans. A. N. Sheridan Smith (London: Tavistock).

Foucault, M. (1970), *The Order of Things* (London: Tavistock).

Fox, F. [1660], *A Battle-Doore for Teachers and Professors to Learn Singular and Plural* (London).

Fox, G. (1975), *Journal of George Fox* [1675], ed. J. L. Nickalls (London: London Yearly Meeting of the Religious Society of Friends).

Fuller, J. (1970), *A Reader's Guide to W. H. Auden* (London: Thames & Hudson).

Fuller, T. (1845), *The Church History of Britain until 1648*, Vol. IV [1655], ed. Rev. J. S. Brewer (Oxford: OUP).

Garfinkel, H. (1967), *Studies in Ethnomethodology* (Englewood Cliffs, NJ: Prentice-Hall).

Goffman, I. (1975), *Frame Analysis* (Harmondsworth: Penguin).

Halliday, M. A. K. (1970*a*), 'Functional diversity in language as seen from a consideration of modality and mood in English', *Foundations of Language*, vol. VI, pp. 322–61.

Halliday, M. A. K. (1970*b*), 'Language structure and language function', in Lyons, J. (ed.), *New Horizons in Linguistics* (Harmondsworth: Penguin).

Halliday, M. A. K. (1971), 'Linguistic function and literary style', in Chatman, S. (ed.), *Literary Style: A Symposium* (London: OUP), pp. 330–65; also in Halliday, 1973, pp 103–43.

Halliday, M. A. K. (1973), *Explorations in the Functions of Language* (London: Edward Arnold).

Halliday, M. A. K. (1978), *Language as Social Semiotic* (London: Edward Arnold).

Hill, C. (1972), *The World Turned Upside Down* (Harmondsworth: Penguin).

Hill, C. (ed.) (1973), *Change and Continuity in Seventeenth Century England* (London: Weidenfeld & Nicolson).

Hill, C. (1977), *Milton and the English Revolution* (London: Faber).

Hoggart, R. (1951), *Auden: An Introductory Essay* (London: Chatto & Windus).

Hynes, S. (1976), *The Auden Generation* (London: Bodley Head).

Jack, J. H. (1964), 'Art and *A Portrait of the Artist*', in Connolly, T. (ed.), *Joyce's Portrait* (London: Peter Owen), pp. 156–66.

Jaquette, J. (ed.), *Women in Politics* (New York: Wiley).

Jardine, D. (1832–5), *Criminal Trials*, Vols 1–2 (London).

Knights, L. C. (1971), *Public Voices* (London: Chatto & Windus).

Kuhn, T. (1962; revised 1970), *The Structure of Scientific Revolutions* (Chicago, Ill.: University of Chicago Press).

Kuhn, T. (1967), *The Copernican Revolution* (Cambridge: CUP).

Lacan, J. (1977), *Ecrits*, trans. A. Sheridan (London: Tavistock).

Laing, R. D. and Esterson, A. (1970), *Sanity, Madness and the Family* (Harmondsworth: Penguin).

Lakatos, I. (1976), *Proofs and Refutations: The Logic of Mathematical Discovery* (Cambridge: CUP).

Lakatos, I. (1970), 'Falsification and the methodology of scientific research programmes', in Lakatos, I and Musgrave, A. (eds), *Criticism and the Growth of Knowledge* (Cambridge: CUP), pp. 91–6.

Lakoff, G. and Johnson, P. (1980), *Metaphors We Live By* (Chicago, Ill.: University of Chicago Press).

Leech, G. N. (1965), ' "This bread I break": language and interpretation', *A Review of English Literature*, ed. A. N. Jeffares, vol. VI, no. 2, pp. 66–75.

Leech, G. N. (1969), *A Linguistic Guide to English Poetry* (London: Longman).

Leech, G. N. (1971), *Meaning and the English Verb* (London: Longman).

Leech, G. N. and Svartvik, J. (1975), *A Communicative Grammar of English* (London: Longman).

Leech, G. N. and Short, M. H. (1981), *Style in Fiction* (London: Longman).

Lyons, J. (1968), *Introduction to Theoretical Linguistics* (Cambridge: CUP).

Lyons, J. (1977), *Semantics*, Vol. 1 (Cambridge: CUP).

McHale, B. (1978), 'Free indirect discourse: a survey of recent accounts', *Poetics and the Theory of Literature*, no. 3, pp. 235–87.

Macharey, P. (1978), *A Theory of Literary Production*, trans. G. Wall (London: Routledge & Kegan Paul).

Millett, K. (1977), *Sexual Politics* (1969; repr. London: Virago).

Nicholson, J. (1958), 'Musical form and the Preludes', in Braybrooke, N. (ed.), *T. S. Eliot: A Symposium for His Seventieth Birthday* (London: Hart-Davis), pp. 110–12.

Palmer, F. (1971), *Grammar* (Harmondsworth: Penguin).

Pascal, R. (1977), *The Dual Voice: Free Indirect Speech and Its Patterning in the Nineteenth Century European Novel* (Manchester: Manchester University Press).

Popper, K. (1977), *The Logic of Scientific Discovery* (London: Hutchinson).

Popper, K. (1979), *Objective Knowledge*, rev. edn (London: OUP).

Quirk, R. and Greenbaum, S. (1973), *A University Grammar of English* (London: Longman).

Quirk, R., Greenbaum, S., Leech, G. and Svartvik, J. (1972), *A Grammar of Contemporary English* (London: Longman).

Rich, A. (1977*a*), 'When we dead awaken: writing as revision', *College English*, vol. 34, no. 1, pp. 18–30.

Rich, A. (1977*b*), *Of Woman Born: Motherhood as Experience and Institution* (London: Virago).

Rowbotham, S. (1973*a*), *Woman's Consciousness: Man's World* (Harmondsworth: Penguin).

Rowbotham, S. (1973*b*), *Hidden from History* (London: Pluto Press).

Ryle, G. (1949), *The Concept of Mind* (London: Hutchinson).

Sacks, H. and Schegloff, E. A. (1973), 'Opening up closings', *Semiotica*, vol. 8, no. 4, pp. 289–327.

Sapir, E. (1956), *Culture, Language and Personality* (Berkeley, Calif.: University of California Press).

Saussure, F. de (1974), *Course in General Linguistics*, trans. W. Boskin (1916; repr. London: Fontana).

Searle, J. R. (1969), *Speech Acts* (Cambridge: CUP).

Showalter, E. (1977), *A Literature of Their Own: British Women Novelists from Brontë to Lessing* (Princeton, NJ: Princeton University Press).

Sinclair, J. McH. (1966), 'Taking a poem to pieces', in Fowler, R. (ed.), *Essays on Style and Language* (London: Routledge & Kegan Paul), pp. 68–81.

Sinclair, J. McH. (1972), *A Course in Spoken English: Grammar* (London: OUP).

Sinclair, J. McH. and Coulthard, M. (1975), *Towards an Analysis of Discourse* (London: OUP).

Spears, M. K. (1963), *The Poetry of W. H. Auden* (New York: OUP).

Spitzer, L. (1970), 'Linguistics and literary history', in Freeman, D. C. (ed.), *Linguistics and Literary Style* (New York: Holt, Rinehart & Winston), pp. 21–39.

Tarski, A. (1956), *Logic, Semantics, Metamathematics* (Oxford: Clarendon Press).

Traugott, E. C. and Pratt, M. L. (1980), *Linguistics for Students of Literature* (New York: Harcourt Brace Jovanovich).

Vološinov, V. M. (1973), *Marxism and the Philosophy of Language*, trans. L. Matejka and I. R. Titunik (1930; New York: Seminar Press).

Waith, Eugene M. (1964), 'The calling of Stephen Dedalus', in Connolly, T. (ed.), *Joyce's Portrait* (London: Peter Owen), pp. 114–23.

Watkins, O. C. (1972), *The Puritan Experience* (London: Routledge & Kegan Paul).

Webber, J. (1968), *The Eloquent 'I'* (Madison, Wis.: University of Wisconsin Press).

Whorf, B. L. (1956), *Language, Thought and Reality*, ed. J. B. Carroll (Cambridge, Mass.: MIT Press).

Widdowson, H. G. (1975), *Stylistics and the Teaching of Literature* (London: Longman).

Selective Subject and Name Index